Praise for *B*

"Saying 'we are investigating' and nothing more is not going to cut it anymore."
— Colonel Ron Replogle, Law Enforcement Commander in Ferguson, Missouri; Missouri Highway Patrol (retired)

"Lance LoRusso knows the law as few do. He proved that with his book, When Cops Kill. Blue News looks at how effectively law enforcement communicates, with itself and with others, in times of crisis. I can't imagine a more timely topic"
— Jim Bohannon, Westwood One Radio (fifty-year broadcast veteran heard nationally on over 300 stations)

"One inaccurate story could destroy a career, a job, a life."
— Paul Crawley, thirty-six-year veteran reporter

"Thank God for the men and women who have chosen law enforcement as a career. Thank God a man like Lance LoRusso is there to represent and defend those officers in their dark times of dire need. I know you'll enjoy *Blue News*."
— James "Moby" Carney (forty-year radio show host syndicated in five states, member of the Country Radio Hall of Fame, five-time winner of Billboard's Major Market Country Morning Show of the Year and Academy of Country Music's Major Market DJ of the Year)

"Lance J. LoRusso, Esq., did an amazing job of addressing the issues and changes that have plagued the police departments in the US. How police departments handle the media has to evolve, or the mainstream media will continue to control the narrative of critical incidents with sensational, misleading headlines. Lance lays down a guide to all public-information offices to manage their incidents and control the media. He also outlines how media successfully uses social media and police departments lag behind. This is a must-have in every chief's office and every public-information office."
— Nathan McCreary, Former PIO

Blue News

Blue News

DARELL,
TELL YOUR
STORY!

Lance J. LoRusso, Esq.

BOOKLOGIX®
Alpharetta, GA

ISBN: 978-1-61005-853-7

Library of Congress Control Number: 2016919681

10 9 8 7 6 5 4 3 2   0 1 2 6 1 7

Printed in the United States of America

∞This paper meets the requirements of ANSI/NISO Z39.48-1992 (Permanence of Paper)

Lance J. LoRusso, Esq.

Author of *Blue Line Lawyer,*
The Legal Blog for Cops

A Blue Line Lawyer publication

www.bluelinelawyer.com

As always, much love and appreciation to my wife, Barbara, who always knows when to speak up and save me, sometimes from myself.

Any fool can know. The point is to understand.

—Albert Einstein

Contents

Disclaimer

This is a guide for law enforcement officers and law enforcement agencies for responding to and effectively handling media events and critical incidents. I will use the terms "law enforcement officer" and "officer" throughout this book. I hope you will interpret this term to mean just that—anyone who puts on a badge and gun and agrees to be a part of that thin blue line that separates order from anarchy. Whether their badges say "police," "sheriff," "agent," "corrections," "trooper," "ranger," "constable," "warden," "marshal," or any other law enforcement professional, they all share the same goal: to fulfill their sworn duties and return home at the end of each shift. Across the United States, their missions vary little in the final analysis and any variations are irrelevant for the purposes of this book. I use the term "journalist" in the same sense— whether writing for the *New York Times* or a local paper, speaking in soundbites on a small radio show in a tiny market, or sitting in the anchor chair of a major news show, journalists are those committed to telling the story of humanity.

The information presented stems from my own research and experiences based upon nearly twenty-five years of interacting with numerous local, national, and international media outlets, as well as the informal media comprised of blogs, nonprofessional media sources and outlets, and social media. At the time of this writing, I have conducted over three hundred interviews with every type of media since publishing *When Cops Kill: The Aftermath of a Critical Incident* in 2012, and at least 150 more as a law enforcement officer and an attorney before then.

Nothing contained herein is proposed or intended as legal advice, which is very fact-specific and may vary depending upon where you live. Put more simply in the vernacular of the ubiquitous social media posts that inundate us: Seriously? Are you expecting legal advice you can apply to specific situations from a book about situations in general? LOL! (Sorry, I couldn't resist!) Careers and reputations are preserved through the expeditious use of legal advice. It is well worth the investment. Get a clue, tighten your belt, and hire a lawyer. Be smart. Individual law enforcement officers of all ranks can and should join the Fraternal Order of Police (FOP) as well as the Fraternal Order of Police Legal Defense Plan. Go to www.foplegal.com for more details. Members of the FOP Legal Defense Plan will find a plan run by current and retired law enforcement officers who are all FOP members. The plan will provide an attorney of your choosing for you and, under most circumstances, the plan will cover your legal fees and expenses without a cap. With few exceptions, the plan is unlimited. You cannot afford to work in law enforcement anymore without this protection.

I also recognize that journalists, producers, journalism students, and editors are also likely to read a book about law enforcement and media relations. To them, I say candidly that I truly respect your profession. The bravery of the journalists working by candlelight over presses in root cellars was just as much a key to the American Revolution that gave rise to the First Amendment and a free country as the soldiers and citizens who fought in the streets. By that same measure, I also believe the printing press was as valuable a weapon as the Kentucky long rifle, the "assault weapon" of its day. The freedoms we enjoy, especially the freedom of the press, would not exist without a combination of the two.

The principles in this book regarding journalists, especially those related to the competitive nature of the media, apply to all journalists throughout the world. One need only watch the coverage of a high-profile officer-involved shooting, use of force, or a highly charged political issue to learn this lesson. Journalists from all over the world will track and report stories that interest their customers and trigger their watchdog instincts. Therefore, the recommendations for law enforcement officers and agencies contained in this book transcend the borders of the United States. It is also a stark reminder to all American law enforcement officers and agencies that the events occurring in your community could be broadcast around the world in minutes.

Through this book, I hope journalists will learn about the law enforcement officers and law enforcement agencies with whom they interact each day, and make a concerted effort to continually increase the depth of their knowledge about the law and police procedure. We all benefit from a broader understanding of the person standing in front of us. I know the law enforcement officers reading this will grow in their understanding of journalists and why they conduct themselves as they do.

Preface

I wrote this book to heighten the mutual understanding of two groups—law enforcement and journalists. They work side by side, sometimes in concert, and often like brothers and sisters riding across the county in a station wagon, fussing at each other at every opportunity. Like those imbroglios that seem important only to the participants, conflicts between law enforcement and journalists often stem from a lack of understanding. My hope is to broaden the knowledge of both and thereby improve their relationships. Hopefully, one day the shouts of "Are we there yet?" will be replaced with the satisfaction of announcing, "We arrived here together."

Acknowledgments

Books are a conglomeration of effort by many individuals. The author's name is on the front for fame or the firing squad, but many build the bones of the critter and give it life. Many thanks to my editors and the staff at BookLogix, and my researchers, especially Kate Craig, as well as those who provided feedback and comments along the way. Many thanks, as always, to Julie "Eagle Eye" Wiedeman. Special thanks to my "editor and spouse" Barbara G. LoRusso, PhD, who has read each and every word I've written several times to ensure that I make sense.

Introduction

When I published *When Cops Kill: The Aftermath of a Critical Incident*[1] in December 2012, I faced criticism over two main issues. First, people wanted to know why I chose to call the book "When Cops Kill." They said, "People will think it's an anti-law enforcement book!" This never bothered me, as the profits from the book support law enforcement charities like the Fraternal Order of Police Foundation.[2] To date, I have been fortunate to have donated over $10,000 to law enforcement charities from the sale of *When Cops Kill*. The profits from *Blue News* will follow the same path.

The second criticism was more direct. "Why use the word 'kill?' You will just incite people." In response, I reminded readers that the word "kill" is a verb meaning "to deprive of life; to destroy the life of an animal or person."[3] The word implies no malice and accurately describes the act of taking a life, so it was an appropriate choice of words for the title. As to inciting emotion, a little incitement is good for the soul now and then. It also sparks and fosters a healthy curiosity—perhaps enough to get more people to look between the front and back covers of *When Cops Kill*. Irrespective of their motivation for buying and reading the book, I am honored people have done so.

Another issue people had with the title was the use of the words "critical incident." I cannot tell you how many journalists, often off the air and off the record, asked me, "What do you mean by a 'critical incident'?" The question caught me somewhat off guard at first. I mean, to me, it was self-explanatory. However, I guess I should have remembered that self-explanatory is an oxymoron. What is self-explanatory to one man is a question for the ages for another. So began my long effort to explain the meaning of a critical incident to non-law enforcement officers; law enforcement officers seem to understand it without hesitation. This book will explore the difference so that readers will not only understand the term, but also empathize with those who have lived through one.

The work of law enforcement officers often forms the basis for media stories, and as such fuels the economy of media outlets. Officer-involved shootings, high-profile arrests, police chases, and the injuries and deaths of law enforcement officers grab and retain headlines. More importantly—and more recently—allegations of law enforcement officer misconduct have dominated headlines and likely sold more advertising space and newspapers than any other real or manufactured scandal. Perhaps the people driving this attention sought to deflect the spotlight, or at least cause it to dim in other areas.

In the middle of these stories, existing before and long after the headlines are popular and the links are trending, are law enforcement officers who wake up and go to work every day. They are like everyone else in that regard. They differ, however, in three critical respects. First, they wear the uniform and badge of their office, clothed with the authority of the State. Second, they kiss and hug their families goodbye, and the people on both sides of the embrace know it may be their last. Third, for some of them it will be their last day on this earth, or their lives will change forever because of the uniform and badge they wear.

Attacks upon and death threats to law enforcement officers are nothing new. I remember reading my first briefing about a group advocating for the open killing of law enforcement officers during a squad meeting in 1990 before beginning night shift as a street cop. It was unnerving to say the least, especially for a young police officer. In 2016, many of those threats came to fruition in Dallas, Texas, and Baton Rouge, Louisiana, and before that in 2014 with the murders of New York Police Officers Ramos and Liu. The current trend of openly bashing and condemning law enforcement, ironically under the guise of calling for an end to judging all people by the actions of a few, has allowed vocal and often ignorant small groups to grab and hold media attention. Although ignorance, like the quest for knowledge, knows no bounds, readers will learn enough to open their eyes. This only works, however, if they are willing to look.

Chapter One

The Critical Incident

Other than random attacks, all such cases begin with the decision of a police officer to do something, to help, to arrest, to inquire. If the officer had decided to do nothing, then no force would have been used. In this sense, the police officer always causes the trouble. But it is trouble which the police officer is sworn to cause, which society pays him to cause and which, if kept within constitutional limits, society praises the officer for causing.[4]

The words "critical incident" seem to strike most law enforcement officers as nearly intuitive. In fact, the marketing materials for my firm announce that I respond to the scene of critical incidents. Never once have I had an officer ask what I meant. Perhaps a critical incident is simply known to those in law enforcement in a manner such as the United States Supreme Court described pornography:

> I shall not today attempt further to define the kinds of material I understand to be embraced within that shorthand description []; and perhaps I could never succeed in intelligibly doing so. But I know it when I see it . . .[5]

Perhaps it is because law enforcement officers accept as routine events, predicaments, and a work day filled with occurrences that the average person would consider critical, but officers handle these situations and move on to the next call for service or request for assistance. They are routine to a point and regarded as such because they happen so frequently. However, every law enforcement officer knows that any call, no matter how routine, can shift classifications from a boring event to a critical incident in a microsecond. So, let's explore the meaning of the words and learn why non-law enforcement officers struggle with the term.

A critical incident is an event that raises the stakes of life and death, as well as liability for the officer. By liability, I mean civil liability as well as the fear and risk of prosecution and incarceration. You see, officers are called upon to take actions that the average citizen finds distasteful, sometimes abhorrent, and often frightening. They drive through dangerous neighborhoods, speaking to children on one street and witnessing drug deals on another. They respond to domestic disputes and see people injured and killed by the ones they love, and remove children from those environments. They respond to crimes in progress and are sometimes forced to take a human life to save their own or the life of a stranger. However, as stated quite eloquently by the quote at the start of this chapter, society calls upon the law enforcement officer to take those actions and reserves the right to judge her for it. Every officer knows that judgment will not take place in the darkness or environment in which the decision was made. Such judgment follows painstaking and laborious analysis in the light of day, in the safety of lawyers' offices, newsrooms, and the conference rooms of politicians. The pressure to pass judgment will be barely palpable compared to the forces demanding action by the officers at the time of the event, and the very same people calling for her head will be praying for her presence when they are in danger.

The United States Supreme Court recognized this dichotomy in the landmark case of *Graham v. Connor* when Chief Justice Rehnquist wrote:

> The 'reasonableness' of a particular use of force must be judged from the perspective of a reasonable officer on the scene, rather than with the 20/20 vision of hindsight. With respect to a claim of excessive force, the same standard of reasonableness at the moment applies: 'Not every push or shove, even if it may later seem

unnecessary in the peace of a judge's chambers,' violates the Fourth Amendment.[6]

Therefore, the calculus that allows an event to become a critical incident arises somewhat from the level of scrutiny the law enforcement officer will likely face from the media, the department, the government for which she works, the district attorney, civil litigants, and the public.

It is important for readers to keep in mind that officers willingly put themselves into situations that may rise to the level of a critical incident. Traffic stops can turn deadly, and an officer may be forced to use deadly force. Any use of deadly force is a critical incident. This is especially true when a suspect is injured or killed. A law enforcement officer may be involved in a traffic crash that causes a serious injury or the death of a motorist. This turns into a critical incident even if the officer is not at fault because the officer and the employing government entity can expect a lawsuit to arise from the occurrence. A suspect who attacks an officer or resists arrest may be severely injured or die even if the officer did not use deadly force or discharge her weapon. This also becomes a critical incident. Finally, the serious injury or loss of life that, when viewed through the wonderful lens of hindsight, could have been prevented by more or less action by the officer also becomes a critical incident. This is true even though the law is clear that law enforcement officers do not owe a duty to protect the public at large. "[N]othing in the language of the Due Process Clause itself requires the State to protect the life, liberty, and property of its citizens against invasion by private actors. The Clause is phrased as a limitation on the State's power to act, not as a guarantee of certain minimal levels of safety and security."[7]

The scrutiny applied to the officer following a critical incident applies to the law enforcement agency, as well. This is an important point and explains why law enforcement agencies find themselves the subject of scrutiny and media pressure that they never expected and for which they are often unprepared. The critical incident frequently seems routine, at least somewhat, to the agency. Even an officer-involved shooting is an expected event in the law enforcement profession.

Even though the public seems to react with shock every time a law enforcement officer shoots someone, to the officer and the law enforcement agency, the event is always reasonably foreseeable and a function of the law of averages. If officers respond to enough calls, in areas with enough crime, and encounter enough people who have been released from prison and committed crimes in the past, sooner or later the officer will find herself in a life-threatening situation and her training will take over. While the public often finds any use of deadly force surprising, as I explained to a *New York Times* journalist, "Private citizens don't get paid to use deadly force; law enforcement officers do."[8] In fact, the opposite is also true. Under certain circumstances, the public would expect sanctions for an officer who did not use deadly force when required to save the life of the officer or a citizen. Therefore, when an officer shoots someone, the law enforcement agency begins an analysis set out in policy that is a function of its mission as a government entity. It is an event for which the agency prepared, and if it were not prepared, the agency would justifiably face scrutiny.

While the law enforcement agency begins the process of investigating the officer-involved shooting, word of the incident begins to reach the public and the media. Do not think for a moment that the agency and the command staff do not recognize the gravity of the matter at hand; far from it. However, the agency, a large portion of it in many instances, is focused on the business of investigating; it is part of the mission of the law enforcement agency. It is what we expect them to do, and their efforts and resources are appropriately focused inward toward that task.

Outside the agency, however, a different type of activity has begun. The public learns of the critical incident, as do the journalists in the local media outlets. The public learns of the critical incident in several ways. They may witness the events, they may hear about it from friends, relatives, or coworkers, or, more than likely, they learned about it on social media. Journalists may hear about the critical incident by monitoring law enforcement radio transmissions, phone calls from members of the public, or "leaks" within the law enforcement agency. I will discuss these leaks in more detail in Chapter Four. Once this occurs, the journalists will be driven to learn details, inform the public, monitor the progress of the investigation, and continue reporting whatever information is available as long as the public is interested in the story. I will discuss the reasons why this path is in the DNA of every journalist and every media outlet in Chapter Three.

For the law enforcement officer, the critical incident marks the beginning of a whirlwind that will change her life forever. The personal struggles and the scrutiny by the department, outside agencies, and the media take the officer down a seemingly endless path toward a far-off promise and hope of eventual resolution. As one law enforcement officer told me fifteen years after he was forced to take a life, "I hope that one day I can go the entire day without thinking about it." As the officer works through this process, she begins each day hoping the next will lead her back to a normal life.

For the journalists, the critical incident presents many opportunities and obligations. There is a basic obligation to report the facts of the officer-involved shooting to the public and customers of the journalist's employer. Journalists see their general role as watchdogs over the functions of the government. This is part of the mission of every journalist. The use of deadly force by a law enforcement officer that leads to the death of a citizen naturally creates a legitimate area of inquiry. The opportunities lie in the desire of every journalist, indeed each member of every profession, to practice their craft to the best of their abilities under stress and in furtherance of the ideals they hold in high esteem. So begins the process through which the tension often builds between the media and the law enforcement agency.

The First Days of a
Long Search for Answers

The first few days following a critical incident are typically filled with unknowns. Law enforcement officers and command staff of law enforcement agencies do not like unknowns. They work constantly to prepare for situations by drafting policies, training, performing drills, and dividing departmental resources into specialized units to avoid being caught unprepared for situations they largely view as foreseeable. For the most part, this process works even in situations that would cause the public—and even some seasoned corporate entities—to panic.

For example, a law enforcement agency prepares for an active assailant on a large mall, a bomb threat or the location of a device in a sports arena, or a barricaded and armed subject in a multi-tenant office building. The agency response to these situations falls, more or less, into a process after the initial three- to five-minute response phase is complete. The officers on the scene of all ranks generally know the plan, execute the plan, and investigate the crime. It is what law enforcement agencies and officers do.

In those instances, the private corporations and civilians affected by the incidents stop any sense of normalcy. Businesses in the area close, employees go home, and people wait for the law enforcement agency to give the "all clear" signal. However, the advantage to these scenarios for law enforcement agencies is that they do not happen often. Additionally, they do not last long. Even though the investigation may go on for months, the actual time on the scene is rarely more than a matter of hours or a couple of days. This is not the case with a critical incident that attracts widespread media attention.

The critical incident is also different for the media outlets. Most often, news events are covered by local media outlets. If the story gains traction beyond the borders of a metro area or a state, local affiliates or local journalists will feed the news to larger networks. Interviews may be done by remote feed to news anchors in other cities, and phone interviews usually will satisfy the customers of the news agencies. Even international news sources will reprint stories of interest they obtain through the Associated Press or internet sources.

The Associated Press,[9] which was founded in 1846, is a source for news around the globe, but most law enforcement officers have no idea how those stories come to be. If you look at your local newspaper or internet news source, you will see the initials "AP" at the beginning of many stories. This indicates that the story, or at least portions of the news story, were provided by the Associated Press (AP). It is also possible that the entire news story was written by the AP staff and copied wholesale, with permission and according to an agreement, by the source you are reading. The AP is a not-for-profit news cooperative organization owned by member news organizations. It is not controlled by a single business entity or any government. The staff is overwhelmingly comprised of journalists and boasts over fifty Pulitzer Prizes for journalism and more than thirty in photojournalism. Based in New York, the AP has more than 280 locations around the world.[10]

So, here is one fact that every law enforcement officer and the head of every law enforcement agency must understand: the AP is interested in news stories that have a larger focus and wider interest than the local news typically covered by your local paper, radio stations, or television news stations. The AP is widely regarded as a professional and ethical news organization. This means that they will make efforts to gather facts and report stories of interest to their member companies and their consumers. As to ethics, the AP provides a long list of its ethical standards, guidelines, and principles. You can find them in detail on their website at www.ap.org under "Company" and "News Values." However, one portion of those values I believe demonstrates their commitment to professionalism and should provide law enforcement officers and agencies with a level of comfort when the AP is involved in reporting a critical incident:

> It means we must be fair. Whenever we portray someone in a negative light, we must make a real effort to obtain a response from that person. When mistakes are made, they must be corrected – fully, quickly and ungrudgingly.[11]

I believe you will agree that fairness is the number-one concern of any person or entity that finds itself the subject of a news story.

While the involvement of the AP may mean that the agency will be dealing with professional journalists, it also signals to law enforcement officers and agencies that the critical incident you are dealing with right now just garnered national attention. This brings a new level of scrutiny and pressure to release information. At the very least, members of the AP will be pressing the law enforcement agency for information and details to feed the stories they are writing. More requests for information mean more demands on manpower and more pressure in the political sense on the governing entity. In short, the city mayor may act very differently to a few requests for information from local journalists than a request from CNN.

On the other end of the spectrum, coverage by the AP may encourage national and international news media to send a correspondent or journalist to the location. This may be done to gain information from local sources like courthouses, law enforcement agencies, or even neighbors, or to just have a person on the ground to increase the credibility of the stories they publish. This is especially important in high-profile incidents and increasingly more common in high-profile critical incidents.

Shortly after George Zimmerman shot Trayvon Martin on February 26, 2012, the story quickly captured national attention. Within a few days, news sources from around the United States were present in Sanford, Florida. Soon thereafter, the story gained international attention. I was even interviewed twice about the murder trial of George Zimmerman by Radio Russia. Once news coverage reaches those levels, the stories seem to take on lives of their own. The news hits a twenty-four-hour news cycle (explained more in Chapter Seven), the requests for information become fluid and endless, and the resources of the law enforcement agency become overwhelmed, often without a clear plan to handle the situation. Unlike a bomb threat or active shooter, it is difficult to write a policy for a situation that at one time occurred so infrequently that law enforcement agencies across the United States had no set of facts upon which they could draft a policy. However, that is no longer the case.

The same pattern emerged in Ferguson, Missouri, following the death of Michael Brown on August 9, 2014; in New York City after the death of Eric Garner on July 17, 2014; and in other high-profile officer-involved shootings in the past five years. Remember, during this time many resources of the law enforcement agency are already engaged in the investigation of the critical incident, as well as meeting with members of the community and preparing for or dealing with threats of civil unrest.

What is happening to the law enforcement officers who were involved in the critical incident during this time period? Well, that depends upon the size of the department, the nature of the critical incident, the location of the law enforcement agency in the United States, and the individual officers themselves. While there is no national standard about releasing the names of involved law enforcement officers, following the death of Michael Brown, there has been increasing pressure to force law enforcement agencies to release the names of involved officers as soon as possible. For example, the City of Philadelphia Police Department has a written policy mandating the release of the involved "officer's name, years of service, assignment, and duty status" within seventy-two hours following an officer-involved shooting.[12] Once those names have been released, the world changes for those officers, their coworkers, their families, and their neighbors. Quiet neighbor-hoods become staging areas for news trucks, people are interviewed while walking their dogs and retrieving their newspapers, and officers may be forced to leave their homes due to death threats.

The department will be under great pressure to release this information, and there have been some efforts to mandate the release in a certain number of days through legislation. However, irrespective of the forms the efforts take, I believe there will be a continued push to release this information quickly. In a few cases involving officer-involved shootings in 2015, the law enforcement agencies acted quickly in releasing available details: the information known to the law enforcement officers before the officer-involved shooting; information about the decedent; and the name and work history of the law enforcement officer. This has not only immediately countered claims that the law enforcement agency was obstructing justice, but also averted a great deal of national media attention. While this is certainly not a laboratory experiment capable of replication, it appears that this tactic has worked. However, I can foresee scenarios in which a quick release of the officer's name would not be appropriate, such as when death threats appear immediately on social media and the agency must take precautions to safeguard the officer and her family. Sadly, such threats have become the norm.

Following up in the Search
for Answers and a Resolution

The critical incident does not fade in a matter of weeks, even though the fevered nature of the news coverage may subside. The news coverage of the death of Michael Brown became just as much an effort to cover the civil unrest as the shooting itself. In Ferguson, an additional officer-involved shooting occurred in a neighboring city a few days after Michael Brown died but coverage of that incident was, to a large extent, overshadowed by the riots in Ferguson.[13] The civil unrest also caused part of the intense media coverage of the death of Freddie Gray in Baltimore, Maryland, on April 12, 2015. I bring this up to remind readers that every officer-involved shooting resulting in national and international media attention will not result in months of intense coverage and scrutiny. However, in the current environment, this scenario is increasingly more likely.

After the first few days of the critical incident pass, several events will bring the events back into the media spotlight. The good news is that the law enforcement agency should be able to anticipate these and nearly schedule the inevitable media attention. However, time and again agencies seem surprised by the upswell of media attention and appear unprepared and annoyed by a renewed round of media inquiries. Perhaps the better practice is to estimate the timeframe for those events as best as possible, provide that timeline to the media during their initial coverage of the critical incident, and prepare to have a press release, press conference, or phone calls made to journalists who you know are following the case. At the very least, the agency's command staff and media team, such as public information officers, must be aware of this timeline.

Here are some examples of the events that will trigger follow-up inquiries and will likely result in news stories. This list is as exhaustive as possible, but not all of the items on the list will apply to every critical incident. It is intended as a guide to perhaps consider some events that law enforcement officers and agency command staff believe are routine and may not, in their minds, trigger follow-up news coverage. I created this list based upon my experience representing law enforcement officers in officer-involved shooting cases, as well as cases that I have followed for my own purposes or to prepare for media interviews. Of course, if the law or agency policies provide specific deadlines for the release of information, you must follow the law or seek a court order with good cause that will release you from that obligation. Otherwise, schedule the release, advertise the release, and prepare for the release of that information.

- ❖ Release of the names of the involved law enforcement officers
- ❖ Death of involved law enforcement officer(s)
- ❖ Death of involved person shot or injured
- ❖ Release of video from the law enforcement agency
- ❖ Discovery or release of video from bystanders
- ❖ Results of toxicology from the person shot or killed
- ❖ Results of toxicology of involved law enforcement officers, including any workers' compensation required testing
- ❖ Results of ballistic tests
- ❖ Results of DNA tests
- ❖ Results of any related accident investigation, such as speed calculations or the download of airbag modules or crash data recorders
- ❖ Filing of any *ante litem* notices[14] or other required pre-suit notifications[15]
- ❖ Completion of the criminal investigation
- ❖ Completion of the administrative investigation
- ❖ Involved law enforcement officers being discharged from the hospital
- ❖ Person shot or injured being discharged from the hospital
- ❖ The law enforcement officer returning to work
- ❖ The law enforcement officer being disciplined or terminated
- ❖ Consideration of the case by prosecutors
- ❖ Decisions by prosecutors
- ❖ Grand jury presentments and deliberations
- ❖ Grand jury decisions (no bill, indictments, or civil determinations)
- ❖ Inquiries by the United States Department of Justice (USDOJ)
- ❖ Results of USDOJ investigations
- ❖ Any other use of deadly force by the involved law enforcement officers
- ❖ Use of deadly force by another law enforcement officer in the same agency or community

❖ Hearings or trials of the involved law enforcement officers, including verdicts and sentencing
❖ Promotions of the involved law enforcement officers
❖ Discipline of the involved law enforcement officers, even if unrelated to the critical incident
❖ Any other officer-involved shooting or use of force resulting in serious injury to the person shot or injured
❖ The anniversary of the critical incident
❖ Filing of any civil suits
❖ Trials on any civil suits
❖ Results of any civil suits
❖ Arrests of any close relative of the person shot or injured
❖ Protests, vigils, or social media events about the person shot or injured, irrespective of the gathering's size, success, or who organized them

For the law enforcement agencies anticipating one of the events enumerated above, it may seem like the media scrutiny will never end. However, it will generally decrease in intensity with the passage of time. In addition, the media will watch the public reaction to certain events and adjust their level of coverage accordingly. For instance, I represented a law enforcement officer in an officer-involved shooting, and after several planned rallies failed to produce more than a handful of participants, the media barely covered them. You will be able to gauge the media response based upon the attention afforded the last significant event. However, you cannot allow your agency's response, or lack thereof, to become the news story.

Every Critical Incident Is an Opportunity to Educate and Advocate

It is easy to look at media inquiries during and following a critical incident as nothing more than a huge distraction for the law enforcement agency. However, I hope that this book will convince you otherwise. Every media inquiry is an opportunity to tell the story of your law enforcement agency: how you select and train law enforcement officers; how you maintain standards; the experience and effectiveness of your investigators; and how you remain responsive to requests for information are only a few examples. Further, every media interaction is an opportunity to educate the media and the public about the laws surrounding the use of force by law enforcement officers, the unlawfulness of resistance to law enforcement commands, and the local and national statistics of those injured and killed in the line of duty.

Agencies should take every opportunity to provide statistics on the types of weapons used against law enforcement officers and the number of law enforcement officers assaulted in their agency, in their county, statewide, and throughout the United States. Agencies should have readily available the daytime and nighttime population of the city or county and the number of arrests made annually by their agency, in their county, statewide, and across the United States. If possible, agencies should have a good-faith estimate of the number of law enforcement officer-citizen contacts annually in their department. Compare the number of arrests to that number, and show that the overwhelming number of interactions between law enforcement officers and citizens are peaceful. The statistics clearly support this fact.

I have used a set of statistics for the past several years in my classes. I will present them below:

YEAR	NUMBER OF ARRESTS[16]
2009	13,687,241
2010	13,120,947
2011	12,408,899
2012	12,196,959
TOTAL	**51,414,046**

These statistics not only give journalists and the public something to consider, they also encourage further research by the media.

In the past several years, there has been a rise in the use of raw statistics by journalists. That is not to say that journalists have not used statistics in the past. However, in the past, the statistics formed the basis of the story and were used to lend credibility to the information presented. Today, there is a trend to make the statistics the story. There are many reasons cited for this phenomenon, but perhaps the answer is quite simple. Young, tech-savvy journalists have learned that the internet and open-record laws provide access to statistics that were either unavailable before or, perhaps worse, not organized and compiled.[17] While researchers have always been performing surveys and bringing the results of studies into the forefront through scholarly articles, those articles only saw the light of day if they were discovered by a journalist and interpreted through the news story. Today, that same researcher can publish the statistics directly to the public via the internet and informal media to millions of people at no cost. Unfortunately, often those statistics-driven stories provide no context for the numbers presented.

Law enforcement officers involved in a critical incident want something simple: support. Even if they are ultimately cleared of any charges and exonerated in every court and investigation possible, my past clients have confirmed to me that the way in which they were treated in the hours and days following the critical incident made the difference for them as to whether they recovered emotionally or whether they remained part of the law enforcement profession. If they will be criminally charged or disciplined, they should still be treated with respect. If you are a chief, administrator, or sheriff who believes that every law enforcement officer should be treated as a suspect following a critical incident, I urge you to make a great contribution to the law enforcement profession and get out. Remember that all of the law enforcement officers in your agency are watching how you treat the law enforcement officer who is currently under the microscope.

I will close this section with a quote from *When Cops Kill: The Aftermath of a Critical Incident*.

> Q: Do you think one of the roles of the supervisors after a shooting is to look after the officer and protect his rights just as they would anyone else?
>
> A: I think it's probably . . . I think it's the primary role, taking care of that officer.
>
> — *Thirty-two-year veteran of law enforcement*

Chapter Two

The Feeding Frenzy

The newspapers! Sir, they are the most villainous, licentious, abominable, infernal—not that I ever read them. No, I make a rule never to look into a newspaper.

The Critic Act I, Scene 2,
by Richard Brinsley Sheridan

At one point, I believe CNN alone had seventy-eight full-time employees living in Ferguson, Missouri. We were also getting daily media requests from international news sources from Japan, Germany, Australia, Canada, Britain. As much as the press was looking for and putting out stories, the social media sources were more of an issue. Information was going out so quickly, and some of it was wrong. It was so hard to correct. The ability to counter the bad info was hampered because traditional media contacts were too slow.

Colonel Ron Replogle, commander of the Missouri
Highway Patrol, retired, commander of law
enforcement operations in Ferguson, Missouri, per
order of Governor Jay Nixon during the aftermath of
the Michael Brown shooting

There is a unique parallel between law enforcement officers and the media. If you have been around law enforcement agencies or watched the news a few nights, you have seen the similarity. Oddly enough, it relates to the manner in which officers and journalists perform their duties on a daily basis. It is the concept of a "beat," and it is critical information for officers interacting with journalists.

Long before law enforcement officers worked in radio-dispatched cars, they worked "beats," or designated areas of patrol on foot, horseback, bicycles, and vehicles. These beats were geographically designated assignments and drove the work of the law enforcement officer and the agency.

For example, a law enforcement officer on the beat in a downtown area would patrol a specific section of the city. If they took a report of a crime, the investigators or detectives who followed up on that crime would also handle crimes in that area. Sometimes, the beat would be patrolled by plainclothes officers. Perhaps the most famous example is the work of Cleveland Detective Martin McFadden on Halloween 1963, when he stopped and patted down Mr. Terry, Mr. Katz, and Mr. Chilton on the corner of Huron Road and Euclid Avenue. This encounter led to the legal foundation of perhaps the most prolific search and officer safety technique: the stop and frisk.[18]

The concept of a beat is part of the DNA of any state and local law enforcement officer. Protectors by nature, law enforcement officers are encouraged to "learn" their beats and the people and businesses within. They are encouraged to "handle" their beats by not only responding to all calls for service in that area, but also actively patrolling to suppress crime and look for and investigate criminal activity and suspicious circumstances in the spirit of Detective McFadden. Many law enforcement officers would be surprised to learn that journalists perform their duties in a similar fashion.

"Beat reporting" is not a new concept. Journalists' duties are divided among beats as well. In any news organization, there will likely be a government beat, a society beat, an investigative reporting beat, and a police beat. Those beats may be further broken down by geographic area. For example, I have been interviewed by the *New York Times* and the *Wall Street Journal* several times. The journalists who interviewed me about use of force by law enforcement officers are not assigned to the international sections of their respective papers. They routinely cover law enforcement matters ranging from high-profile arrests of criminals, law enforcement techniques, allegations of police corruption, government investigations into police conduct, and officer-involved shootings. These two publications allow me to illustrate my point as they routinely cover events and news from around the world. However, both divide the world and topics into segments and regions. The goal is to match an informed journalist with the story she is investigating and ultimately reporting.

Much like the law enforcement officer on the beat, the journalist is expected to learn their beat from the top down. The advice below is quoted from Sonya Smith's article featured on the Society of Professional Journalists' website entitled, "Beat Guide: Your First Beat." Her advice should sound familiar to law enforcement officers.

Learn all about the beat.
Spend extra time in the first few weeks reading up and learning about the beat. Find experts to meet with and learn from. On my beat, for example, growth is a big issue—so I met with a city planner who explained to me how city planning, development and building work.

Find good sources.
Finding quality sources doesn't happen overnight—but they are invaluable to your beat-building. Meet, face to face, each person on the beat—exchange business cards and talk about what information they can provide.

Ask for cell phone and home phone numbers to contact them after hours. Be fair to the sources—work hard to give them adequate time to call back and the ability to say "I don't know"—then they'll understand when there is breaking news.

Find a good mentor.
Finding a good mentor will help make your journalism career. Try to find someone who will give frank advice on your ideas, reporting, writing and journalism future.[19]

To me, this sounds a lot like the advice I received in the police academy—learn the beat, learn the people in it, be ready to respond quickly under stress, and be responsible for your beat. Want more parallels? The field training officer is the counterpart to the senior journalist and acts as a mentor within the news agency. The law enforcement officer's informants and sources correspond to the people the journalist meets, and often seeks out, in advance of needing specific information. This is akin to the officer who stops his patrol car and speaks to the street vendor or store owner before information is needed on a suspect. Both the officer and the journalist are working toward a common goal: building relationships.

Different Goals Lead to Different Definitions of Success

A critical incident, especially an officer-involved shooting, generally triggers two law enforcement investigations. An administrative investigation will determine if the officer violated policy, if their training was adequate, and if they were properly equipped to perform the task. A criminal investigation will go forward just like any other with the goal and sworn charge to determine if probable cause exists that a crime took place and if a specific person committed that crime with an arrest to follow, if appropriate. If the use of force was justified under the law, then no crime was committed.[20]

Both investigations rely upon the benefit of time and diligence. One well-respected text on homicide investigation states that a basic principle of homicide investigation is "you've got one shot to get it right."[21] This drives the course of action of the investigators and means three basic tenets are always at play. First, the investigation will be deliberate. Second, the investigators will be diligent and persistent. Finally, the investigation, although moving at an appropriate pace, will not be rushed. Anyone who has ever worked with investigators— especially homicide investigators—knows they do not become warm and fuzzy when pushed to close an investigation before it is appropriate to do so, to make an arrest before they are ready, or to take the investigation in a direction not dictated by the facts, their evidence, and their experience. The same is true of administrative or internal investigations, although in my experience they are sometimes subjected to pressure to complete their investigations in a timely manner, often in the interests of due process or to preserve reputations. The investigators are nonetheless just as diligent as their counterparts involved in the criminal investigation.

So, it is fair to expect that law enforcement officers are not in a rush to provide information to journalists to assist them in meeting their deadlines. From their perspective, and the perspective of their supervisors and chain of command, their first obligation is to their sworn duties. Often part of those sworn duties is to keep information very close to the vest in order to properly vet potential witnesses.

Media goals are far different during and after a critical incident. The critical incident sparks an assignment of the story to journalists. Some stories are assigned to journalists based upon the regions to which they are assigned, and others are assigned to journalists who typically work with law enforcement officers and agencies. Irrespective of which journalist picks up the story, they have a set of obligations and, more importantly, a set of bosses who will hold them accountable. So when the journalists respond to the scene, which they typically do, they will be focused on getting as much of the required information as possible.

So now you have an image in your mind of dozens of journalists driving up to the crime scene tape, setting up cameras and tape recorders, and running up to the tape, shouting questions. Fortunately, with very few exceptions, that is not accurate. Most journalists will look for an opportunity to interview a law enforcement officer while simultaneously working their contacts within the law enforcement agency for information. They will also likely be in contact with the public information officers, or PIOs, for the involved agencies, of which there may be several, looking for a press release, an organized or impromptu press conference, or some official word of what occurred. Simply put, the journalists want to be able to tell their customers, the public, what happened and what will likely happen next.

However, the journalists are not likely to be standing around, patiently waiting for officers and agencies to respond. This means they will look to other sources of information, including bystanders and witnesses. This should be expected for several reasons. First, the journalists are in competition with other news outlets. They are part of a profession that seeks to be first in reporting news. They are just like any other private corporation; they have a desire to be better than their competition. Second, depending upon the time of day that the critical incident occurs, the journalists will be under added time pressure to meet the deadlines of their respective employers. For radio and television journalists, this may provide them with a very short window in which they must gather what they can, prepare a story known internally as a "package," and get ready to be on the air with the story. That story will be short. A time allotment of more than a minute or two is unusual, especially for breaking news.

At the outset, we see the potential for conflict. The law enforcement officers and the agency are driven by a goal to be diligent, complete, and proceed without allowing the clock to drive the outcome. On the media side, in many respects, the clock is the driving force. Many times, especially with a high-profile officer-involved shooting, the desire to be first with the facts and to meet production deadlines places the clock as the *only* driving force, second only to a concern for liability for reporting inaccurate facts. Can you see the inherent conflict of goals and the potential for friction? Can you also see the stage is set for frustration on an individual level? After all, on both sides of this equation there are people doing their jobs, answering to bosses, and hoping to be viewed as not only competent, but excelling beyond their peers.

Let's explore the difference in goals. We'll keep the sides the same to be consistent. The law enforcement officers and the agency are focused on the prosecution and possible civil cases. Both of those potential events most likely will occur years after the critical incident. However, on the media side, their story is over when it is published. They may—and likely will—report follow-up stories, but their responsibility is to their bosses and their customers, and it generally ends when they report that story. Of course there are exceptions, as when the story itself sparks interest from broader news sources, management, or the journalist. However, this, in my opinion, is the biggest difference between law enforcement on one side and the media on the other. It also may be the biggest reason why journalists will go to press or in front of a camera with information supplied by neighbors, people in the area, coworkers, or other sources who have no indicia of reliability.

Law Enforcement Activities Following an Officer-Involved Shooting	Media Activities Following an Officer-Involved Shooting
Diligent, deliberate, and driven by procedure	Driven by deadlines and competition
Thoroughness is more important than speed	Speed and content are priorities
Sources of information must be vetted and scrutinized	Sources of information are likely trusted with little or no vetting process due to time constraints
Activities are subject to review by courts and the chain of command	Activities are subject to critique by customers and superiors
Maintain careful and detailed documentation of the information gathered and the sources	May keep notes on sources for the purpose of follow-up stories or for liability purposes
Must keep details confidential to vet potential witnesses and suspects	Rewarded for disclosing as much information as possible as quickly as possible
Investigate, document, and take action, expecting eventual scrutiny in criminal and civil court proceedings	Investigate and document enough to obtain the facts for a story and shield themselves and their employers from liability
Focused on the future use of the information, evidence, and findings they make	Focused on the next deadline and obtaining information for follow-up stories
Lawsuits for false arrest, false statements about individuals, mistakes in procedure are anticipated and highly likely in the event of an error	Lawsuits based upon inaccuracies are rare and typically easily defended based upon case law[22]

Most media training for law enforcement officers is focused on providing details when the law enforcement agency and officers are not the focus of the story, like a bus accident, multiple burglaries, or the search for a wanted or missing person. In those cases, the agency provides information and responds to questions pointed at someone else. Was the driver intoxicated? Is the suspect in custody? How many people are injured? In these instances, there is a comfortable exchange of information because the law enforcement agency has the information at hand and desires to share it as soon as they are able to do so. Journalists in this scenario find themselves asking straight forward questions and receiving information, sometimes from multiple sources within the law enforcement agency. The end result is that everyone is generally happy. The law enforcement agency is able to satisfy its obligation to get information out to the public, and the journalists are able to draft and report fact-filled and compelling stories.

However, the formula changes when the law enforcement agency or individual law enforcement officers become the story. I suspect part of this tension is primal. No one wants to be the focus of a potentially negative, or more accurately, "non-positive" media story. It is uncomfortable, it can be embarrassing, and it can make you feel like the story is omnipresent. I know, as I have been the subject of one driven by a person with a broad, negative agenda and carried by a journalist who surprisingly was not able to understand that he was being played. I say this only to let you know that I understand the temptation to build walls, push away trusted journalists, and just hide while wishing the story would take another direction. I heard one person who was in the middle of a grueling media campaign focused on him wonder what natural disaster or manmade catastrophe would be big enough to pull the spotlight in another direction. Sometimes, it seems that is what it will take.

This is why law enforcement agencies must prepare for these events and learn how to respond. I discuss this planning and preparation in detail later in the book. If you and your agency have never truly been the focus of a negative news story or series of stories, I can assure you it is an experience. Expect constant media inquiries, rapid calls for follow-up stories and information, a barrage of requests pursuant to your state's disclosure laws, and the physical presence of journalists and news trucks at precincts, headquarters, and sometimes at the homes of law enforcement officers.

The frustration of being the focus of a news story can be further exacerbated by a lack of understanding of the guiding principles of journalists and having unrealistic expectations. Everyone will agree that media outlets are comprised of the people who do the work of the corporation. As such, they are not perfect and never will be—neither will law enforcement officers. Journalists will misunderstand, mistakenly misquote your words, and report information that later is proven to be inaccurate or false. One of the reasons this occurs is the human factor referenced earlier, but another is the fact that journalists may rely upon sources that are, or prove to be, unreliable, even if they seemed trustworthy at the time. Sometimes, the journalist relied upon those sources because no one else was available or willing to provide any information.

Another factor is that journalists and law enforcement officers have one huge thing in common, and this trait is shared by millions of people. Both professions tend to trust people in their own profession more than anyone else. We do not think twice about this concept when we discuss other professions, but strangely, law enforcement and journalists are suspicious of this concept. Perhaps it is because of the myth that law enforcement officers distort the truth in some huge conspiracy forming the "thin blue line." Perhaps it is because officers speak with other officers about critical incidents more candidly, because they feel that only another officer will truly understand the issues and their feelings. Irrespective of the reason, everyone involved must acknowledge and keep this basic truth in mind when interacting with each other.

I want to point out two real-world examples of this phenomenon. In the first, I sat in my office with a journalist from a large metropolitan Atlanta television station. She sought the interview following a high-profile officer-involved shooting in Atlanta. I represented the law enforcement officer who fired the shots, and after my media statements had been made and all of the interviews were finished regarding the officer-involved shooting, journalists began contacting me about "the general investigation process," or at least that is how the interview requests were framed. This was my first time working with this journalist, but I did a bit of background and, like most, she was college educated, had experience in other markets prior to working in Atlanta, which is considered a big market, and was given general field assignments as opposed to focusing on a specific area such as government, consumer issues, or law enforcement.

She was, as are most journalists, prepared with a list of questions about the use of deadly force. I answered her questions and pointed her to Georgia statutes by number and United States Supreme Court cases by name, citation, and year. I could tell from her body language and facial expressions, which were off camera, that she was getting frustrated. Finally, she asked me to talk about the "clearly illegal shootings" involving law enforcement officers. When I pressed her to tell me what makes an officer-involved shooting "clearly illegal," she replied, and I quote, "You know, when they shoot someone in the back." I was prepared for this and could see that this interview was about this issue and nothing else. I provided the law, state and federal, that justifies shooting a person in the back, as well as the tactical and training issues that might necessitate shooting a suspect in the back. After I answered, it was clear that her frustration only grew. I then asked her this question: "It is clear to me that you are well educated and prepared for this interview. Who told you that a shooting in which a law enforcement officer shoots someone in the back is 'clearly illegal'? Did you hear that in the newsroom?" Her face turned red, her eyes dropped, and she indicated several cues that anyone trained in interviews and interrogations would recognize as a person who was caught. She was so embarrassed that she could not answer my question. I was prepared to let her off the hook and change the subject. However, she tried to cover for her embarrassment by asking me a question: "Well just because they can legally shoot a person in the back, does that mean they should?" At that point, even her cameraman recognized she had lost credibility.

The lesson from this interaction is that sometimes the information that you provide journalists in the best of efforts and in good faith is outweighed by the information, accurate and otherwise, they receive from their coworkers. Now, I do not fault the coworkers. At the essence, they are no different from any other person who is untrained in the mechanics and laws controlling the use of deadly force. I suspect that the discussions in that newsroom that led to her belief and her questions were no different, and no more founded in research, than the conversations and comments law enforcement officers try to avoid at parties. However, it is said that in the land of the blind the one-eyed man is king. In the newsroom, the coworker with more experience with officer-involved shooting cases, who once worked the police beat, or who perhaps read more detective novels than anyone else, will have some credibility. Do not get frustrated when this happens to you. Expect it, prepare for it, and have the law and the facts ready to trump the rumor mill. View it as I saw this situation: an opportunity for education.

As an aside—and I discuss this in my book, *When Cops Kill: The Aftermath of a Critical Incident*—journalists are not the only people who are swayed and intoxicated by the fragrance of fruit from the rumor mill and quaint sayings or concepts propounded by the uneducated. In the course of a six-and-one-half-hour hearing wherein the family of a deceased suspect was trying to have my law enforcement–officer client arrested for murder via a Georgia procedure that allows a private citizen to seek criminal charges, the attorney for the family asked the investigating special agent with the Georgia Bureau of Investigation this question:

[Isn't it] standard procedure for an officer, before he fires a gun, to just give a warning to tell people, "Get your hands up, I'm going to shoot you"?[23]

This question, which caused the special agent to look a bit perplexed, should not surprise you. Nothing in law school teaches attorneys about the laws and the mechanics of the use of deadly force. Putting aside the fact that this particular attorney took it upon himself to represent the family and still did not properly learn the law or police procedure, if an attorney would make this statement in court on the record, you should not be surprised that journalists who do not read the law on a regular basis might also be completely uninformed and incorrect. Do not allow a question that indicates ignorance lead you to condemn a person as biased. However, their reaction to factual information and the law should be an indicator as to their potential bias as well as their willingness to admit the deficits in their knowledge.

In the second example, two newspapers contacted me in reference to their investigations regarding the number of officer-involved shootings in two regions: one in a metropolitan Atlanta county and the other in a large city in another state. The investigation was proffered to me as an objective look at the number of shootings as compared to the number of law enforcement officers prosecuted for their use of deadly force. After listening to both journalists—and both interviews were long and involved extensive back and forth—it was clear that they were starting their research and beginning their efforts with a premise: if law enforcement officers shoot enough people, a percentage of those law enforcement officers should be prosecuted. It took me a while to get to the root of their premise, but once I discovered it, I posed two questions:

If we train law enforcement officers in the academy on the laws of the use of deadly force; teach them the mechanics of the use of deadly force on the range; force them to demonstrate their proficiency in the use of deadly force; put them through shoot/don't shoot scenarios called "judgmental use of deadly force," then retrain and evaluate them annually, why are you surprised that when they use deadly force, they do so in accordance with the law?

Given this information and reality, shouldn't we expect that none of the officer-involved shootings resulted in criminal charges against the officer?

In both cases, with both journalists, my questions were met with silence. It was clear that neither journalist had ever considered these concepts. Because I have been interacting with journalists for more than twenty years, I was not surprised. I was also prepared to provide the journalists with the facts surrounding law enforcement training, the law that required the training I mentioned, and other resources they could use to not only verify what I said, but also educate themselves. The journalists were well trained, experienced, and driven to draft professional stories. However, their basic premise likely began with a discussion among their peers.

These examples and concepts underscore the reason and importance for law enforcement agencies to build professional relationships with media agencies and individual journalists. Law enforcement officers should take advantage of every opportunity to provide journalists with the law, court cases, training—such as judgmental use of force—and any other experiences that will either raise their knowledge level and awareness, or increase their desire to learn more about law enforcement procedures and the realities of the profession.

Not All Relationships Can Be Repaired or Improved

Despite the efforts of law enforcement agencies, there are some journalists who will not support the mission, tactics, or philosophies of law enforcement agencies and officers. The goal should be to recognize these individuals as quickly as possible and use caution when working with them. In reality, these folks will be rare critters in the forest, although this may vary somewhat geographically. While many journalists will be noncommittal and quiet about their true beliefs, this does not mean that they are anti-law enforcement. Law enforcement officers must recognize that not everyone is as open about their beliefs as they tend to be. Off-duty officers, with few exceptions, are generally open about their beliefs regarding politics, current events, and, ironically, the media. However, I am discussing the truly anti-law enforcement journalist.

This bias is generally discovered one of three ways. The first is rare, but they may state it outright. Statements like, "It doesn't matter what you say, that use of force was wrong," are clear red flags, as is any indication that a person refuses to listen to facts. Second, you may read, hear, or watch a story written by the journalist that rocks you back on your heels. Some examples are clear decisions to ignore facts that you know the journalist had, the inclusion of facts that the journalist knew or should have known were suspect at best, an outright dismissal of facts or questioning the integrity of the facts that have been established, and the use of the facts to make an argument or create the impression that the law enforcement agency or officer is lying. Finally, the journalist may refuse to receive facts, law, information, or experiences offered and accepted by other journalists. While there may be a valid reason that a journalist would "respectfully decline" a raised letter invitation to be exposed to a conducted energy device, an invitation to attend a training class involving PIT maneuvers or judgmental use of deadly force would generally be accepted overwhelmingly. The journalist who is steadfastly anti-law enforcement will be concerned about being perceived by peers as subjecting one's self to "indoctrination" by law enforcement. This gets back to my previous discussions of journalists naturally trusting their peers and coworkers over others and wanting to avoid being viewed as soft or subject to being swayed.

Once you discover that a journalist belongs to this small group, keep that issue present of mind whenever you are dealing with him. Remember that you still must work with him and similar-minded journalists, and the worst thing you can do is treat them differently or decide to tell them "no comment," which is something you should NEVER say to any journalist. I recommend that you still offer them the law, the cases, and the experience opportunities, because the best way to get them to at least be fair is to use peer pressure to your advantage. Sooner or later there will be a conversation among journalists, and other journalists will likely come to your defense—or at least question why the anti-law enforcement journalists would refuse information or an opportunity to learn. You will likely never hear such conversations, but you may see the results.

Like any other set of entrenched beliefs, there are a plethora of reasons why a journalist would become firmly anti-law enforcement. Perhaps they had bad experiences with law enforcement officers; perhaps their family had those experiences; or perhaps, and I have seen this, the journalist has been arrested in the past. It is possible they distrust the power provided to law enforcement officers and agencies on a philosophical level. Whatever the cause, there is a clear truth about firmly held beliefs: they take a long time to develop and may take years to change.

"Information from an Unidentified Source . . ."

More than once, typically following an officer-involved shooting, I've contacted an agency head or city or county attorney to give them the bad news that they have an information leak in their agency. These were difficult conversations. Some of those agency heads and attorneys were my friends, and I could hear the disappointment in their voices.

The unauthorized release of information from inside a law enforcement agency is the subject of much debate. Journalists hold their sources to be sacred and the law supports that position. The aptly named "Reporter's Privilege," also known as the "Newsman's Privilege" or "Shield Laws," is intended to allow reporters to protect sources when legal efforts force them to disclose such information.[24] The concern for the law enforcement agency is several fold. First, without knowing the identity of the source, there is no guarantee that the information being shared is accurate. Second, if the information is accurate, there may be a valid reason why it was not being released through standard channels. Third, if the source is close to the investigation, they should be releasing information only through official channels and their motivation to do otherwise is concerning. Fourth, without an official release of information, there is no way for the agency to ensure that all journalists are receiving information fairly. It would be improper for one journalist to receive information that is not available to others, especially the journalists who "follow the rules" and may truly support the law enforcement agency on a regular basis. Finally, information passed on to journalists from unofficial sources rarely contains only facts. In my experience, such statements are filled with opinions and conjecture.

There is no dispute that a news leak in a law enforcement agency is a problem and in the end can cause serious harm to the relationships between the agency, media outlets, journalists, investigations, and the public by eroding the trust between the entities. So what can be done to avoid these issues? First, it is important to understand that leaks are not limited to law enforcement agencies. A quick scan of breaking news will reveal facts attributed to "a source," "someone who was not authorized to speak on the record," and other indications that the information was not obtained through official means. These leaks occur in government entities, hospitals, private corporations, political campaigns, and the military. I've heard critics of the media accuse journalists of making up the "source" as a way to give credibility to information that the journalist fabricated or extrapolated from officially released or available facts. I do not share this belief. I believe that in any organization, there will be someone willing to break the rules and speak to journalists without proper authorization.

After many years working in a law enforcement agency and practicing law, I have met people who seek out journalists to provide information. Some people who leak information to journalists clearly have an agenda. They may be disgruntled, they may be whistleblowers, or they may be concerned citizens who are unhappy about the events that give rise to the news story. Perhaps the most well-known leak was the infamous Deep Throat, who provided information on the Watergate scandal to journalists Woodward and Bernstein in 1972. His identity remained a secret until 2005, when his name and position were revealed in a *Vanity Fair* article.[25] Deep Throat was Mark Felt, a high-ranking FBI official cultivated as a source by Woodward. Interestingly, Woodward was adamant that Felt only confirmed a great deal of information the journalists obtained from other sources.

People may contact journalists with information because they have a personal relationship with them or because they are related by blood or marriage to them. The leak may also be from an employee in the media industry. In one instance, I represented a law enforcement officer following an officer-involved shooting who arrived at church one Sunday to find a news truck and a journalist out front. He left before he was discovered, but in that moment, he lost the one refuge he had during a particularly high-profile and contentious media storm about his shooting. We later learned that a producer with a local station attended church with the officer. My client knew the person, but did not know about her connection to the media. When the media contacted his pastor, the pastor believed he would be helping the officer by doing an interview on camera explaining the toll the shooting was taking on him. The result was that the law enforcement officer, who was pursued at his home for weeks and had to sneak out, felt like he was without any safe place. I had a very direct conversation with the journalist involved years later when he sought an interview on a separate officer-involved shooting. We discussed ethical boundaries, the effect of his decisions, and basic human boundaries. His apology, received after a lengthy one-sided portion of our phone call, was somewhat genuine, although I believe he realized if he did not apologize, I was not going to speak with him. However, I believe he never truly understood the impact of his decision. Perhaps it was because he was not aware that the officer had nowhere else to feel safe and comfortable; the journalist did not understand how deeply religious the law enforcement officer was; or perhaps it was a basic truth that I have come to understand—people often do not see law enforcement officers as vulnerable. Looking at this situation, the producer was hoping to increase her standing within her company by providing information to the journalist. She also likely knew the journalist and saw him as a coworker she could help. She made a poor decision, but I understand her reasons even though I vehemently disagree with them.

For journalists, sources are part of the job. An excellent and succinct article discusses the role of leaks as well as the obligations of journalists who receive them. I recommend reading the entire article, which was printed in part in the *Los Angeles Times* in 2006. One quote from the article is particularly germane to this discussion:

> *In general, leaks will always be part of a free society, and even more so in the era of so many competing news sources, including blogs and dueling websites. We also need to have some caution about claims that unethical leaks have occurred. British Lord Northcliffe had it right when he said that "news*

is what someone, somewhere does not want printed. The rest is advertising."[26]

The article cautions journalists to vet their sources not only for accuracy, but also for motivation. I believe journalists are taught, formally and informally, to be leery of sources who seem far too eager to provide information, even when their efforts may have devastating results. However, we cannot and should not deny that a major function of the media in general is to serve a watchdog function, especially over government. Although we can point to some examples of journalists arguably overstepping the bounds of their own ethics and decency, sources help journalists fulfill this role. It is hard to believe that the drafters of the First Amendment to the United States Constitution did not recognize the unique ability of the media, both published and underground newspapers at the time, to affect change, inform the public, and be a persistent source of aggravation for corrupt leaders, when necessary. It is also important to note that *The Washington Post* received a Pulitzer Prize for the work of Robert Woodward and Carl Bernstein on the Watergate Papers in 1974.[27] The Pulitzer Prize, awarded in 1973 although also reported as being conferred in 1974, was in the area of Public Service.[28] I believe this underscores not only the role of the media, but also the vigor with which individual journalists will seek out and protect sources to fulfill their watchdog mission.

A law enforcement agency must work to reduce or eliminate leaks. Typically, this is done through the implementation of written policies and procedures as well as general orders regarding contact with media sources, the release of information, and the establishment of procedures for the dissemination of information to journalists. Here are some examples:

Employees will not grant interviews or answer questions from media representatives regarding any work-related activities or incidents involving the Atlanta Police

Department without prior approval from the Chief of Police or the PAU except as provided for on the initial scene of an incident.[29]

H. Personnel will not release any of the following information to the news media:

1. The existence or contents of any statement or confession given by the accused, or their refusal to give a statement or to take tests (i.e., breathalyzer, polygraph)

2. Any statements as to the merits of the case

3. The possibility of a guilty plea

4. The home address and/or telephone number of any:

   a) Member of the police department

   b) Complainant

   c) Witness of a crime

5. The identity of a person under eighteen years of age taken into custody, unless charged as an adult

6. The identity of a complainant or relative

7. The identity of a homicide victim prior to proper notification

8. The identity of a neglected or abused child

9. The identity of a victim of a sex crime

10. The identity of any deceased person or accident victim prior to proper notification of a relative

11. The identity of any deceased or injured police officer prior to proper notification of the officer's relatives[30]

The Public Information Officer (PIO) will generally be the source of information about the Bureau to the press/media. However, a member may be contacted by the press/media requesting official records. Because press/media requests regarding official records (e.g. police reports, photos, videos, etc.) must be made in writing and reviewed in accordance with applicable public record law, members will direct any press/media requesting official records to the Records Division, in accordance with Directive 614.50, Release of Information. Members should direct press/media requests for booking photos to the Multnomah County Sheriff's Office.[31]

V. Media Interviews

Media interviews are permitted with members of the Department concerning incidents/investigations they are assigned to or law enforcement topics about which they have direct knowledge. **These interviews may be conducted after receiving permission from their supervisor or the scene supervisor**. Limit answers to known facts and avoid expressing opinions or hypothetical comparisons.

A. Individual Interviews

The appropriate personnel to answer journalist questions at a **minor** crime/accident scene **may be** the first responder or their supervisor. Regarding a major incident, the appropriate personnel to answer journalist questions are the scene commander, the precinct commander, division commanding officer, chief investigator or the Media Relations Officer. The Media Relations Officer shall be notified of all media interviews given by an employee of the Department. This notification should precede the interview when practical.[32]

As you can see, there are many ways to articulate the basic concept that all releases of information should be coordinated through appropriate channels. However, as with many policies and procedures, they are difficult to enforce. This is especially true in an age of electronic mail, texting, social media pages which all journalists maintain, and smartphones. In short, it has never been easier for an employee of a law enforcement agency to reach out to a journalist and for the journalist to cultivate sources in a confidential manner. Further, it is nearly impossible to detect or stop this flow of information.

Law enforcement agencies must use caution in their efforts to uncover and punish employees responsible for leaking information to media sources. Depending upon the job description and the motivation of the person leaking information, the task and process of investigating and disciplining the employee may be fraught with peril and should be conducted with the advice of legal counsel.

If the leak is from a member of the investigative team and the law enforcement agency can easily articulate that the leak did have or had the potential to undermine the integrity of the investigation, then the efforts to root out the leak and discipline the employee will likely be on solid ground. A law enforcement agency has an obligation to ensure that investigations are conducted in a fair and impartial manner, as the failure to do so could result in failed prosecutions, wasted public resources, the destruction of the reputation of a suspect who is eventually cleared, and the deprivation of due process rights of the accused. So, when an employee close to an investigation compromises the investigation, the law enforcement agency is likely on solid ground when taking action. The air gets foggy as the source of the leak moves away from the investigators, and the motivation of the source diverges from embarrassing the agency, having a personal relationship with the journalist, or fame seeking, and more in the direction of whistleblowing. Of course the farther the source from the investigation, the less reliable the information they provide will be.

A whistleblower is a person who brings a problem out into the open, usually through media disclosure or a formal complaint outside of the normal channels of communication in an agency.[33] The act of whistleblowing may be protected under federal law and many state laws.[34] While the protection for the whistleblower may be narrow if the statutes apply, the law enforcement agency and individual officers may land in the middle of a lawsuit facing civil damages, individual liability, injunctions, and a loss of immunity if the situation is not handled properly.

If a law enforcement agency is contemplating an investigation to find and discipline a leak source, I recommend that legal counsel be involved at the outset. Whistleblower laws apply in several contexts and areas and have many exceptions as well. It is critical that you are aware of the applicability of these statutes before you begin the process of uncovering a leak within your agency. Many of these statutes are triggered by a person claiming to expose waste or corruption. Therefore, an employee who claims they leaked information in an effort to alert journalists about improper expenditures by the agency, typically the use of grant funds, may not only be protected in that activity, but your efforts to discipline them may expose the law enforcement agency and individual officers to injunctions, money damages, and a great deal of embarrassment. This is an area of law in which law enforcement officers typically do not involve themselves. If you need further convincing, consider that some attorneys focus their practices and specialize in this area, so proceed with caution.

Journalists Will ALWAYS
(Well, Almost Always) Protect Their Sources

As discussed above, journalists rely upon sources to be effective. Not all of their sources are like what Hollywood movies depict, with shadowy figures meeting in dark parking lots to pass along unmarked manila envelopes. The overwhelming majority of sources are everyday people who provide fairly innocuous information to journalists with whom they develop a relationship. For example, a journalist may develop a relationship with a clerk in the office of the city manager. From time to time, the journalist may check on the status of hearings and meetings and confirm the agenda by calling the clerk. In addition, the clerk may call the journalist to advise that protestors are expected at a city council meeting. In the overwhelming majority of cases, the journalist's source will not be subject to any risks in speaking with the journalist, and at worse, the source may provide information a few hours before it is released to the public. This is especially true with government employee sources. However, that two-hour heads up may allow the journalist to change her schedule, secure a photographer or camera operator, and advise her producers and editor that a story is waiting to be told at the city council meeting that night. For the journalists, that information is invaluable.

Sources also save journalists time in knowing where to obtain information. For example, a journalist who is new to your state may find that an employee in the police department's records room will assist in knowing how to send requests for documents, where some records are physically located, and what division of the department handles specific investigations. Once again, this is information the law enforcement agency would readily disclose to anyone, as it is public and not privileged in any way. However, the source makes the journalist more efficient.

So what happens when the source becomes the focus of the news story or court case? While it does not happen often, there are times when the journalist may be pressured to identify a source. Keep in mind that editors routinely work with journalists to vet sources, especially in high-profile or sensitive cases. While the editor and managers may not know the names of sources, they will typically learn the position of the sources and other information that gives credibility to the information provided. In addition, as with law enforcement sources, a journalist's source who consistently provides accurate information will be trusted more often, specifically regarding stories that present a higher potential liability for the journalist and the news agency.

The disclosure of a journalist's source typically takes three paths. First, law enforcement officials may require the information to discover victims, locate evidence, discover the source of inappropriate disclosures in violation of policies, or to exclude the source as a suspect, especially if the source has demonstrated knowledge of facts that have not been disclosed. Second, a court might order the disclosure of a source because the testimony of that source is critical to a criminal or civil case. The case may be an action against the journalist for libel or slander or completely unrelated to the reporting. For example, the information attributed to the source may demonstrate that the source must be called as a witness in order for the parties to have a fair trial. Finally, and this is extremely rare, the journalist may disclose the identity of the source. Generally, this will only occur when the journalist has permission from the source to do so.

In the first two scenarios, the matter will eventually come before a judge. This may occur in response to a subpoena to the journalist for a trial or deposition, a civil notice to produce documents or information, or a subpoena to appear before a grand jury. Many states provide statutory protection that allows a journalist to refuse to divulge the identity of a source except under extremely limited circumstances (see Appendix B). The protection of a journalist's source is entrenched in American law, but the punishment of the journalist may hinge on whether or not the information was unlawfully disclosed to the journalist or the source. A law enforcement agency or person seeking the identity of the source will likely bear the burden of proving to the judge's satisfaction that the disclosure is required, especially if your state has a statute or constitutional provision that protects the journalist's information. You can expect that the journalist will be represented, often quite ably, by attorneys who focus their practices on media-related issues and remain on retainer for news agencies.

Lawyers have a saying that, generally in civil contempt, "the person holds the keys to the jail cell," meaning that the journalist may remain incarcerated until they provide the information. However, even if the court orders the journalist to disclose the source, many journalists have faced jail and paid fines for civil contempt in an outright refusal to disclose the identity of a source. In those cases, the credibility of the journalist may actually increase.

There are several famous cases involving journalists and sources. In 1980, *Washington Post* journalist Janet Leslie Cooke wrote a story entitled "Jimmy's World" about an eight-year-old heroin addict.[35] The description of Jimmy was replete with detailed descriptions of the needle marks on his body. Naturally, law enforcement officials and child welfare groups were quick to respond and began looking for Jimmy. However, they were unable to find him. In response to pressure, then Mayor Marion Barry publicly declared that Jimmy was known to officials and in treatment. Later, Mayor Barry's office eventually declared, no doubt with appropriate sadness, that Jimmy died. When Ms. Cooke won a Pulitzer Prize for Journalism in 1981, having been nominated by one of her editors, Bob Woodward, the veracity of the story and her academic credentials were called into question by the Pulitzer committee, and eventually she confessed that Jimmy was a complete fabrication. Publicly disgraced, *The Washington Post* delivered a very public apology. Cooke resigned and blamed the high-pressure environment of *The Washington Post* for her deeds. She eventually sold the rights to her story for a reported price of $1.6 million. There is little information as to why the authorities did not seek an order requiring Cooke to disclose Jimmy's full name, location, and any other information that could have been used to locate him. Perhaps the environment of Washington, DC, along with the sheer force of the reputation of *The Washington Post*—at the time so soon after the publication of the Watergate Papers—dissuaded such efforts. However, the fact remains that the source for the story did not exist, and the system that shields journalists from disclosing sources allowed the perpetration of the fabrication. As to Mayor Barry's role, his escapades provide sufficient explanation.

In 2005, *New York Times* Washington Bureau journalist Judith Miller famously spent eighty-five days in jail for refusing to reveal her source when she refused to appear before a federal grand jury in connection with a leak that identified Valerie Plame's connection with the Central Intelligence Agency.[36] She was eventually sentenced to eighteen months in jail for contempt by United States District Court Judge Thomas Hogan, and the sentence was upheld by the United States Court of Appeals for the District of Columbia. The United States Supreme Court declined to hear the case. She was ordered to prison to begin her sentence on July 7, 2005.[37]

In 2004, WJAR television journalist Jim Taricani refused to divulge the source who provided him an undercover surveillance video that depicted a public official accepting a bribe from an FBI informant. The tape was evidence and sealed in the prosecution case of the officials. Taricani refused to disclose his source when subpoenaed and was found in civil contempt. Following his unsuccessful appeal, Taricani's station reportedly paid $85,000 in fines. Taricani was sentenced to six months of home confinement and served four prior to being released early. He never revealed his source.[38]

When considering how journalists handle sources, the question always arises about the difference between statements made on and off the record. As an attorney, I will tell you that I find this question a bit amusing. Lawyers, at least litigators, are constantly "on the record." We ask questions and defend clients in depositions and appear before courts for hearings and trials with a court reporter taking down everything we say. We constantly document telephone calls and meetings with letters and emails to confirm what was said. This, however, is not the world of the journalist.

Generally, statements made to journalists should be considered "on the record." This means that the journalists will feel free, and in some instances will be obligated, to quote you or use the information you provided. Whenever you are appearing on camera, speaking through a radio interview, or are being recorded, you should assume that your statements will be used. The reason for this, in my opinion, is that the journalist generally does not own the recording. Even if the journalist agrees not to use the information or the quote, a producer, editor, or boss of the journalist may decide otherwise. If this occurs, the journalist may have little say in the matter.

A statement made "off the record" is one that the journalist will not quote or use in the story. Examples of off-the-record statements may be information that the person has heard thirdhand and does not feel comfortable verifying or is unable to do so; a belief that a set of facts exist but the source has not yet been able to verify; or a statement that the source is quite certain of but the use of the information will likely expose the source. As I will explore, off-the-record statements are the source of much controversy.

Many instructors, publicists, and media experts will tell you, "There is no such thing as an off-the-record statement." This is probably good advice, especially for the novice, in dealing with journalists. However, as you work with journalists, you will receive questions that clearly call for off-the-record responses. Here is an example:

Journalist: Thanks for speaking with me today. I really appreciate that you took my call.

Police Chief: No problem. If I'm available, I'm happy to help.

Journalist: Do you think the public safety director will take my call?

Now, that could be a loaded question. Perhaps the police chief was designated to field this call by the public safety director who wanted nothing to do with this story or, worse, this specific journalist. It's also possible that the public safety director is out of town visiting a sick relative, but this information is not public. Finally, the public safety director may not enjoy speaking with the media in general. This later scenario is not uncommon, by the way. Many law enforcement agencies have commanders and directors who prefer not to speak with any media sources and delegate those duties as appropriate. As an aside, for many this is a wise decision, as I will discuss in Chapter Six. So how should the chief respond?

Well, our police chief has a few options. She can tell the journalist the truth, but letting the journalist know that the public safety director prefers not to speak with journalists is not good for the law enforcement agency, the agency's relationship with the media in general, nor the career of the police chief's boss. The police chief can say, "I couldn't tell you, give it a shot." This is also probably not a wise choice, as the public safety director may refuse to speak with the journalist and the journalist will waste time making fruitless phone calls. Finally, the police chief can make a statement off the record. It will be a simple one of little consequence and can be done without exposing too much information. A simple statement to this effect will not only improve the relationship between the journalist and the police chief, but also spare the public safety director from being contacted.

> Police Chief: You can certainly try to contact the public safety director, but we spoke about this issue and agreed that I could provide you with all of the details we just discussed. You may also find it hard to reach him right now. Feel free to contact me if I can provide anything else to help you with your story.

At this point, the journalist will likely understand that you have been designated as the point of contact for the law enforcement agency and accept your answer. She is not likely to publish in a story that you advised her that the public safety director was hard to reach. First, it is not part of the story, and second, you likely did her a favor by saving her the time of reaching out to him.

If the off-the-record statement contains simple statements like this that can really do no harm, the decision is easy to give an off-the-record answer or statement. The tougher issues arise when the facts are more sensitive or when the journalist *asks* for an off-the-record statement. In my experience, it is rare for a journalist to ask for a statement off the record, and this should put you on alert. More often, the discussion with the journalist leads to a place where a question calls for information that you are not authorized to disclose, either because no one anticipated the question, or because a full and complete answer could lead to the disclosure of information that is not authorized. In these scenarios, the conversation can quickly lead to a discussion of what the journalist may and may not publish.

If you have no experience with the journalist, you must consider whether or not to direct the interview to a different topic or simply state that you are not prepared to respond to that question. To do otherwise can be a very dangerous choice.

If, however, you have experience and perhaps even a professional relationship with the journalist, you may speak frankly and ask the journalist if she is comfortable receiving information off the record. If the answer is no, then revert to the recommendation in the preceding paragraph. If the answer is yes, you must go a step further and confirm with the journalist that you will answer the question only if they agree that they either will not attribute the information to you, will not use the information, or will only use it at a later time based upon a deadline you give them or when you contact them at a later date.

The agreement to keep information off the record is just that: an agreement between the two parties. If at any time you have any indication that the journalist will not keep his word, is hesitant about agreeing to keep the information off the record, or just makes you feel uncomfortable, do not make the statement. You can deflect the question by agreeing to revisit the topic at a later date and state simply that you cannot answer the question at this time.

The final caution about speaking off the record is a simple truth that many people may not realize—journalists often record interviews to protect themselves and ensure the accuracy of quotes. This practice varies greatly by journalist and geographic region, as some states may require the consent of both being recorded. However, if you consider that any and all interviews and statements are being recorded, you will be appropriately more cautious.

Next we will discuss situations in which journalists have revealed their own sources. While they are rare, the results can be devastating for the source and the journalist. Courts have held that a *mutual* agreement to keep information off the record is binding on the journalist, and a failure to abide by that agreement can expose the journalist and media outlet to liability. In a famous case, *Cohen v. Cowles Media Co.*, two journalists contacted a source about a story. The source wanted to cooperate but feared retaliation in the form of being terminated from his job if he provided information. The journalists promised not to use his name and to keep his comments off the record. During the course of the drafting of the story, two newspapers used his name and exposed him as the source of the information. As the man feared, he was terminated, and he filed suit for promissory estoppel, or breach of a promise. The case was a unique claim. Nothing was reduced to writing about the agreement between the source and the journalists. However, it was clear that he would not have shared the information absent the assurance that it would be off the record and that his fears were justified. The man took the case to the United States Supreme Court, and he won. The Court held that the agreement between the man as a source and the journalists was a binding agreement and the publisher could be held liable for money damages for breaching that agreement.[39] So, the bottom line is this: lawsuits aside, use extreme caution about speaking off the record, especially if you do not have a longstanding relationship with the journalist.

Throughout the past twenty-five years, I consider myself fortunate to have fostered relationships with several journalists. The relationships are professional only—they are not sitting at my house for Thanksgiving dinner—but they are strong. I know they will contact me if they need a quote or if they just need background information for a story. I have strengthened those relationships and built new ones by being a resource for the journalists. Something as simple as explaining a complicated legal procedure, providing a copy of a statute or court case, or pointing them in the direction of other sources of information goes a long way. This should come as no surprise. People in all professions appreciate assistance.

Recently, I did an interview with a well-known journalist for a national news source. As always, the conversation flowed easily. He is a very pleasant person and a professional. We know from past experience that we do not likely see eye to eye on some political topics, but like most professionals, we work around those differences and, most importantly, *we respect each other's opinions.* Well, we worked through the questions that he had for the story he was covering and we finished up with the quotes he expected to use. When we were done, he asked if he could chat with me about another topic. I immediately recognized that he was in need of information for a story he was either considering and researching or that he planned to publish in the near future. In fact, he asked me if we could have a discussion off the record. I agreed. We discussed several aspects of this new topic and, as usual, I pointed him toward several sources, some law, and gave my thoughts on some interesting aspects of the topic that he had not considered. Not only is he a pleasure to speak with, he is extremely bright. It is enjoyable to watch a true professional working in his field. I know when this story nears publication, he may or may not call me for quotes or information that he can attribute to me. However, if he does contact me, that will be a different conversation and it will be clear that my statements will be fair game for him to publish. It is important to remember that even though the conversation was off the record by agreement and his request, I was cautious about what I said and did not act in an unprofessional manner.

Is There a Road Map for This Interview?

I cannot tell you how many times law enforcement officers have asked me questions like, "How do you keep journalists on topic and prevent them from asking anything they want?" While I would like to give them the impression that I have the ability to control the path of the interview as it goes forward, this is obviously not the case. The way to keep an interview moving on a predictable path with questions that not only don't surprise you, but that you can anticipate is to have a frank conversation with the journalist in advance before the camera is on, the recorder has started, or they begin asking questions. This may seem like an awkward way of handling this, but most journalists expect it and, quite frankly, it is the only way to handle the issue irrespective of your experience or relationship with the journalist. So how do you get them to tell you what information they are looking for and separate out the topics with which you do not feel comfortable? Let's go through it.

Journalist: Thanks for taking the time to meet with me. We want to get this story on the news this evening. As you know, a lot of people are talking about it.

PIO: Not a problem. I'm glad our schedules were able to line up. So tell me, what information are you looking for?

Journalist: Just background information on the procedures going forward now that a suspect has been arrested.

PIO: Okay, happy to help. Remember that I'm not a lawyer, so I can only address what will happen from the perspective of the sheriff's office. I also may not be able to answer questions about the specifics of the crime scene, the autopsy, if there are other suspects, and those types of questions, as much of that has not been released. Are there specific questions you want to ask on those topics? If you let me know now, I may be able to point you to the appropriate person to save you some time.

At this point, the journalist knows the boundaries of what you cannot and will not answer. Further, he knows that you are not qualified to answer a whole set of questions pertaining to criminal procedure, so asking you those questions will not be productive. By asking for specific questions, the journalist is put on notice that you want a road map prior to beginning the interview. Your offer to help direct the journalist is, in every sense, an offer to help. Rarely is an offer to help seen as anything negative. As you can see, this conversation is not awkward or unprofessional. In fact, the PIO is establishing herself as a resource for future stories.

If the journalist steps outside the boundaries set out and agreed upon prior to the start of the interview, you will have to decide if it is a minor oversight, if the journalist is attempting to catch you off guard, or if they are going back on their word. For minor oversights, I would answer the question and add a qualifying statement that another person may be better suited to answer that question.

Journalist: So now that an arrest has been made, when will the bond hearing take place, or will he even get a bond?

PIO: I know the law provides for bonds in most cases, but that is a question for the district attorney.

For the questions that you believe are meant to catch you off guard, you can respond as follows:

Journalist: Weren't there witnesses who said there were other suspects who could have fired the fatal shot?

PIO: The detectives who investigated the case routinely search for witnesses and they will make every effort to investigate any and all leads and information. In fact, we encourage anyone who believes they witnessed any part of this incident to call the tip line.

If the journalist goes back on your agreement, and honestly this is rare in my experience, there is a simple way to handle this.

Journalist: Our sources are saying that there were drugs on the scene and that one of the suspects interviewed by your homicide detectives has worked as an informant in the past. Is that true?

PIO: Well, before we began, I specifically told you that I was not able to discuss specifics about the crime scene and other suspects. As we discussed before we were on camera, the detectives working the case have not finished their reports, so some information is not yet public.

Rarely have I had a journalist completely breach the agreements they made with me before the start of the interview. They know that if this occurs, you will likely not return their calls next time, or worse, you will call them after you have called every other journalist. Further, they know that if an issue is breaking, they will only get a heads up if you have pleasant experiences with them and trust them. Although I do not recommend this and specifically counsel you <u>not</u> to do this, the journalist always runs the risk that a group email or fax with a press release might not reach them if they are inadvertently left off the list.

I had an experience with a journalist when I first began handling media issues for the police department. I was asked to meet with a journalist following a very high-profile murder case. Central to the case was the suspected failure of an alarm system, or that the perpetrators were able to access the home completely undetected even though the doors were locked and the alarm was armed. Now, I was aware of the facts of the case, but he did not know that. I also knew that he had been told repeatedly that certain facts would not be released. So, he approached the department with a crime prevention story reportedly aimed at increasing awareness and safety following a heinous crime that had many in the community frightened. I had secured a home to walk through with him to point out various recommendations about making the house more secure by upgrading locks, adding equipment to the alarm system, and trimming landscaping. As you may imagine, it was a long distance from the location of the homicide. However, he had an interesting alternative plan. He suggested we go to a subdivision and named it. Well, what a coincidence, the subdivision he named was where the homicide occurred. At that point, and we had been meeting in my office for over half an hour prior to getting on the road, I looked at him and told him that we were not going anywhere near the house. His face blanched a bit and his cameraman smiled. He had been caught. At that point, though, he was stuck. If he did not follow through with the story he pitched to my chief and to me, the same one for which I had done some homework and lined up a home, his credibility would have been shot. So, we went with my plan and the police department was able to get some great exposure about basic crime-prevention techniques. When we finished filming, he got into his van, then passed me his business card with his home number on it. He looked me in the eye and told me he would be very appreciative of any information I could give him about the homicide, especially before anyone else knew it. I thanked him and his cameraman and watched them drive away. This was clearly an invitation for me to speak with him off the record about confidential information that he correctly surmised that I knew. However, I had no intention to do so. I worked with that journalist many times after that, but I never trusted him. I suspect he knew it too. He also probably knew that I was not the only law enforcement officer who felt that way about him.

This was a great example of the main reason why journalists attempt to breach the agreements they make before the camera starts. As I suspected, and verified when I returned to headquarters, this same journalist had been bugging anyone he could reach in the department with the same questions he asked me. At every turn, he ran into a brick wall. Most of the time when a journalist asks you a question that you advised you cannot answer or explicitly said you would not answer, it is because they have already asked other sources and were told the information was not available.

As to the information that you cannot answer, there is no harm in essentially saying, "I'll help, but there are some things that either I do not know, or there are people who are better qualified to answer those questions." I routinely tell journalists if a topic is outside my wheelhouse or if I feel uncomfortable commenting based upon my involvement in a case or a related matter. I know they appreciate my candor and knowing up front where the rocks are. This allows them to seek another source with sufficient time to meet their deadlines. On several occasions, I have either suggested sources for them or provided information that led them to credible sources.

How Can They Contact Me?
Let Me Count the Ways . . .

Following a critical incident, most people are amazed at the number, types, tenor, and timing of media inquiries. Journalists are very good at working sources, as discussed earlier. They are also very good at being persistent; that is their job and part of their training. You can expect journalists to push to get the information they believe they need for the story they are writing. If you want an analogy, a good journalist is like a well-motivated law enforcement officer looking for a bad guy; do not expect them to give up easily.

Journalists will use confidential sources, as outlined earlier. They will also use public sources and methods of contacting the law enforcement agency, and today there are many more than when I started in a public relations role in 1992. At that time, facsimiles, written requests, telephone calls, pagers, letters, and personal delivery of written requests were the only methods available to journalists to reach out to law enforcement agencies. Much has changed, and you should expect multiple requests through multiple channels.

Until the late 1990s, although email was available, many law enforcement agencies did not disclose email addresses widely, and certainly not through public directories. One reason was the inability of the email servers to handle large quantities of email. Another reason, of course, was that email was viewed either as a means of internal communication or as a portal to the law enforcement agency that could be used to steal data or introduce a virus. In fact, I specifically recall when the county I worked for allowed employees to send and receive emails to people and entities outside the organization. That was 1997. Prior to that, as a fraud investigator, I had to get time on a county computer with internet access and a special email system to correspond with suspects.

Obviously, although the risk of data theft, corruption, and viruses has increased exponentially, today's email servers can accept extremely high volumes of incoming messages. In addition, the proliferation of law enforcement websites and the drive to make law enforcement agencies more accessible to citizens means that anyone can send an email to most any agency, and sometimes individual officers, by using the agency directory found on the law enforcement agency's website. As a result, you can and should expect to be inundated with emails following a critical incident. Not all of those emails will be from journalists. Therefore, it is important to have a system to separate the nonsense email from the legitimate inquires, and further separate out the journalists who are contacting you for information. In many states, an oral or email request for open records is binding on the law enforcement agency.[40] Do not miss one because you were unable to sift through the hundreds if not thousands of emails that you will receive. The failure to properly respond can not only lead to litigation and an assessment of attorney fees and expenses for the failure to disclose public information and records, it could also lead to a public relations nightmare for a law enforcement agency accused of hiding documents, ignoring the law, or simply violating it. You will have enough on your plate. Do not create additional dragons to slay.

Email requests can be a particularly difficult problem to solve. It is important to get your information technology (IT) support folks on this problem way before the critical incident occurs. As you meet with them, you must critically analyze their skills and determine if they are the best folks for the job. The IT person considered a genius in your city or county because they seem like a wizard with Windows may not be the right person to protect your agency from an attack by hackers, denial of service (DOS) attacks, ransomware, and viruses, and your email system is the quickest way to attack your computer system. Following the death of Michael Brown in Ferguson, Missouri, on August 9, 2014, the computers of the Ferguson Police Department, the City of Ferguson, the State of Missouri, and others were hacked, shut down, or otherwise compromised.[41] In addition, the personal email accounts of law enforcement officers and their families were hacked and their identities stolen.[42]

Email systems contain many features people never use. For example, in Outlook there is a way to flag emails from certain people with a different color to ensure that you will see them. This is an excellent tool to ensure that the journalists you expect to contact you will receive prompt attention. Simply enter the email of the journalist in your contacts and select it for a flag. You may choose from several different colors. I use this system for clients who typically contact me and my firm with emergent matters. When I look at my email following a meeting or phone call, I can quickly scroll through and scan my incoming messages for email from these individuals and review them as necessary. You can add new journalists to the list very quickly and will soon have a quick method of making sure you do not drop the ball. You may choose one color for local journalists, another for national journalists, and yet another for international. You can also use this system to code for "informal media" journalists, as defined earlier. This is an invaluable tool for command staff[43] and PIOs who may need to either open and respond to the email or forward them quickly to ensure proper handling. Unfortunately, this technique does not appear to work yet on every smartphone, but the technology is evolving.

Email also allows you to verify that you sent information. You can also ask for verification that the email was received, opened, and read. Although this last feature can be bypassed or declined, in my experience, most people do not have a problem acknowledging that they read your email. You can store and save these verifications and they can become quite useful, especially if you are sued or publicly criticized for failing to respond to a request for public information.

Email systems are designed to receive, send, and store email. This may seem intuitive, but remember that email systems are not intended to protect you from those who mean to use your email system as a portal to your servers. A law enforcement agency without use of its computer systems for even one day can find itself fighting crime in the Stone Age. Computer-aided dispatch systems, records management software, evidence logging and storage systems, and simple word-processing programs have become the life blood of effective law enforcement in the United States. Losing them would be catastrophic. Therefore, you must supplement your email system with programs that sift through incoming messages and remove suspicious messages or known viruses. There are many on the market, and they are usually implemented systemwide. I have experienced great success with a program that sends me and my staff an email every morning with email messages that were blocked the day before. If I see an email that was blocked in error or through the program protecting me, I can release the email to come through to my inbox and tell the program that future emails from this person are acceptable. The daily message also lets me know the viruses that were blocked each day. Sometimes, that part of the daily email is quite sobering. There are many systems on the market, but you must have at least one. Do not let the finance folks try to tell you it is unnecessary or, worse, it should come out of your budget. If the law enforcement agency is under attack, a person will find a way in and put the entire government entity in peril.

It is critical to remember that the weakest points in any email system are the users. Employees must be educated to carefully look at their email messages and avoid opening any with attachments, including photographs or movies, from anyone they do not personally know or from a source from whom they are not expecting such messages. It is important to have a system through which any employee can have a suspicious email properly screened. It is also important to be supportive if they call for help unnecessarily. Build an environment that encourages caution. At the very least, this may not only avoid a problem before it grows, it may help isolate the entrance point for a virus and assist in the eradication of the offending program.

Finally, the sheer volume of email you will receive can be staggering. It seems that anyone with an opinion will contact you to share it. Some will not be warm and fuzzy and may rise to the level of criminal activity. I believe any threats should receive attention—some more than others. If nothing else, put them on someone's radar within your agency. Many of the people who contact the agency may have words of support. Those people deserve, and must receive, a response. A simple "thank you" will go a long way and can be done by support staff. Others may contact you with the answers to all of your difficulties, the names of the perpetrators of every unsolved crime in your files, as well as the answer to who really killed Jimmy Hoffa! One of the chiefs in my department, during a particularly high-profile murder investigation, routinely received calls from a pleasant woman who announced with pride that she had solved the case! She explained that she was "a TV detective" who spent all day consuming any and all news coverage on the murder. She advised that her unique role allowed her to discern fact from fiction, hype from hysteria, and solve the crime. While her intentions were honorable and she may have increased stock prices of tinfoil producers around the world, her contacts with the police department were a waste of resources. I guess she never considered that the source for most of what she was binge watching was the police department itself. Bless her heart.

While facsimile, or "fax," communications are still alive and well in law enforcement agencies in the United States, most have gravitated to other methods of communication. Electronic fax services allow the sender to transmit documents to the law enforcement agency directly from a computer without the use of a fax machine. This is an easy way to send requests for reports, crime statistics, and press releases. Fax machines have also evolved a great deal. It is now easier than ever to send press releases and other information to multiple journalists with the touch of one button. As strange as this might sound, most media outlets still rely heavily on fax machines. I routinely use them to communicate press releases and other information, in large part because they are effective and also provide a method of verifying that you sent information and it went through properly. Although the other end of the fax might reach the journalist in an email, you should think about using fax communication in order to take advantage of the ease and speed of reaching multiple parties. You can program large numbers of phone numbers into a fax machine or program to "blast" documents to set groups. Part of the reality is that it is often easier to correctly enter a ten-digit telephone number than a long or confusing email address.

Many departments now have computer systems that grant citizens access to records. Programs such as www.policereports.us and www.sungardps.com have citizen-to-police communication, also known as "C to P" portals, that allow private citizens to access public records. The Cobb County Police Department in Georgia allows citizens to obtain reports and crime data through a website.[44] The advent of these systems was intended to relieve the record staff of responding to a constant flow of information, such as the number of burglaries in a given area, the number of false alarms handled by the law enforcement agency, or copies of documents such as motor vehicle accident reports, which are routinely released to citizens who are entitled to receive them. It is important to look critically at these programs for two reasons. First, they provide another portal for those with ill intent. Second, they will likely receive far more requests following a high-profile critical incident than they do on a regular basis. If your agency proudly boasts the use of one of these systems, make sure it can handle a rapid and severe increase in the number of queries. Journalists will likely use these systems to gain quick access to information, and you should support that effort to avoid unnecessary requests flowing to your agency in other formats.

Social media sites have become a standard method for law enforcement agencies to disseminate information to the public—including, of course, journalists. Facebook, Twitter, Instagram, LinkedIn, and others form a vital and prolific network throughout the world. The release of information is not one way, of course. Information can and will rapidly spread over this network, part of what I call the "informal media," irrespective of the accuracy of that information. Even though law enforcement agencies are gaining a significant presence on this network, to an overwhelming extent, they fail to use it properly and to their advantage.

Social media sites can be configured to push information out from the law enforcement agency to the public, including journalists. This is an invaluable resource, as an agency with an active site already has viewers and followers who look to the site for information. While some agencies have social media sites, some are much better than others at using them to keep the public updated. Make no mistake, the local media in your area monitor your agency's social media sites—all of them. They rely upon the sites to give them a heads-up about events and issues. Unfortunately, many law enforcement agencies set up social media sites only to pat themselves on the back, believing they are "wired," then fail to devote any resources to maintain and develop them. Having a social media presence usually means that a live person must be monitoring and updating the sites—all of them—on a regular basis. In the social media world, a day is equivalent to a year. Therefore, all social media sites must be updated with information on a daily basis. This is not as difficult as it seems, but it requires a commitment from command staff and, most importantly, a delegation of autonomy for the person authoring the posts. This sometimes proves to be a difficult concept for many law enforcement agencies.

Updating social media sites can be done in a natural method that will not seem stilted or forced. For example, I routinely follow several law enforcement agencies that keep their sites updated several times each day by posting road closures, significant wrecks or road construction, and arrests of importance to the community. You can also post information on job openings within the agency or the governing body, upcoming firearms classes for civilians, awards, commendations, promotions, wanted persons, missing persons, and information on new hires. In short, think of the social media sites as a newsletter that pushes your message out instantly.

As stated previously, many law enforcement agencies allow their chain of command to interfere with the flow of information on social media sites by attempting to control every word. Let's be frank for a moment; the officers you trust to use deadly force every day in a lawful manner consistent with the Fourth Amendment of the United States Constitution can also be trusted to disseminate information on wrecks, classes for the public, and other information without getting approval from the chief or sheriff! Just give the officer in charge of this process a list of "fair game" topics and guidelines, and turn them loose. Your agency will be better off in the long and short term.

One of the best law enforcement agency examples of this principle is the Georgia Department of Natural Resources (DNR). Their Facebook page includes photographs of hunters and anglers exercising their rights and lawfully using Georgia's natural resources. These are activities that form the core mission of the Georgia DNR. In one of my favorite posts, two DNR rangers posted pictures and photos of a deer hunter they discovered in a field. He was hunting lawfully and had a great day! This left him with a huge buck he had to drag back to his truck alone. The DNR rangers helped him get the deer out of the woods and bragged on his success, thereby promoting the DNR's mission. The posting framed these law enforcement officers and the law enforcement agency in a great light and set the stage that the Facebook page was not a trophy case for captured poachers. It was a resource for the public and a way to stay in contact with the law enforcement agency.

The Kentucky State Police is also a shining example of social media presence. The agency maintains a Facebook page, Twitter, Instagram, and an active YouTube channel. Information Office Supervisor Sherry Bray advised that the agency began the program without a specific budget to do so. She told me the Kentucky State Police successfully used the social media platforms during several natural disasters to keep the public informed, and that the YouTube channel has helped their recruiting efforts. Although the agency started the project using video and photo equipment and personnel from divisions within the Kentucky State Police, her unit has been able to acquire specialized equipment through grants. At times, the social media efforts have produced unexpected results. Following an Instagram post of the agency's canine officers on National Dog Day, a company contacted the agency offering to provide free Kevlar vests for the canine officers. "We never expected that, but it was amazing to see the response from a photograph and post that did not seek any funds or assistance," said Bray.

There are many other examples of law enforcement agencies that are properly taking advantage of the power of social media. Take a look at the City of Dunwoody, Georgia, the Cobb County Georgia Sheriff's Office, the New York Police Department, the Federal Bureau of Investigation, and others. Whether the agency is small or large, the potential exists to make an impact and social media is a bean counter's dream—free!

When a critical incident occurs, the public, including the local journalists, will look to the social media sites they view every day to obtain information. They will check the sites at least as frequently as they do on a normal day, and you should expect that your social media sites will attract significant traffic. That is why it is important for the law enforcement agency to keep posting the traditional information and get something out specific to the critical incident. National and international media attracted to the critical incident will check these highly public and easy-to-access sources first. If they do not see any information on a critical incident that has attracted their attention, they will start calling and emailing the law enforcement agency. That is how the cascade leads to an avalanche of requests, and at some point, any agency will get overwhelmed. If there is information available, journalists can process and assess their interest in the critical incident. If they decide to follow up, their requests will be more targeted. A simple social media statement that reads as follows can keep the command staff free from interruptions:

> For more information about the officer-involved shooting that occurred this afternoon on 5th Avenue, please direct all inquiries to Sgt. Alice Info in the Public Information Office via email at PIO@YOURLEA.gov, fax 777-777-7777, or private message through social media. You can also continue to follow the department on the following social media sites, where we will release information as we are able: Facebook, Twitter, Instagram, LinkedIn.

Such messages resonate with producers working in the media who are following and assessing dozens, if not hundreds of stories every day. As stated earlier, a wall of silence when something is clearly going on in your jurisdiction is the like rolling out a red carpet for all types of journalists to push harder and oftentimes speculate about what is happening. Avoid the information vacuum.

YouTube is another type of social media site that is vital to every law enforcement agency. YouTube is a site that hosts videos from users and also gathers videos from around the internet. In essence, it acts as a repository of videos with a built-in search engine. The site also allows people and organizations, including law enforcement agencies, to have a dedicated YouTube "channel" that essentially acts as a central location for storing the videos that you upload.

A dedicated YouTube channel is a must for every law enforcement agency. Consistent with the theme of this section, when the agency is not involved in a critical incident, the channel allows you to upload videos of officers helping others, going through training, arresting severely impaired drivers, and public service announcements. In addition, the law enforcement agency can upload video messages to the public from the chief of police and PIOs, as well as videos of 911 operators and other footage that will give the public and journalists a sense of what the agency is all about. The videos should be short, normally less than five minutes, unless the topic or story requires a longer video, such as a story about agency's efforts to reduce teen arrests for impaired driving. According to Sherry Bray, the information office supervisor with the Kentucky State Police, troopers are generally excited about working with the program and the response from the public has been very positive.

During and after a critical incident, the agency can post mini press conferences that pass along information. These are critical, as the print media sources can quote them, the television media can use the clips, and radio stations can use the audio. The vetting of information going out over the agency's YouTube channel can be done through the same process for a written press release. In essence, this is just a video press release with a face of the law enforcement agency appearing rather than a white piece of paper with dry words. We have all seen the words of these press releases on the nightly news, and they look terrible. The video gives all media outlets the information they need and allows them to choose the format. In addition, the PIO can have a couple of chances to get the information, the lighting, the tenor, and the body language of the video perfect. When appropriate, the agency can release body camera, surveillance footage, or patrol car video relevant to the critical incident in an instant through a YouTube channel. This is far more effective than creating dozens, if not hundreds, of DVDs to disseminate to media outlets and individual journalists, as well as the public.

The videos uploaded to YouTube do not require special equipment. You can go to the YouTube channel for my law firm to see the video blogs I record from time to time. Simply go to www.youtube.com and search for Lance LoRusso or LoRusso Law Firm. You can also find the videos by checking my blog at www.bluelinelawyer.com. A simple smartphone will provide sufficient video capabilities. However, you can use a tripod-mounted video camera with an external microphone if you want to get a more professional quality video but keep the size of the video file manageable. High-definition cameras may record videos that are too large to upload to YouTube or otherwise disseminate. Watch for bright lights behind the person speaking and shadows on the person's face. Remember that this is a moving video, so the same nonverbal cues we are concerned about with live interviews are a concern in this medium. The videos are more powerful because there is a personal connection between the viewer and the agency representative. They're easy to make and look professional. Remember to train people to look at the camera and to smile when appropriate. I have a face made for radio, and even mine receive compliments.

One final note on YouTube channels: You can remove videos as well when they are no longer timely, or edit and reload them. While there is always a chance that the video will be copied or uploaded to another website, the law enforcement agency can manage what is available for the public on a daily basis with little effort.

An important part of your strategy must be to protect your web assets. If a critical incident involving your law enforcement agency garners national or international attention, expect a tremendous strain on your agency's website and any other asset online. Without proper protection, websites can be hacked, shut down through a massive overload of information—called a denial of service (DOS) attack, which is usually accomplished through the use of robots—rerouted to a false website, replaced with a pirated site, and any number of other nasty outcomes subject to the imagination of someone who will likely remain unidentified or outside the jurisdiction of United States law enforcement authorities. Your law enforcement agency should assess the ability of the government IT personnel and make arrangements to hire your own if you do not have a comfort level after such consultation. You should spend the money to evaluate your agency and news media websites. Both are vulnerable.

The final social media outlet available to law enforcement agencies is perhaps the most delicate: a blog, which is like an online newsletter. Video blog posts are often referred to as "vlogs," which is short for "video blog." A blog post can be quite lengthy, however the most effective blogs keep the postings to a length of three hundred to five hundred words. One of the most prolific bloggers, Seth Godin, whose blog has been one of the top blogs in the world for some time, typically posts daily blogs of less than one hundred words. Blog articles or videos allow the department to disseminate original information, pass on information from other sources, or comment on current events. For example, if news stories about carjackings are filling the nightly news and newspapers, the blog can provide helpful hints to avoid becoming a victim, statistics on the number of carjacking crimes in your jurisdiction compared to the surrounding areas or nationally, and descriptions of suspects. A blog is just another tool for passing on information. Although viewers and subscribers can leave comments, which the law enforcement agency can regulate, it is generally not as conducive to two-way communication as Twitter, Facebook, Instagram, or LinkedIn. Nonetheless, a blog can be a powerful tool to keep the public and journalists informed, especially during a critical incident.

Social media is a critical way for law enforcement agencies to tell their stories. Those stories are comprised of the lives of the citizens you serve, the law enforcement officers who put their lives on the line for strangers every day, and the world around your community. If you provide material and information, journalists and the public will consume that information. If you do not, someone else will tell your story for you. Do not expect someone else to be kind or objective. Take charge, take a stand, and take over the social media presence of your agency.

Lance LoRusso

What Is Fair Game during the Coverage of a Critical Incident?

There are several sources available that allow us to examine the ethical guidelines and aspirations of journalists. As stated previously, this is a profession defined as journalism. Merriam-Webster's online dictionary defines journalism well and expresses the broad nature of the term.

1 *a*: the collection and editing of news for presentation through the media
   b: the public press
   c: an academic study concerned with the collection and editing of news or the management of a news medium
2 *a*: writing designed for publication in a newspaper or magazine
   b: writing characterized by a direct presentation of facts or description of events without an attempt at interpretation
   c: writing designed to appeal to current popular taste or public interest

I like this definition because it describes the traditional role of the journalist—gathering information and publishing news stories—as well as the academic side of the term. Further, this definition expresses the idea of the traditional, old-school journalist who presents the facts without interpretation juxtaposed with the last section, "writing designed to appeal to current popular taste of public interest."[45]

One organization, the Society of Professional Journalists, founded in 1909, boasts 7,500 members in broadcast, print, online journalists, journalism educators, and students. Members gather for conferences, prepare articles that are both scholarly and informational, and seek to share information as a profession.

One bone of contention for law enforcement officers and law enforcement agencies during riots and other types of civil unrest is the focus on lines and groups of law enforcement officers in riot gear or driving specialized vehicles. There are several reasons why the news is filled with these images. Some have to do with the audience or media customers. Some of it has to do with the journalists themselves. Some of it is the fault of law enforcement agencies.

Images of law enforcement officers in riot gear or driving specialized vehicles appeals to a wide variety of customers. For journalists, it is a no-brainer to post the videos, photos, and descriptions whenever possible. These images appeal to antipolice activists who believe that every law enforcement officer is working hard in a concerted effort to deprive every citizen of their rights, if not their lives. They appeal to the anticop viewer who would not attend a protest if their life depended on it because they are the ones who sit at home or yap in the office about how bad the police are, but still call them whenever there is any type of unrest or imbalance in their personal world. Antigovernment consumers will also soak up these images. Also enthralled by these images are the law-abiding people who are frightened by protests and civil unrest. There are also people who will want to see these pictures who are law enforcement supporters, including officers and their families. Soon after they see the images, you will hear them say they cannot believe the officers were placed in those positions, or that they admire their bravery. Finally, these images also appeal to other media sources that, for all of the reasons stated above, want to promulgate such images to their customers. So, with such a variety of interest, you know where the cameras will be pointed at the next sign of civil unrest.

The journalists taking the images, the producers directing the cameras, and the editors who decide what is shown are also part of this matrix. While you will see images of people looting and destroying police cars, the images will quickly return to the lines of heavily armed or helmeted law enforcement officers. Perhaps the news coverage of the unrest in Baltimore in 2015 is the best example of this concept. The now iconic images of law enforcement officers in riot gear eclipsed the disgusting video of a man throwing a cinderblock at a firetruck that was responding to a fire set by protesters. Take the context from civil unrest to a football game and you will understand why.

Sunday afternoon football is a tradition in the United States. Imagine you are a journalist tasked with getting footage of the game that not only will entertain people watching the game right now, but also those who see the snippets of coverage on the news hourly throughout the evening, the people who read the paper in the morning, those who peruse the internet the next day looking for information about the game, and the station's social media sites. You cannot place cameras on the players. You also do not have an unlimited budget to have twelve camera operators and photographers around the field. So, what is your game plan? Well, if you know anything about football, and despite the belief of some of my friends I know a little bit, you will marshal your resources to obtain the best pictures and footage during the most important points in the game. You will identify the quarterbacks, the key receivers, the coaches, and anyone known to do anything outrageous on the field in terms of athletic ability or showmanship. Then, you will identify the points at which those individuals are likely to do something, or have something done to them, that will be exciting and of interest to your customers. When an event in the game coincides with the presence of one of the people you identified, the cameras will roll and the shutters will snap. Yes, it's really that simple. Don't believe me? Let's look at two examples. Watch any game where Michael Vick is playing in 2016, which he advised will be his last season.[46] Cameras follow him all the time when there is no specific action on the field because people want to see him for a variety of reasons. Also look at the media focus on Clete Blakeman, the referee of Super Bowl 50. He is a lawyer who also works as a referee in the National Football League. Cameras focused on him only when he made calls, until he was dubbed the "hottest ref in the NFL" and became a media sensation with the hashtag #hotref. You can count on cameras being focused on him for quite a while.

The journalists at the scene of civil unrest will obtain footage of events in the area. This is akin to the footage of the fans in the parking lot and the player signing autographs. They will also capture images of the people on the street complaining about law enforcement in general or the issue that surrounds, or many times has provided the excuse for, the civil unrest. The game analogies are the fans holding banners and the shirtless guys, and there are usually three of them standing together, wearing body paint and yelling while holding their hands up to display the fact that they are consuming alcoholic beverages. Thanks, but we already knew that. The rest of the footage goes back to the law enforcement officers in riot gear and the specialized vehicles. These are the quarterbacks and receivers in the NFL game. Simply put, if you stay focused on these people and items, you will obtain images that your consumers want. A prime example is the image of a young man, Devonte Hart, hugging Sergeant Bret Barnum at a Ferguson-related rally in Portland, Oregon.[47] The officers were dressed in riot gear and Devonte was thanking them for being there. The cameras were focused on the officers in riot gear waiting for something to happen and when Devonte Hart approached them, the photographer was ready. Yes, it's that simple.

One element to point out is the truly rare biased journalist. There are likely to be more of them present at a civil disturbance. We have all seen and heard them. To them, virtually no law enforcement action is appropriate, justified, or reasonable. Short of officers handing out puppies, they will always be the bad guys. That is just part of the equation, however, you can expect more of them to gather in your community during times of unrest.

Finally, some of the reason for this focus on law enforcement officers in riot gear and specialized vehicles is the fault of law enforcement agencies. I know some of you will take offense to this, but this book should challenge you to correct these problems that may haunt law enforcement agencies for decades if efforts are not undertaken to remedy the problem.

Prior to civil unrest, I have never seen a news story or an effort by a law enforcement agency to meet with members of the media to show them why the use of riot gear and specialized vehicles is important. Agencies have traditionally kept these items in the proverbial basement, and many do not even park the specialized vehicles in public view. Most journalists have no idea why a law enforcement officer would exchange their softball cap or campaign hat for a Kevlar helmet. *Show them*. Tell them about the frozen water bottles that were thrown at law enforcement officers in Ferguson, and demonstrate what happens when those bottles hit a window, a piece of plywood, or some other representation of the damage they can do. Demonstrate why the shields are important by showing photos of people spitting on officers. Show them what happens when a protester throws a brick or a Molotov cocktail at a mannequin dressed in a law enforcement officer uniform, especially one made of polyester, then demonstrate what happens when the brick or Molotov cocktail hits an armored vehicle.

Part of the reason that journalists focus on riot-gear-clad officers and specialized equipment is that it is new to them, and that is partly the fault of law enforcement agencies. There are plenty of opportunities for agencies to invite journalists to see, hold, get into, and learn the purpose of that equipment. Let them stand behind a shield while two or three people push them. Let them wear a helmet and see how hot it gets in July in Atlanta. Allow them to see the damage done to helmets and shields from bricks, bottles, and stones under controlled circumstances and through photographs from prior events in your community and around the United States. Finally, allow them to see the inside of the armored vehicles owned by your agency. Have them lay on the ground and experience an extraction into the vehicle. If journalists only see this equipment in the middle of tense and often chaotic circumstances, you can expect they will portray the equipment with a sense of fear and a lack of understanding of why they are deployed, their purpose, their limitations, and how they keep officers and civilians safe.

The fervor surrounding specialized vehicles has become fanatical. Motor vehicles with engines and a chassis that happened to have armored bodies were the subject of legends. To read the media reports and listen to some politicians, you would believe they were filled with everything from 20mm guns to unicorns. In reality, they are empty hulls compared to what they were as military equipment. The varieties built specifically for law enforcement purposes are generally uncomfortable vehicles that can withstand bottles, rocks, bricks, and Molotov cocktails better than a standard police vehicle. Let the journalists see them, get inside, look at the empty slots where military equipment once resided, and educate them. Help them to understand why law enforcement agencies seek out surplus military equipment, and that one reason is cost. A surplus military, armored personnel carrier may cost a law enforcement agency $3,000 to $4,000 in shipping costs, engine work, and initial repairs before it is ready to be used. A special-purpose law enforcement vehicle with armor plating typically costs $300,000 to $400,000.

Before the civil unrest, let them know that your goal is to disrupt the snowball effect of riots. Show them footage and photos that demonstrate failure of law enforcement officers to contain dangerous protests that led to the destruction of large sections of cities in the past and many deaths. Show them that you are aware of precedent from the United States Supreme Court, but also point out state laws that limit unlawful actions cloaked in free speech. In short, let them know that there is a plan in place, law enforcement officers are not working as a reactionary force, and the clashes with protestors are driven by defined goals. Do not assume they know. The most famous example of media ignorance was a journalist who posted a picture of foam earplugs to his social media site, asking if they were rubber bullets. Use this as the standard when you are wondering if you've put out enough information.

Chapter Three

Understanding the Media as a Profession

The central dilemma in journalism is that you don't know what you don't know.

Bob Woodward

Journalism will kill you, but it will keep you alive while you're at it.

Horace Greeley

News is what somebody does not want you to print. All the rest is advertising.[48]

Alfred Lord Northcliffe

It is nearly impossible for law enforcement officers and agencies to work with the media without understanding the profession. Officers see a constant stream of reporting that often seems inaccurate to them. They were on the scene of the shooting, the civil unrest, or the car wreck, and the facts as reported do not match what they observed firsthand. This leads, often incrementally, to an adversarial relationship. In Chapter Five, I discuss the effects of this distrust and how it can spiral into a worsening divide. The purpose of this chapter is to give some insight into the "other side of the camera," the radio, or the pen. I hope officers will learn that the media as a profession has its challenges like any other. However, there are efforts underway, longstanding efforts, to bring about more ethical approaches to journalism. Like any other profession, journalists are not homogenous and their practices are influenced, and in some cases controlled, by those occupying the midground as well as those at the ends of the political spectrum.

It would be difficult for law enforcement officers to learn how to interact with journalists if they are not familiar with the training, beliefs, core mission, and ethics of their profession. If you already interact with journalists on a regular basis, I hope this chapter will expand your understanding and in turn improve your communications and professional relationships.

Journalistic Ethics

Like law enforcement officers, journalists are constantly placed in situations that are not covered in classrooms, textbooks, and perhaps within the collective experience of the journalists in the office or the entire community. The tremendous challenge is understanding that what is printed, stated, and recorded today will have an effect on the public, law enforcement officers, and other journalists forever. This is especially true in the current age of technology. Stories appear and may be accessed without regard to their age, and quotes are used, truncated, and misappropriated with few ramifications, if any. The professional report compiled by a professional journalist in the hours following an event is accessed, quoted, and kept in the forefront by the "magic" of the internet and search engine optimization long after the facts contained therein have been disproved or elaborated on. The inability to purge or link stories in chronological order to prevent this effect has led to the destruction of careers and unwarranted disparagement of law enforcement agencies and officers, some of whom are my clients.

Many people have this idea of journalists as young people being thrown into their roles with little or no training and even less guidance about what is ethical and appropriate. While that may be the case with the informal media that I discuss in Chapter Six, this is not the norm with established media outlets. In my experience, journalists have degrees in journalism and related areas as well as mentors within their profession and their employment who guide them and "bring them up" in the profession. I have heard journalists speak very plainly of the elders in their profession who helped them along, taught them how to be good journalists, and also taught them about fairness and how to be a professional. Like any other profession, sometimes those mentors found the journalist through the hierarchy of the news outlet, and other times the journalist sought out their own mentors. The problem is, many times the situations presented are unique and require judgment calls by both the journalist and management. Here is one example:

> Seconds after a Northern California jury convicted Richard Allen Davis of murdering twelve-year-old Polly Klaas, a press-pool photographer took a picture of Davis, who held up both of his middle fingers. *The San Jose Mercury News* decided to publish the picture on its front page, accompanied by a "Dear Reader" box soliciting reader response and explaining its reasoning for running the controversial photograph.
>
> *Mercury News* Executive Editor Jerry Ceppos told readers that the picture showed Davis's "contempt for the system that convicted him."[49]

This was obviously a judgment call, and many law enforcement officers may be surprised to learn of the decision to publish the photograph. In researching this book, I have come across many such ethical dilemmas. This one is quite illustrative for many reasons.

The murder of a child is horrific, and the reporting of the crime alone, which is essential for many reasons, likely conjures up ethical quandaries. The end consumer of news is the public at large, and we do not, thankfully, live in a world where newspapers, radio broadcasts, and television or internet news shows are selectively disseminated to a chosen few or kept from others. You will not find a local newspaper being sold in the United States in a brown paper covering. This means that all consumers of all ages, beliefs, experiences, and sensitivities will see the photograph described above. The conviction of this child killer was an important historical event, had meaning for the community, and understandably brought closure to many people.

However, the courtroom probably had a seating capacity of less than one hundred, and even if more people wanted to attend, they were going to work, taking care of their own children, and living their own lives. The outcome of the trial was nonetheless important to thousands who never set foot in the courtroom.

Was it enough to simply print a headline that read "Jury Convicts Killer of Polly Klaas"? Was the fact that the victim here was twelve years old a critical part of the story? The journalists were not likely to get an immediate interview with the now convicted murderer, so how could they convey his response to the verdict? What about the adage that a picture tells a thousand words? In addition, except for radio broadcasts, media is a visual forum. Newspapers use bold fonts as well as photographs to not only tell the story, but to attract people walking by newsstands. Television broadcasts entice viewers to watch through commercial breaks with snippets, known as "teases," of what will appear next. Finally, what photograph would have conveyed the evil contained in the killer more than this picture? A photograph of Polly Klaas's parents reacting to the verdict would have shown the pain and impact of the crime, but not the man who brought about this tragedy. So the paper, through the photojournalist, the journalist who wrote the story, the editors, and management, made a judgment call. I have confidence that this was not an easy decision, and while the demands of deadlines placed limits on the time available to discuss the issue, I believe there was a great deal of debate.

Judgment calls are made by the editors and management. J. K. Murphy, managing editor and vice president of content, and Otis Brumby III, publisher, both of the *Marietta Daily Journal*, *Cherokee Tribune*, and *Neighborhood* newspapers, made it clear that both news stories and photographs require judgment calls. Both stressed that there is no rulebook to guide them. "We are always conservative about protecting young readers," says J. K., a man with about thirty-six years of experience. He stressed that many times the standards for judgment calls may vary by region or by publication. A photograph may appear in one paper and be rejected by another. However, it depends upon how compelling the photograph is. "The picture may be the story," Otis told me. For me, those words sum up the dilemma.

There are often questions of what should be captured on film or on video. Law enforcement officers should be relieved to learn that this is a source of a great deal of discussion within news outlets. The discussion does not end when the photos are taken. There is a road between taking the photo and publication that may often contain curves and bumps that the public never sees. This is not unlike the struggle courts find themselves in regarding crime scene photographs and pictures of perpetrators and victims. Is a photograph, although illustrative of a point, too graphic to show to a jury? In court, we expect the intervention of a professional, a judge, to make a decision. As you can see, professionals make the decision in the context of news every day.

Anytime decisions or judgment calls are made, you can be assured of two things. First, people will disagree on the result. Second, people will make mistakes. I have seen the selective use of photographs to enhance the public appeal of a news story. I have also seen photographs "deselected" by media outlets. Although I try to give the benefit of the doubt to members of any other profession, in many cases, I have a difficult time reconciling the decision in light of the outcome that was eminently foreseeable. Let's discuss one example.

On February 26, 2012, George Zimmerman shot and killed seventeen-year-old Trayvon Martin. The shooting followed a physical confrontation between the two, therefore the relative height and weight of the men was pertinent to the analysis and discussion. It also became a factor in the criminal trial, because there was no dispute that Trayvon Martin was not armed with a weapon. Trayvon Martin was five-feet-eleven-inches tall. His weight was reported as anywhere from 158 pounds or higher, and George Zimmerman was reported to be five-feet-eight-inches tall and approximately 200 pounds.[50] Although a recent photograph of Trayvon Martin was posted shortly after his death, the national media began to run an old photograph of him that appeared to portray him as much younger and smaller in stature.

In addition, although they were available on the internet if one chose to search for them, photographs of George Zimmerman's head cut and bleeding from impacts with the concrete curb were rarely published. I recall pointing to these photographs during the many interviews I provided during the trial and found many journalists unaware of them. The jury ultimately made a decision based upon the evidence. However, the photographs used may have sparked a great deal of unnecessary controversy and increased tensions. *The Orlando Sentinel* reported that one group put out a $10,000 reward for the "capture" of George Zimmerman, who was either in custody or out on bail at the time.[51] Famously, Spike Lee tweeted the incorrect address of George Zimmerman,[52] reportedly causing the elderly couple who lived at the address to leave their home in fear.[53] Lee settled with the couple, apologized, and retracted his Twitter post.[54]

The decisions, and more importantly the judgment calls, made in the newsroom have profound effects on how the public views the media in general. Law enforcement officers have many times found themselves scratching their heads or just plain angry at those decisions. Let's explore the ethical rules of the media as a profession.

The Society of Professional Journalists publishes a Code of Ethics for members.[55] The preamble is enlightening and reads as follows:

Members of the Society of Professional Journalists believe that public enlightenment is the forerunner of justice and the foundation of democracy. Ethical journalism strives to ensure the free exchange of information that is accurate, fair and thorough. An ethical journalist acts with integrity.

The Society declares these four principles as the foundation of ethical journalism and encourages their use in its practice by all people in all media.

The four principles are listed below and are expanded upon in the actual code.[56]

1. Seek Truth and Report It
2. Minimize Harm
3. Act Independently
4. Be Accountable and Transparent

The Society of Professional Journalists was founded in 1909 as Sigma Delta Chi and today boasts 7,500 members.[57] There are certainly other professional groups of journalists, including the American Society of News Editors[58] and the National Press Club.[59] The *New York Times* also publishes and makes available to the public a guide for its journalists.[60] I include this information from the Society of Professional Journalists to show you that journalists, like law enforcement officers, belong to groups, have organized training classes and conferences, and aspire to a common code of ethics. The law enforcement equivalent of the ethics code is the law enforcement officers' oath of office, although I am aware that some law enforcement agencies and professional organizations also employ ethics codes.

I have never worked as a journalist, and I am not formally schooled as a journalist. My experience with over three hundred media interviews since publishing *When Cops Kill: The Aftermath of a Critical Incident* in December 2012 added to my experience with all types of media that began in 1992 when I was assigned to the Crime Prevention Unit and Training Unit at the Cobb County Police Department. I would say that throughout my law enforcement and legal careers I have easily given more than four hundred interviews. Through those interactions with various media sources, I have learned a great deal. However, for the purposes of this chapter, I reviewed several journalism books and texts in an effort to gain more insight into the profession. I also interviewed working journalists with decades of experience. I have known some of them for many years. I selected them with two criteria. First, they were widely respected as having a tremendous amount of experience. Second, I knew they would speak plainly with me.

A profession is defined in many ways. *The Merriam-Webster Dictionary* defines a profession as "a type of job that requires special education, training, or skill."[61] It is also said that a profession has certain characteristics associated with it. There have been many efforts to further refine this definition and explain what constitutes a profession. In his paper, "Attributes of a Profession," Earnest Greenwood stated the following:

> Succinctly put, all professions seem to possess (1) systematic theory, (2) authority, (3) community sanction, (4) ethical codes, and (5) a culture.[62]

Journalism meets all of these criteria except, arguably, community sanction. We will discuss this anomaly later in this chapter. However, I believe that in any analysis, journalism qualifies as a profession.

As a profession, there are standards of practice that the public can and should expect of journalists. However, we must be careful to point out that we are dealing with professional journalists who work for media outlets on a full-time basis and many others who work part time or outside the normal media outlets in what I referred to in *When Cops Kill: The Aftermath of a Critical Incident* as the "informal media." I discuss this term more thoroughly in Chapter Six.

There are more than five hundred journalism schools, or schools that offer a minor in journalism, in the United States.[63] Those schools teach writing, research, and ethics. However, like most academic institutions, graduates rely upon their first jobs to instill in them many skills they will need to be successful.

The watchdog role of the media is embraced in every journalist, whether they work in the formal media space or make up the informal media. In his book *Ethics in Journalism*, Ron Smith discusses the impact of this role.

> American journalists—particularly newspaper journalists—overwhelmingly embrace the watchdog role. A large-scale survey found that about two-thirds of American journalists said investigating government claims was among their top priorities. British and Australian journalists are even more committed to the watch-dog role, with more than 80 percent of them listing it among the most important roles for the news media.[64]

Therefore, it would be naïve to believe that journalists will not be interested in the areas of law enforcement that involve the public trust. You might say that everything law enforcement officers do involves the public trust, and that is true to some extent. However, there are six areas that will trigger the watchdog instinct in every journalist who is worth her salt. When these issues are at play, you should expect assertive, if not aggressive coverage. I would argue that in a democracy, law enforcement agencies should not only expect the scrutiny, they should prepare for and welcome it. As you can see from this quote, most journalists would likely agree with me.

> *Journalists are obligated to gather information as best they can and to tell the truth as they find it. They must be undaunted in their pursuit of truth and unhampered by conflicting interests.*[65]

The six areas are as follows in no particular order:

1. Use of force
2. Expenditures of public funds

3. Intrusions and searches of "persons, houses, papers, and effects,"[66] including computers and cell phones, especially following the case of *Riley v. California*[67]
4. Seizures of private property, especially the seizure of assets prior to conviction
5. Selective enforcement of the law or favoritism shown toward individuals or groups, especially law enforcement officers, or the perception of such
6. Violations of the law by law enforcement officers

In each of these scenarios, the first test will be whether or not the story is newsworthy—if the public will be interested. However, the watchdog instinct is triggered by the fact that law enforcement officers in these scenarios have authority and power not granted to citizens, and any potential abuse of that power could be a sign of and lead to corruption.

This brings us back to the ethics code promulgated by the Society of Professional Journalists (SPJ). As stated above, the code expounds upon the four principles. I am producing it here for your review.

Seek Truth and Report It

Journalists should be honest, fair and courageous in gathering, reporting and interpreting information. Journalists should:

❖ Test the accuracy of information from all sources and exercise care to avoid inadvertent error. Deliberate distortion is never permissible.

❖ Diligently seek out subjects of news stories to give them the opportunity to respond to allegations of wrongdoing.

❖ Identify sources whenever feasible. The public is entitled to as much information as possible on sources' reliability.

❖ Always questions sources' motives before promising anonymity. Clarify conditions attached to any promise made in exchange for information. Keep promises.

❖ Make certain that headlines, news teases, and promotional material, photos, video, audio, graphics, sound bites, and quotations do not misrepresent. They should not oversimplify or highlight incidents out of context.

❖ Never distort the content of news photos or video. Image enhancement for technical clarity is always permissible. Label montages and photo illustrations.

❖ Avoid misleading reenactments or staged news events. If reenactment is necessary to tell a story, label it.

❖ Avoid undercover or other surreptitious methods of gathering information except when traditional open methods will not yield information vital to the public. Use of such methods should be explained as part of the story.

❖ Never plagiarize.

❖ Tell the story of the diversity and magnitude of the human experience boldly, even when it is unpopular to do so.

❖ Examine their own cultural values and avoid imposing those values on others.

❖ Avoid stereotyping by race, gender, age, religion, ethnicity, geography, sexual orientation, disability, physical appearance, or social status.

❖ Support the open exchange of views, even views they find repugnant.

❖ Give voice to the voiceless; official and unofficial sources of information can be equally valid.

❖ Distinguish between advocacy and news reporting. Analysis and commentary should be labeled and not misrepresent fact or context.

❖ Distinguish news from advertising and shun hybrids that blur the lines between the two.

❖ Recognize a special obligation to ensure that the public's business is conducted in the open and that government records are open to inspection.

Minimize Harm

Ethical journalists treat sources, subjects, and colleagues as human beings deserving of respect. Journalists should:

❖ Show compassion for those who may be affected adversely by news coverage. Use special sensitivity when dealing with children and inexperienced sources or subjects.

❖ Be sensitive when seeking or using interviews or photographs of those affected by tragedy or grief.

❖ Recognize that gathering and reporting information may cause harm or discomfort. Pursuit of the news is not a license for arrogance.

❖ Recognize that private people have a greater right to control information about themselves than do public officials and others who seek power, influence, or attention. Only an overriding public need can justify intrusion into anyone's privacy.

❖ Show good taste. Avoid pandering to lurid curiosity.

❖ Be cautious about identifying juvenile suspects or victims of sex crimes.

❖ Be judicious about naming criminal suspects before the formal filing of charges.

❖ Balance a criminal suspect's fair trial rights with the public's right to be informed.

Act Independently

Journalists should be free of obligation to any interest other than the public's right to know. Journalists should:

- ❖ Avoid conflicts of interest, real or perceived.
- ❖ Remain free of associations and activities that may compromise integrity or damage credibility.
- ❖ Refuse gifts, favors, fees, free travel, and special treatment, and shun secondary employment, political involvement, public office, and service in community organizations if they compromise journalistic integrity.
- ❖ Disclose unavoidable conflicts.
- ❖ Be vigilant and courageous about holding those with power accountable.
- ❖ Deny favored treatment to advertisers and special interests and resist their pressure to influence news coverage.
- ❖ Be wary of sources offering information for favors or money; avoid bidding for news.

Be Accountable

Journalists are accountable to their readers, listeners, viewers, and each other. Journalists should:

- ❖ Clarify and explain news coverage and invite dialogue with the public over journalistic conduct.
- ❖ Encourage the public to voice grievances against the news media.
- ❖ Admit mistakes and correct them promptly.
- ❖ Expose unethical practices of journalists and the news media.

❖ Abide by the same high standards to which they hold others.

As you can see, this is not a cursory set of aspirations. Great effort has been expended to create a set of guidelines for journalists.

The Society of Professional Journalists' code is certainly not the only set of journalistic ethics codes. I include several in this chapter for your review. Not only will reading these codes bring more understanding, law enforcement officers will learn what behavior is acceptable to journalists, what is outside of the realm of acceptable behavior, and be able to intelligently raise issues of impropriety with journalists and management.

The Radio-Television News Directors Association adopted this set of standards in 1987.[68]

The responsibility of radio and television journalists is to gather and report information of importance and interest to the public accurately, honestly, and impartially.

The members of the Radio-Television News Directors Association will accept these standards and will:

1. Strive to present the source or nature of broadcast news material in a way that is balanced, accurate, and fair.
   a. They will evaluate information solely on its merits as news, rejecting sensationalism or misleading emphasis in any form.
   b. They will guard against using audio or video material in a way that deceives the audience.
   c. They will not mislead the public by presenting as spontaneous news any material that is staged or rehearsed.

    d. They will identify people by race, creed, nationality, or prior status only when relevant.

    e. They will clearly label opinion and commentary.

    f. They will promptly acknowledge and correct errors.

2. Strive to conduct themselves in a manner that protects them from conflicts of interest, real or perceived. They will decline gifts or favors that would influence or appear to influence their judgments.

3. Respect the dignity, privacy, and wellbeing of people with whom they deal.

4. Recognize the need to protect confidential sources. They will promise confidentiality only with the intention of keeping that promise.

5. Respect everyone's right to a fair trial.

6. Broadcast the private transmissions of other broadcasters only with permission.

7. Actively encourage observance of the Code by all journalists, whether members of the Radio-Television News Directors Association or not.

This set of standards comes from the National Press Photographers Association.[69]

The National Press Photographers Association, a professional society dedicated to the advancement of photojournalism, acknowledges concern and respect for the public's natural-law right to freedom in searching for the truth and the right to be informed truthfully and completely about public events and the world in which we live.

We believe that no report can be complete if it is not possible to enhance and clarify the meaning of words. We believe that pictures, whether used to depict news events as they actually happen, illustrate news that has happened or to help explain anything of public interest, are an indispensable means of keeping people accurately informed; that they help all people, young and old, to better understand any subject in the public domain.

Believing the foregoing, we recognize and acknowledge that photojournalists should at all times maintain the highest standards of ethical conduct in serving the public interest. To that end the National Press Photographers Association sets forth the following Code of Ethics, which is subscribed to by all of its members:

1. The practice of photojournalism, both as a science and art, is worthy of the very best thought and effort of those who enter into it as a profession.

2. Photojournalism affords an opportunity to serve the public that is equaled be few other vocations, and all members of the profession should strive by example and influence to maintain high standards of ethical conduct free of mercenary considerations of any kind.

3. It is the individual responsibility of every photojournalist at all times to strive for pictures that report truthfully, honestly, and objectively.

4. Business promotion in its many forms is essential, but untrue statements of any nature are not worthy of a professional photojournalist and we severely condemn any such practice.

5. It is our duty to encourage and assist all members of our profession, individually and collectively, so

that the quality of photojournalism may constantly be raised to higher standards.

6. It is the duty of every photojournalist to work to preserve all freedom-of-speech rights recognized by law and to work to protect and expand freedom-of-access to all sources of news and visual information.

7. Our standards of business dealings, ambitions, and relations shall have in them a note of sympathy for our common humanity and shall always require us to take into consideration our highest duties as members of society. In every situation of our business life, in every responsibility that comes before us, our chief thought shall be to fulfill that responsibility and discharge that duty so that when each of us is finished, we shall have endeavored to lift the level of human ideals and achievement higher than we found it.

8. No Code of Ethics can prejudge every situation, thus common sense and good judgment are required in applying ethical principles.

Public Radio News Directors Incorporated also promulgates a set of ethical standards.[70] This set of standards was published in July 27, 1991.

Whereas Public Radio News Directors Incorporated (PRNDI) was formed in December 1984 to enhance news and information programming, and
Whereas PRNDI was formed to encourage professional development, and
Whereas PRNDI is to foster events to pursue developmental goals of journalists, producers, editors, independent

contractors, students, and volunteer news and public information aides, and

Whereas PRNDI members serve many communities and interests that deserve news programs of the highest standards of honesty, fairness, integrity, balance, compassion, and technical quality;

Now, therefore Public Radio News Directors Incorporated does advance and call upon members to follow this code of ethical conduct . . .

1. Prepare and deliver news programs accurately to maintain public trust. All errors of fact, bias, or omission must be corrected immediately.

2. Strive to eliminate personal, station, or community bias and balance matters of race, religion, ethnic origin, gender, and sexual preference.

3. Recognize, understand, and vigorously pursue our public's right-to-know laws. Members must evaluate the merit and news value of materials provided by anonymous sources. After deliberation, members must insure the sanctity of those sources based upon right to privacy and guard against its violation.

4. Make efforts to name those who provide newsworthy information and avoid all sound presentations not generated at the news site.

5. Responsibly evaluate the newsworthiness of all broadcast items and guard against undue pressure from non-news personnel.

6. Honor legitimate requests to hold or embargo newsworthy material provided in advance.

7. Avoid making false representations to obtain materials from those who might otherwise object to discussing matters with journalists, editors,

producers, independent contractors, student aides, or volunteers under your direction.

8. Inform news sources when conversations are being taped.

9. Make no promises or guarantees to report, promote, or advance materials without true news value.

10. Avoid the reality or perception of all conflicts of professional and personal interests. These include rejection of gifts, favors, commissions, privileges, or special access that cloud perception.

11. In every case possible, maintain a separation of duty during station pledge drives and other fundraising efforts. If possible, this separation should include all news-related personnel.

12. Reconsider the associations with community events, service projects, boards, councils, or commissions when conflicts of interest arise and to work to assign stories on those organizations to journalists.

13. Avoid employment that involves work for politicians, corporations, companies, sponsors, underwriters, or station donors that strain professional obligation and public trust.

14. Avoid participation in any event (marches, demonstrations, picketing, rallies) that compromise professional integrity and future news or public information assignments.

15. Maintain and upgrade these standards as circumstances require.

16. Require all new employees, independent contractors, producers, editors, talent, aids, and volunteers under member direction to adhere to these standards.

And, upon acceptance of these standards, members should advance them by personal action. By doing so, members maintain a standard of excellence which enhances the value of the news delivered. Members doing so provide worth to their stations, their communities, and the employees under their direction. This provides the public with a trustworthy product that is beyond reproach.

My research indicates that these guidelines truly guide the efforts of working journalists. In preparation for this book, I interviewed Paul Crawley, a retired television journalist with a bachelor of arts degree in radio, television, and motion pictures from the University of North Carolina Chapel Hill. He had wise words for young journalists and shared principles and practices that he lived by over his nearly forty years in the media profession.

One inaccurate story could destroy a career, a job, and depending upon the story, a life. I always envisioned what it would be like on the other side of the camera. There is a lot of power in being in the media. Be wary of the witnesses standing around and too eager to get on camera. The true witnesses were probably the ones who were removed from the crowd so that they could be interviewed in private.

Go to the crime scenes and wreck sites. Verify that the witness statements first make sense, and second, that they could have seen what they told you. This is the equivalent of police officers reconstructing crime and wreck scenes. You must verify witness statements. I never reported information I could not verify. This was a function of my experience and professional ethics.

Paul Crawley reported on news in the Atlanta area for more than thirty-six years and covered everything from multiple homicides, serial murders, plane crashes, public corruption cases, and the murder of law enforcement officers. Although he was quick to hold a law enforcement agency's feet to the fire over access to crime scenes, documents, and information, his perspective on the relationship between law enforcement officers and journalists was instructive.

> I met with the police chief and district attorney on a regular basis. I wanted them to know who I was, understand that I was a professional, and to create a professional rapport with them. My hope was that if I was covering a news story, they would trust me enough to know that I would be fair while doing my job.

Paul is proud of the relationships he developed and equally proud that he reported the news without favor, irrespective of those relationships.

Paul pointed out that as a journalist, he did not make his political views known to anyone. He felt that this might create a sense of bias if he was forced to investigate a story on a friend, political candidate he supported, or a political opponent of an acquaintance. In addition, he explained the delicate balance of his personal feelings toward law enforcement officers and his role as a watchdog over government action.

> With regards to law enforcement officers, the news media's job is to hold them accountable, be skeptical, and verify. But we must respect anyone who would take a bullet to protect us for so little money. We expect law enforcement officers with relatively little education to be lawyers, judges, or kung fu artists, and do it when making split-second decisions.

Paul's reports were direct, professional, and impactful. Even though he reported many stories that were not favorable to law enforcement officers and agencies, he always had—and continues to have—a tremendous respect for the law enforcement profession, despite several less-than-pleasant interactions regarding access throughout his career. However, the journalistic principles he learned in college and in his profession guided his conduct and his decisions.

It is axiomatic that publishing and even pledging adherence to ethical codes does not ensure ethical conduct. Indeed, many journalists would be quick to point out that an oath has not prevented many public officials and law enforcement officers from committing crimes. However, it is worthwhile to remember that journalists do not take an oath of any kind to perform their duties. In the next section, we will explore how the ethics codes provided above are enforced.

Who Watches the Watchdogs?

In the past two years, there has a been a great deal of emphasis upon law enforcement officers and agencies investigating the actions of officers, particularly involving the use of deadly force. Some of this criticism came from various grossly uninformed groups and politicians. When I began the research for this book, I sought insight into how journalists "police" themselves. I was aware that ethical guidelines and professional societies existed, but I wanted to understand how journalists as professionals maintained these standards and effectuated the task of what Earnest Greenwood called "community sanction," mentioned earlier in this chapter. What I found was surprising, intriguing, and somewhat concerning.

It is easy to locate examples, in some cases high-profile examples, of questionable conduct by journalists. With all of the ethical standards in place, I wondered how the offending journalists fared in the fallout. We have all seen law enforcement officers in the crosshairs of media attention. Even when they are eventually cleared of any wrongdoing, the effects of the scrutiny alone have been enough to destroy careers. Here are a few examples of questionable media conduct taken from an excellent book entitled *Doing Ethics in Journalism: A Handbook with Case Studies*, by Jay Black, Bob Steele, and Ralph D. Barney:[71]

> The image had come to be seared into the collective consciousness of America as a portent of terror: a yellow Ryder rental truck parked in front of a bustling federal office building. Only this time, there was no bomb, no explosion, at least not in the literal sense. On this day, March 31, 1997—by no mere coincidence the opening day of the trial of Oklahoma City bomber Timothy McVeigh—the Ryder truck in question was rented to a Tampa Bay-area television news team and parked in front of a building in downtown Tampa.

> If the idea and the journalists' news judgment were questionable, at least the action taken by government officials and building security personnel was swift and decisive. As viewers of that evening's WTVT-TV newscast witnessed, a station journalist climbed out of the parked truck and started walking down the street. Security personnel quickly emerged from the federal building, detained the journalist and searched the truck. All of this activity was recorded by a WTVT photographer and aired in that evening's newscast.

> No legal steps were taken, but law enforcement officials were quick to criticize the station for staging the event. WTVT-TV news director Daniel Webster—who was not involved in the planning, production or airing of the story—told the *St. Petersburg Times* the story was a test of the "status of public safety in Tampa." Offering that "if the scenario played out differently . . . we might have

done a piece that protected people's lives and led to a change in policies." Webster added that "if you had a belief that if you pulled a fire alarm and it didn't work, you might be exposing an issue of public concern."

U.S. Marshal Don Moreland, however, was quoted in the *Times* report on the stunt as saying, "In this case, I think a line was crossed." And officials at another local TV station were skeptical of the way WTVT approached the story, saying their own report on courthouse security was handled without having to stage an actual test on it.

I have not been able to locate any news stories about any sanctions levied against the journalists or management involved in this incident. Perhaps such actions took place behind closed doors, and that would not surprise me in the least. These are private corporations, not public entities, and personnel matters are largely kept confidential. However, the lack of transparency in the media due to the fact that the entities are private corporations leads to quite a different outcome compared to the public nature of reports eventually available from the internal affairs or office of public standards present in every law enforcement agency.

If there is no division of the media profession charged with enforcing standards, how are these ethical standards upheld or even reinforced on a regular basis? This question extends beyond situations like the one noted above. What about statements made off the record to a journalist? Who enforces the journalist's promise to hold information in confidence? Should journalists be required to identify themselves when speaking with people? What about undercover operations?

Some media outlets have created an ombudsman program, although this appears to be more common in Canada and Britain. Ron F. Smith writes:

Ombudsmen

Many newspapers have turned communicating with readers into a full-time job. They have ombudsmen, also called reader representatives or public editors. In addition to dealing with readers' concerns, more write columns explaining how news decisions were made. Occasionally, the columns are brutally honest. The ombudsman at *The Boston Globe* bashed one of the paper's columnists for making unsubstantiated charges about a political candidate.

Ombudsmen are more common on Canadian newspapers and in many European countries. *The Guardian* hired Britain's first ombudsman in 1997, although other British papers have been slow to join in.[72]

Although this is a noble step, it is not clear that the ombudsmen in place have significant authority to sanction anyone. In fact, in response to complaints, an ombudsman with the *Boston Globe* published this statement:

It's a fact of life: Journalists are after news and specifics and names. If you don't want to see yourself quoted, or talk about sensitive issues, say so and hang up or walk away. Get the ground rules straight at once. Don't talk first, and then decide to go "off the record."[73]

This statement appears to define the role of the ombudsman as a sounding board for the public as opposed to a standard bearer.

Perhaps the most concerning aspect of reporting to law enforcement officers and agencies is fairness and objectivity. Many readers will be surprised to learn that debates in the journalism profession have created a great deal of friction concerning objective reporting. On one side of this debate are journalists who believe they have an obligation to report both sides of the story and to dig equally for the facts in support of those sides. On the other is another school of thought that believes objective reporting is simply an abdication of the journalist's duties and ethical obligations.

This debate filled the pages of several books and articles I read while researching this book, and the full scope of those opposing views is well beyond this text. However, I will present a few quotes to illustrate the conflict.

> Geneva Overholser, former editor of *The Des Moines Register* who now teaches journalism at the University of Missouri, is a longtime advocate of shifting away from objectivity. "All too often, a story free of any taint of personal opinion is a story with all the juice sucked out," she has said. "A big piece of why so much news copy today is boring as hell is this objectivity god. Keeping opinion out of the story too often means being a fancy stenographer." Although she said that she understands the concerns of editors who believe that moving away from objectivity "will open the floodgates of opinion writing," she argued that a greater danger is posed by the boredom of "wishy-washy, take-it-or-leave-it writing that is wholly objective."[74]
>
> Can balance produce lazy journalism? Presenting both sides may provide a more complete story than the single-source stories of the past. But it may not help society get at the truth of complex issues. Instead, journalists may settle for easy-to-do, balanced stories when more detailed reporting and thought are needed.[75]
>
> When the Society of Professional Journalists rewrote its code of ethics a few years ago, the word "objectivity" was dropped from the document entirely.[76]
>
> CNN's Christiane Amanpour applied a similar under-standing of fairness when she covered the war in Bosnia. She wrote in *Quill*:

"I have come to believe that objectivity means giving all sides a fair hearing, but not treating all sides equally. Once you treat all the sides the same in a case such as Bosnia, you are drawing a moral equivalence between victim and aggressor."[77]

Given this trend, it is clear that objectivity, in the traditional sense, is less of a priority for professional journalists than it may have been in the past. There is no reason to believe this trend will slow or change course in the near future.

Another area of concern for law enforcement officers and law enforcement agencies is accuracy in reporting the facts and the quotes provided to journalists. This is another area of study for those who examine journalistic ethics. Some of the errors are humorous and point out that, irrespective of the best efforts of some bright people, innocent mistakes will occur. One of my favorites is a correction:

Our newspaper carried the notice last week that Oscar Hoffnagle is a defective on the police force. This was a typographical error. Hoffnagle is, of course, a detective on the police farce.[78]

You can find more errors at www.regrettheerror.com.

Some errors are no laughing matter, and most professional journalists are not amused by them. As you will see, no institution is immune.

On the same day that the *New York Times* announced on Page 1 that it had won a record seven Pulitzer prizes, it ran four corrections on Page 2. Most of the mistakes are the result of journalists proving that they are human. ("Doctors bury their mistakes," some editor once said. "We print ours.")

Professor Scott Maier reviewed years of studies and found that the percentage of stories with errors ranged from about 40 to 60 percent. When he gave copies of news stories from 14 newspapers to sources names in the articles, they found factual errors—mistakes in dates, places, titles, spellings, and so on—in about half of them. They also found lots of "subjective errors," meaning they disagreed with the emphasis or context the journalist gave to some parts of the story.[79]

A fact-checker for *Columbia Journalism Review*, which publishes articles written by leading journalists and journalism professors, said that in her three years with the magazine, she has found mistakes in every article she has edited.[80]

Surveys by the American Society of Newspaper Editors found that "even seemingly small errors feed public skepticism about a newspaper's credibility." Readers told the researchers in one study that they saw lots of small errors:

- ❖ 35 percent see spelling or grammar mistakes in their newspapers more than once a week;
- ❖ 21 percent see them almost daily;
- ❖ 23 percent of the public find factual errors in news stories at least once a week.[81]

As stated above, these errors were made by well-educated and experienced journalists. Everyone reading this book has proof-read a document only to have someone else find errors. It is frustrating and the reason why I use professional editors. You are virtually pinky swearing to notify me immediately if you find a typographical error in this book. In short, any writer, professional or otherwise, in any environment is prone to produce a product that contains errors that may drastically change the meaning of the words. But what about the errors that evidence more than just the failure of a keen eye for spelling and grammar?

The desire, and professional admonishment, to avoid close relationships may also lead to errors and inaccurate reporting.[82] The failure to "mix and mingle" may lead to isolation and perhaps the worst trap of all—surrounding oneself with other journalists above all others. This is a danger to all professions. Attorneys are cautioned against associating only with other attorneys. Like attorneys, journalists benefit from the opinions, beliefs, thoughts, and ideas of those outside their profession. As discussed in this book, having a professional relationship with a law enforcement officer or the head of an agency will not impair the objectivity of the journalist. This is part and parcel of a maxim I live by: If you surround yourself with people who agree with you, you'll never know when you're wrong.

Telling the Story

Journalists tell stories that are important to their customers and their communities. As I walked in the hallway of the *Marietta Daily Journal*, which published its first newspaper in 1866, I saw examples of headlines that told the story of the City of Marietta, the metropolitan Atlanta area, the State of Georgia, and the United States. The framed front pages carried photographs and stories of everything from national and international tragedies to significant political events and local disasters, like the massive flooding that took place locally in 2009. "Our job is to report the daily history of the community," Otis Brumby told me.

This need, and perhaps mission, to tell the story leads to several undeniable truths about the reporting of critical incidents. As Otis Brumby said, "The story is going to get told." J. K. Murphy had some specific advice for law enforcement officers and PIOs addressing journalists: "We're going to ask all the questions and answer what you can—explain what you cannot answer and why. Journalists will be aggressive and they compete with each other. Have answers ready when facing the press." He also had some of the best caveats I have read or heard on this topic: "We are going to get the story and the facts we believe the public deserves and needs."

Paul Crawley provided similar advice. He described that journalists tracking down information will speak with people who have varying degrees of information to offer, and some will not be able to add anything to the story. Some people were less than interested in speaking with him when he approached them, and Paul was surprisingly accepting of this reaction. When he met resistance, he would say this to the person he wanted to interview:

> You don't have to talk to me, but you can help shape what happens by what you say and how you say it.

He explained that journalists are trained and committed to getting information.

> If you slam a door and say "no comment," it makes you look guilty and makes us suspicious.

He went on to provide some advice for law enforcement officers and agencies that found themselves unable to answer questions.

> Give a reason if you cannot release info. Journalists should work with officers to know what can be said and to get something to show.

Over time, he explained that the relationships he formed, and his candor with people, allowed him to report the story without making enemies.

Paul also had some interesting words about the inaccuracy in news stories coming from law enforcement agencies.

> There is a problem relying on PIO alone as they are likely providing thirdhand information. They were not on the scene or if they were, they were not performing the

investigation. They may also receive information from a commander who also may not have been on the scene. Thirdhand information will contain errors. Journalists must look for eye witnesses.

His words explained why journalists will continue to pursue sources through official channels to verify the information they receive from a law enforcement agency. At the very least, a journalist concerned for any errors that may occur through the passing of information from the detective handling the case, through the detective's supervisor, and on to the PIO will drive that journalist to verify the accuracy of the facts they receive. Therefore, the agency and the PIO should not view the journalist's efforts as distrustful.

Once you apply this lens to the analysis, every officer should understand why journalists press for information on stories, even when they seem mundane. The decision as to whether the story deserves space and time is clearly driven by the perceived needs and desires of the community.

Listen to how the editor of a major southwest newspaper decided what he thought belonged on the front page. "To me, it comes down to two questions: Is this story boring or interesting? Is this story relevant or irrelevant to our readers?" He added, "Some stories may be boring but still have to be reported because they're important."[83]

This series of explanations should hopefully satisfy law enforcement officers that the journalists are not asking questions or pursuing a story with a goal to inconvenience officers or the agency. They are getting information out to the people whom they believe want to know it.

Imperfections in the Human Element

Many times, law enforcement officers and others will become irate when they are misquoted or when the facts are out of sequence, unclear, or inaccurate. My explanation for this is that journalists are human. While some have begun using recording devices to ease in the takedown and add to accuracy, it is neither required nor a professional standard. Irrespective of whether or not journalists use a recorder, they will make mistakes. Officers should not be surprised, as they do it too. The visual identification number on a vehicle may be transposed incorrectly, the year of a vehicle may be incorrect on an accident report, or the make and model of an item stolen during a burglary may be reversed when the information is entered into the National Crime Information Center.

A controversy exists as to whether a journalist should agree to read back all quotes and facts or review a story with a source prior to publication. There are folks standing firm on both sides of this issue. Many believe it is inappropriate to request or demand to see the story in final or near-final form. I make the analogy of a law enforcement officer writing a report. The complainant and witnesses take it for granted that you will get their quotes correct. However, officers do not offer, nor would they tolerate a demand for, the complainant and witnesses approving the report prior to filing. There is a degree of trust that must develop between the journalist and the person providing information. Like any other relationship, it will take time to develop, and if you simply do not trust a journalist, do not speak with them, or have a witness present when you do. Hopefully, this will be the rare occurrence.

Chapter Four

The Informal Media

Distracted from distraction by distraction. Filled with fancies and empty of meaning.
"Burnt Norton," T. S. Eliot (1936)

The informal media is comprised of social media, blogs, and comments to traditional news sources. They are largely unregulated and uncensored.
When Cops Kill: The Aftermath of a Critical Incident
Lance LoRusso (2012)

There are many things of which a wise man might wish to be ignorant.
Ralph Waldo Emerson

I've always been amazed at the things people will say to each other, either by words or gestures. After investigating claims of road rage, watching people drive in rush-hour traffic, and observing social media posts for close to ten years, I've come to believe there is no end to what passes as useful communication. If it's worth saying to someone somewhere, someone will say it. That is a low bar, and often it is the speaker who decides what is worth saying. So begins the cycle of nonsense founded in a basic truth of human behavior: few people will edit themselves.

Social Media

Social media is a phenomenon, and thousands of books have been written in the past ten years about it. How to participate, how to use social media for business, how to streamline your use of social media, and even how to stop obsessive use of social media. Between Facebook, Twitter, Instagram, Snapchat, LinkedIn, and others, people spend millions of hours communicating their thoughts. Some are deep, intimate thoughts; some are trite, such as detailed descriptions and photographs of their most recent meal; and many are critical of something. It is easy to view many of the angrier posts as rebels in search of a cause, as they always seem to find something agitating about the world around them. Winning a multimillion-dollar lottery would probably prompt a post complaining about the parking when they picked up their winnings. As strange and prolific as social media posts are, the informal media is a much bigger world.

Social media has the power to make an individual famous among strangers. A person posting thoughts, opinions, comments, photographs, or ideas inserts their efforts into an endless and permanent media. The post may garner responses and approval from strangers and has the potential to "go viral" in minutes. While there is no standard definition of "going viral," a popular post or video can receive millions of views or hits in a matter of hours. Prior to the advent of social media, it was virtually impossible for a person who did not control or own a radio, television, or newspaper outlet to reach that many people that quickly. The true power of social media is that both entry into the arena and posting is free.

Blogs

Blog is short for "logging the web" or "weblog" and is essentially a running diary or online journal. The term was shortened to "blog," and the word was added to mainstream dictionaries in 2004.[84] Name a topic and you will find someone writing a blog about it. A person who writes a blog is called a "blogger." Many times, a person will manage a blog and write on it, but they will also invite others, known as "guest bloggers," to post articles. When I released my book *Peacemaking*, I promoted the book through a "blog tour" of book sites and those that specifically promote Christian-based books. The audience for blogs varies depending upon the topic, the author, and the timeliness of the topics. However, blogs are a big part of the informal media, and law enforcement agencies must be involved. As you will learn from this chapter, involvement means active participation.

The number of blogs has exploded since the first blog, published by a student, appeared in 1994. In 1999, Technorati.com, a website that hosts blogs, estimated that there were twenty-three blogs and by 2006 that number exceeded 50 million.[85] In December 2005, experts estimated that 32 million Americans read blogs. In 2016, many bloggers have some of the same press credentials as those provided to journalists employed by traditional news sources.[86] Today, there are an estimated 173 million or more blogs.[87] Some are written by accomplished journalists. Michelle Malkin is a syndicated columnist, accomplished author, and blogger. Charles Krauthammer, MD, is a syndicated columnist, a blogger, and a Pulitzer Prize-winning author.

Blogs are posted in nearly every language in countries all around the world. In 2016, WordPress.com estimated that 209 million people read more than 22.6 million blog pages each month and there are 58.6 million new blog posts garnering 49 million new comments each month.[88] Some blogs are very interesting and are filled with well-researched information. Many attract advertisers, and some bloggers make a living mainly through advertising revenues.

Blogs vary in the length of their posts. Some are short in the length of the post, and others can be quite long. In fact, the truly tech-savvy consider Twitter and Tumblr to be "microblogs" or "tumblogs" that limit the amount of text or other content but still provide a format for people to post their comments and opinions about different topics. Other blogs are quite banal or more suited for the narrow-focused, navel-gazing folks attuned to a particular topic. In the "blogosphere," there is something for everyone.

The biggest lesson to be learned from the rise and success of blogs is this: if the content is relevant, if the posts are well written, and if the posts are pointed, the blog will likely be effective. Many effective blog posts are less than three hundred words. While there is much debate in the blogosphere about this topic, the general rule is simple: you need not write two-thousand-word blogs to be effective. Get to the point quickly, be concise, and leave the reader with good information. I once published long posts that were more akin to articles on my blog www.bluelinelawyer.com. As I changed my thinking on this through research, my blog posts became more concise, more effective, and easier to write. If I had a lot to say on a topic, I just divided the thoughts into separate blog posts. If I am writing about a technical legal topic, such as a new case on search and seizure from the United States Supreme Court, it is difficult to be accurate and effective in less than a hundred words.

Blogs are great for any law enforcement agency. Think about it: you can have a free platform to tell your story and put out positive information about your law enforcement officers, your law enforcement agency, and your community. There is no start-up cost, no fee for entry, no censorship by third parties, and the information is available to *everyone* with an internet connection, including media sources. You can also direct people to your agency blog posts from your agency website, social media posts, media interviews, and community presentations. A blog is an invaluable tool for any law enforcement agency to push positive information, educate the public, and provide background for anyone doing research about the agency, the law, your training process, your equipment, and your dedication to your community.

Some city and county attorneys, and some agency heads, will scream out loudly against putting this information on the internet. I have heard the statements "they'll just use that information to sue us," or "why should we tell them anything they can use against us in court?" Well, that is just silly. I say that not as an author, but as a former law enforcement officer and now an attorney who defends officers. What could possibly be wrong with telling the public and news media that you train your officers to prepare for active-assailant scenarios, that you've put all of your officers through the Crisis Intervention Training[89] (CIT) certification, or that your agency provides a handgun-safety class and a citizen police academy? You control the content. As an attorney, the arguments against my position are naïve. Any litigant filing suit against your agency will get this information through the formal discovery process anyway. Why not use it to educate the public and journalists?

The biggest obstacles to law enforcement agencies setting up and maintaining blogs are ignorance of the subject, resistance to change, and the chain of command getting in the way of the free flow of information to the designated department blogger. As you can see, and as I discussed in more practical terms in Chapter Two, your agency blog will become an invaluable tool following a critical incident. As to ignorance of the subject, there is enough information in this book to get you past that hurdle. If you still need more information, there are currently more than six thousand books on Amazon about blogging. As to resistance to change, hang up your flintlock pistol and put your department-issued horse out to pasture. Get with the program. If you are one of the folks who fought using fax machines and email, perhaps you should either retire or delegate these tasks to the myriad of competent folks in your law enforcement agency.

As to the chain of command as an obstacle, this just requires education and courage. I understand that your city manager may be the problem, but keep pushing hard. Buy them a copy of this book. I guarantee when the city manager is hiding in his office afraid to walk to the parking lot due to the journalists and protesters on the property following a critical incident, they will be begging for a way to get out the city's story and some positive information about the department. By then, it may be too late.

The last obstacle, the free flow of information, is the easiest to resolve. You can create, maintain, and promote an informative blog for your law enforcement agency by publishing the information you are required to release to the public. This will also lighten the load for the person designated to respond to requests for this information. Here is a list of information your agency can post on a weekly or monthly basis that it would likely be required to release to the public upon request. Some agencies are uneasy publishing crime statistics, and some politicians believe it will lead to negative publicity. First, it is public record and is available from several secondary sources. Second, setting out the problem, such as an increase in burglaries, allows for better crime prevention efforts. This may also help when budget cuts pit hiring officers against improvements at the city park. The agency will have a group of informed citizens ready to support more funding for the agency to make the community safer.

Information	Frequency of Publication on a Blog
• Number of vehicle crashes investigated • Number of arrests • Number of law enforcement officer-citizen contacts • Number of stranded motorists assisted by law enforcement officers (i) • Number of citizens contacted by law enforcement agencies' crime prevention programs with a breakdown by program • Number of car crashes worked (total, with injuries, with fatalities) • Number of burglaries reported (and number cleared) • Number of seatbelt citations issued along with the results of any seatbelt-use surveys • Number of 911 calls • Number of nonemergency calls for service • Number of media interviews by PIOs and command staff[i] • Number of miles driven by patrol units • Number of lost children and adults located • Number of homicides and deaths investigated along with the number of cleared cases • Number of reports of child abuse or molestation investigated • Number of alarm calls received and investigated along with the number of false alarms • Number of wanted persons located • Number of requests to assist other agencies received • Types of drugs seized • Number of armed and strong-arm robberies investigated and cleared • Number of commendations and letters of appreciation received	Monthly, quarterly summary, and annual summary
• Population of your jurisdiction (day and night if this number differs)	Monthly with annual reports of changes
• Law enforcement officers hired	As academies finish
• Law enforcement officers completing FTO training • Law enforcement officers promoted	As appropriate

(i) This figure should be tracked as part of the law enforcement agency's process of monitoring and improving interactions with journalists. See Chapter Five for more information.[90]

This list alone provides enough information to post twenty-five blogs. That is nearly one half of a year posting weekly. If you add informational blogs and videos for crime prevention purposes, like how to trim shrubs around a house, keeping valuables out of sight in parked vehicles, keeping doors and windows locked, and other topics such as recent law enforcement officer training, the agency can easily fill a year with weekly blogs. You can also link to other blogs and articles that would be of interest to citizens, journalists, and your officers.

The rise of blogs has been troublesome for traditional media sources. They provide sources of information for topics that were traditionally explored only in professional media sources like politics, religion, foreign affairs, sports, and current events. Gone are the days when the cost of setup barred all but the organized or wealthy from creating a widespread news source. Now, all it takes is a computer and an internet connection. If what you are writing or the videos you are posting, often called vlogs, are popular, you will attract readers, viewers, and advertisers. I analogize the rise of blogs and their effect on traditional media sources to the rise of self-publishing companies. At one time, getting a book published required an agent and years of thick skin to handle rejections. Now, an author can write, edit, and publish a book in a matter of months without the intervention of any third party who can quash or severely hamper that effort. There is another important part of this parallel: while there are professionals working in self-publishing and blogging, there are some very unskilled amateurs putting out inferior products and materials.

Informal Media Changes the Rules and the Game

Informal media changed the paradigm of the mainstream media controlling the message. Don't believe me? Why does every major news agency and local media outlet have a sophisticated social media presence? I recently watched a video on the *New York Times* website.[91] This includes a presence on every major social media platform and blogs. Often the individual journalists have their own presence in the informal media space. Although journalists often wrote books, it was unheard of that they would publish their own material on a daily or hourly basis. Perhaps this is why the balance of power seems to have shifted to the big-name journalists and away from the media outlets that employ them. Although I have been unable to verify this, or perhaps no one in the profession has been willing to admit it, this also has the effect of creating some semblance of job security for journalists who can not only build their own popularity, but can also demonstrate their ability to bring readers, listeners, and viewers to any station that employs them.

The traditional and professional news sources no longer control access to the public, and therefore they no longer control the message. If you are old enough to remember the Sears catalog, you remember that there were two ways to shop at Sears—visit a store, or place an order by phone or mail. Now, in an age of Amazon and other online retailers that do not have a physical store, there is no way to steer, guide, or control how consumers obtain what they desire. The same is true of the news.

As stated above, in order to keep up with societal changes in how people consume news, traditional and professional news outlets have taken to competing by not only using social media and blogs, but also having "comment" sections to stories they post on their websites. These comment sections are no doubt used to rate the popularity of stories and journalists. However, they are quite problematic. In most cases, they are largely unmonitored and uncensored. From my conversations with journalists and my research about journalism regarding this lack of control, I suspect this stems from a desire to let people speak freely. Journalists and editors truly struggle with the line between inappropriate speech and giving free rein to those who desire to comment. The First Amendment guides their decisions, and I suppose we are all better off for that. However, I have represented law enforcement officers who were unfairly and viciously attacked in these forums.

One left the state over the informal media coverage of an officer-involved shooting. He was eventually cleared of any wrongdoing in the case, but the comments remain online in perpetuity.

The proliferation of informal media, and specifically the use of informal media by law enforcement agencies, is having an effect on the way journalists do business. First is the frequency with which news can be disseminated. As Paul Crawley told me, "No one wants to wait for the news anymore." It is clear that there is no reason to do so.

The frequency of publication is not the only change. There is also a new drive to be succinct and powerful. I found a very interesting article regarding so-called "data journalism" that outlines how media outlets and journalists are learning to gather data and use that data to drive their stories as opposed to incorporating some data into a story to lend credibility, prove a point, or foster discussion. This trend is being driven in part by the need for journalists to relate the work of law enforcement officers to their customers. The traditional method in which journalists relied upon law enforcement officers for information and the law enforcement agency relied upon journalists to tell their story is becoming ineffective.

> Journalists are being shut out as police craft their own "news" by going directly to the public on social media.

> "Most journalists don't have much contact with cops anymore," Johnston told me. "They don't know them by name. We don't even go to police stations, and that means you don't have the detectives or the patrol guys telling you stuff that you wouldn't otherwise hear about."[92]

This proves, from the perspective of a journalist, that the principles outlined in this book are critical and effective. If social media, blogs, and other direct vehicles are so effective at helping law enforcement agencies tell their stories, keep in touch with the communities they serve, and keep the public informed, why is your agency not maximizing the potential of this media?

Informal Media Wars, Tactical Plans, and How to Survive the Body Count

It's hard to have a plan to handle informal media issues if you do not understand the battlefield. You would not think of sending four police recruits into a house to remove a barricaded suspect, so why do you think you are prepared to handle and respond to attacks and negative information in the informal media world if you do not understand the terms?

The formulation of a plan and policy cannot be abdicated. I once read a joke to the effect that a man did not need to hire tech support for problems with his electronic devices because he had grandchildren. It was cute, but that is not a great strategy for a law enforcement agency. Sadly, this is how many law enforcement agencies deal with this issue. They put an eager and willing young officer in charge with little or no supervision or training because "they know that stuff better than anybody in the department." This statement is often made without vetting the skills of the officer, finding out if they have any formal training or sending them to receive it, or checking to see if someone else in the department knows more. To many agencies, having a presence in the informal media is a nuisance with some marginal benefit. Hopefully, I am convincing you otherwise.

The most important thing to know about the informal media is that it is ALL connected. Blogs reference Twitter posts, and Twitter posts appear on Facebook and Instagram. Hashtags, otherwise known to anyone over the age of thirty as "the number sign," are used on the internet to link or "string" topics and informal media posts. In a sense, all posts on informal media that use the same hashtag are linked together. They can be searched as a hashtag, they can be referenced by the hashtag, and the use of the hashtag provides a running "conversation" consisting of all of the comments that employ the same hashtag. In fact, an agency can create a hashtag to link all agency posts, such as #LAPD or #NYPD.

Some hashtags are composed of a single word like "#yankees," which produces over 72 million search results on Google. Others are sets of words written without spaces. The words need not be a formal title, and it is not uncommon for people to spontaneously string together words in a phrase such as "#copseatdonuts," which incidentally garners nearly two hundred results in a Google search, including a Twitter page by that name. The hashtag serves as an identifier or reference point signaling that all information posted to the internet using that same hashtag and the same language is related. While that is generally a true statement, it gets a bit confusing because the hashtag system does not care whether or not the people writing related posts agree with each other. This leads to some interesting exchanges. For instance, people using #ferguson include journalists covering events related to the shooting of Michael Brown in Ferguson, Missouri, on August 9, 2014, peaceful protestors, radical and violent protestors, and law enforcement supporters. All of them share a common goal; they want anyone reading their informal media post to understand it is related to a larger issue, they want to join the discussion on the topic, and they want people to read the other related posts.

If you are sitting at a computer, try running a Google search for your law enforcement agency with a hashtag in front of it. Try a few variations, as people may shorten the name of the jurisdiction or the law enforcement agency for ease of typing. Some are easy, like #NYPD, which yields over 20 million results. A search for my old department, #cobbcountypolice, yields over three hundred results. As predicted, some are supportive of the law enforcement agency and the law enforcement officers working in it, and some are, well, less than warm and fuzzy, including the genius who believes the department is more of a threat to her than ISIS. I'll allow a few moments for you to stop laughing. Despite her publicly stated beliefs, I'll bet she will call 911 at the first sign of a terrorist attack. Employing your own agency hashtag allows you to link your internet and social media presence as well as monitor and influence the dialogue about your agency.

It is important to see what is being said about your department. Until you know and understand how the system works, you cannot formulate an action plan to respond and work to protect your law enforcement officers and your agency. You can join the conversation, disseminate information to dispel rumors, and give updates regarding topics being discussed simply by posting in the informal media space using the same hashtag. The sooner you correct the inaccurate information in the informal media space, the less damage to your law enforcement agency and officers, and the better your chances of having the accurate information become the "facts" everyone knows to be true.

I've had officers call my office and get upset about an informal media attack on their agency and want to sue for some sort of copyright infringement. Sorry, that will likely not happen any time soon. The names of government entities can generally be used without restriction, as they belong to the people in general, not any one individual. Further, the informal media space is largely untested waters when it comes to defamation lawsuits. Being the test case may be necessary in some instances, but it certainly is not preferable.

Hashtags cannot be "owned" in the traditional sense, although you can register a hashtag at www.twubs.com. However, as stated above, this will not prevent anyone else from using your hashtag to post negative, and often false, information about your agency. It is not the same as a trademark or copyright that can be enforced through the courts through an injunction or other legal remedies to prevent someone from using your intellectual property. The simple fact and the rule of the internet is this: the speed of the postings using any hashtag are so quick and so voluminous that it would be impossible to regulate anyway. The best defense in the social media space is a strong and extremely diligent offense.

Let's look at an example of how to respond and turn the tide on an attack in the informal media space. One of the first things to remember is that the informal media space, like any other publication vehicle, is used by professionals as well as bottom feeders. By bottom feeders I mean the sensationalist, unprofessional people who seem to reside at the fringes of the spectrum. They are the ones that always make outrageous claims, and no one expects them to be correct. They may be well funded, but they are still wrong. The same is true in the informal media world. You will find comments, posts, and other statements about your agency that are pure nonsense. If that information was placed there by a fringe source, ignore it. For example, the genius who wore a shirt following the death of Michael Brown advising that he would rather meet up with a terrorist than a law enforcement officer in his jurisdiction should be left to his own devices. Perhaps he will get his wish and will no longer be involved in the discussion. However, other comments, posts, or statements should not be ignored. Below is an example of the strategy in a hypothetical situation.

Following an officer-involved shooting, there is a tsunami of informal media posts regarding the fact that the body of the decedent, James Roberts, was left on the street, and people are blaming the officers who investigated the officer-involved shooting, claiming they had no respect for the decedent or the family. You will recall that this was a powerful issue following the death of Michael Brown. Let's say that after an internet and social media search, your PIO sees that the hashtag #5thstreetjustice[93] is the most common one being used about the officer-involved shooting. Some of the posts may look like this:

No one should lay in the street when they are dead. Police don't care! #5thstreetjustice

Cops walked over his body for hours. No respect. #5thstreetjustice

I bet no one ever let a cop's body stay in the sun for hours. Not right. #5thstreetjustice

If your law enforcement agency remains silent, this conversation will continue for days, weeks, months, or longer. I received questions in interviews months after the death of Michael Brown asking why law enforcement officers did not remove the body. Instead of waiting for the attacks to end, which may never happen, be proactive. Here is a post that is factual, does not take a position, and changes the dialogue.

#ConwayPD respects families. Officers cannot move a body without Medical Examiner OK. ME was busy on a natural death. #5thstreetjustice

Note the use of the hashtag for the law enforcement agency so the post will connect with other hashtags that reference the law enforcement agency. Also note that the post does not have to follow strict grammatical rules. For example, it is perfectly acceptable to use the initials ME without explaining the term because the letters are capitalized in the words Medical Examiner. There is no need to use the name of the decedent because the hashtag #5thstreetjustice is associated with the death of James Roberts. A critical part of this post is the fact that it is 140 characters, the limit for a Twitter post. Whether or not your law enforcement agency posts this on Twitter, which it should, someone invariably will share it, and if the post fits the Twitter format, there will be no need for anyone to shorten it. Make the post easy to pass on in the form you want.

The most crucial part of writing such a post is to make certain, and double check, that the facts are correct without exception. Posting inaccurate information will create a firestorm. You should also check with the parties involved in any way with the post. For example, in this hypothetical case, you should contact the medical examiner and ensure that she is aware of the post. In a high-profile case, you can expect that the logs and activity sheets of the ME investigators will be sought by journalists through open-record requests.

Finally, you should expect that the media, professional and informal, will not only fact-check your post, they will also follow up. You may want to draft another post containing the state statute that prohibits law enforcement officers from moving a body without permission from the medical examiner. As I've stated throughout this book, never miss an opportunity to educate and inform. Here is an example of a follow-up post:

> OCGA § 45-16-29 prevents the movement of a body until the investigation is complete and the ME approves. #ConwayPD #5thstreetjustice

The follow-up post also references the hashtag for the law enforcement agency and the James Roberts officer-involved shooting. This post is also fewer than 140 characters. You can bet some members of the public and every journalist will look up this code section and read it. If this is a growing issue in your community, you should have copies of the code section available at the law enforcement agency and the medical examiner's office. You may even decide to post the statute on your agency website.

It will take some time to write and rewrite posts to keep them under the 140-character limit. Remember that this limit includes the hashtag, punctuation, and all spaces. I spent about ten minutes editing both of the posts included above. It is a small investment of time that will reap many benefits. You can also link the post to your own blog content, press releases, or videos on your YouTube channel. You can even include hashtags in the description of your YouTube videos. Control the message and tell your own story.

Are Your Agency's Social Media Policies Protecting the Agency and the Officers?

Beginning several years ago, many law enforcement agencies began drafting and implementing social media policies for the agency. I considered including several examples, all of which are available through open-record requests, however, the goal of this book is to educate, not embarrass anyone, and many of the policies are problematic. The social media policies I reviewed vary—a lot.

Some have precautionary statements that protect and provide some good, general advice. They remind officers that what they post is generally not private, and despite all of the privacy settings on your social media account, you cannot be guaranteed that the information posted will not become widely distributed. Often, the information is leaked from "secure" accounts for which all security precautions have been taken by a person who was an authorized recipient. I have defended several law enforcement officers who lost their jobs due to a post on a "locked-down" social media account that was provided to the law enforcement agency by a "friend" on that account.

Another caution is to avoid providing personal information on the same site that identifies you as a law enforcement officer. While a lot of officers properly set the privacy protections on their social media sites to protect their personal information, I am amazed at how many have pictures of themselves in uniform and profiles that provide access to their dates of birth and cell numbers, as well as the names and photographs of their families. Most of this is a function of failing to learn the particular social media site and using the tools it provides. The instructions can be a bit technical at times, making it difficult to use. It seems that some social media sites often change the security features and do not want to encourage people to restrict access to their sites. Others, like Instagram, make it easy. Remember, pretty much everything on Twitter is public.

I have represented law enforcement officers who were disciplined by their agency for social media posts. Some of the discipline was extremely petty and a function of ignorance on the part of the command staff. In those cases, I found the command staff tended to think in terms of absolutes, making statements like, "Once it's out on Facebook, the whole world sees it," or "You have no right to criticize the department in any forum." The first statement indicates a lack of understanding about social media, the second a lack of understanding of the First Amendment. In several of those cases, the officer restricted posts to "friends only," so while it may be shared without the user's permission, they were not publishing it to the world. In the second case, recent case law may prove them wrong. The National Labor Relations Board (NLRB) has ruled that social media posts are protected as part of the right to criticize working conditions and organize.[94] The law is still catching up to social media. This is especially true of First Amendment jurisprudence. Command staff would be well advised to be cautious regarding discipline stemming from social media posts. Check with counsel before taking any action, including searching personal cell phones and storage devices, and always consider a counseling session over discipline. You do not want to be cross-examined in a hearing and admit you were not familiar enough with social media or the law to make an informed decision. Do not assume that the city or county attorney is well versed in the law in this area. Take your time and proceed with caution.

Before you draft and implement a social media policy, speak with other law enforcement agencies and consult an attorney. You must also keep in mind that the social media world is rapidly evolving in terms of technology and volume. Several popular social media sites did not exist five years ago. This means that any policy you develop should be reviewed frequently and perhaps annually. Further, the law surrounding the ability of a law enforcement agency to control social media posts of employees and the protections afforded those employees is rapidly evolving as courts receive these cases and judges get up to speed on the technology. Be very cautious of anyone who provides you with advice framed in absolutes. The law evolves slowly based upon a principle of *stare decisis,* meaning that court decisions should rely and build upon previous case law.[95] This makes the law more predictable. However, in new areas, this process can take a while, and it is more difficult to predict how courts will handle a given situation.

As a final word on this issue, consider that officers are going to defend other officers, they will speak out when the profession is attacked, and they are entitled to have opinions. This is part of who they are. When you draft your policy, you must expect that they will post and comment on posts that describe officers being injured, killed, or treated improperly. This is no different than someone asking their opinion at a party, family gathering, or a coffee shop. For a large segment of the younger generation of officers, this is how they communicate with their friends, coworkers, and relatives. Obviously, there are inappropriate ways to do so. However, the law enforcement agency must be cautious about punishing comments on social media that would result in no response or perhaps a verbal counseling in any other forum. Remember that challenges to discipline based upon First Amendment protections can be very costly to defend. If the agency loses, you could be faced with a loss of immunity as well as paying attorney fees and court costs.

The Informal Media World
Is Here to Stay and Is Growing Stronger

The world of informal media is growing faster than traditional news outlets and shows no signs of stopping. Like any other changing technology or societal paradigm shift, law enforcement agencies and officers must learn to adapt and work within the new parameters. Take some training, get on the internet, and see what is out there, then dive on in. The benefits of participation far outweigh the dangers.

Chapter Five

The Law Enforcement Agency

At one time, we could count on the media to tell our story for us. Those days are over. We must be in charge of our own narrative.

Law enforcement officer with over thirty years of service with the majority in command positions

Put out the facts that will not change; put them out as quickly as possible. Make sure the information is correct. Saying we are in the investigation phase and cannot release any information is not going to cut it anymore.

We knew the "Hands Up Don't Shoot" was a fallacy and that there were no shots in the back. We were unable to shut down that false narrative, and look what they morphed into.

Colonel Ron Replogle, retired superintendent of the Missouri State Patrol, placed in charge of the City of Ferguson and St. Louis County Missouri area from August 14 through the second week of September 2014

Given the choice, most senior leadership in law enforcement agencies would rather have a root canal than deal with journalists following a critical incident. This is understandable when we look at the age of those typically in command. A police chief or sheriff who was born between 1950 and 1970 saw a very different slate of journalists than we see today. First, there were far fewer media outlets when they grew up. For example, in 1960, there were no cable news sources, and in a large city like Chicago, New York, Miami, or Los Angeles, there may have been five news stations.[96]

The number of stations also multiplied, despite an FCC freeze in the issuing of station licenses from 1948 to 1952. In 1946, there were six stations in only four cities; by

1952, there were 108 stations in sixty-five cities, most of them recipients of licenses issued right before the freeze. When the freeze was lifted and new licenses began to be issued again, there was a mad rush to establish new stations and get on the air. By 1955, almost five hundred television stations were operating in the US.[97]

The journalists on the news were anchors who read the stories prepared by field journalists or copy editors.[98] It was rare to have a journalist in the field providing information through what is now known as a live feed.[99]

Broadcasts can be classified as "recorded" or "live." The former allows correcting errors, and removing superfluous or undesired material, rearranging it, applying slow-motion and repetitions, and other techniques to enhance the program. However, some live events like sports television can include some of the aspects including slow-motion clips of important goals/hits, etc., in between the live television telecast.[100]

For example, during the 1968 Democratic National Convention, people tuned in to watch Dan Rather report live from Chicago, which, at the time, was ground-breaking coverage.[101]

The nightly news, typically at six o'clock p.m., was delivered by well-known, respected anchors like Walter Cronkite and Edward R. Murrow who provided formal and often quite stilted readings of the news fed to them on scripts. In fact, the famous footage of Walter Cronkite informing the world that President John F. Kennedy was dead, which can be seen on YouTube and other internet sites, marked a change in the way news hit the airways. Walter Cronkite appears in a button-down short-sleeved shirt with a tie but without a jacket in a broadcast that interrupted all programs uttering those now famous words: "From Dallas, Texas, the Flash apparently official. President Kennedy died at one p.m. Central Standard time, two p.m. Eastern Standard time, some thirty minutes ago."[102]

This was the world in which most command staff and agency heads grew up and learned about the media and journalists. Compare their experiences with those of the youngest officers in their agencies. Law enforcement officers in their twenties and thirties grew up with reality shows, breaking news coming to them on their cell phones or smartphones, searching the internet—including social media sites—for news, and posting their own impressions of the news. News to these officers, and journalists of the same or similar age, is extremely fast-breaking, always changing, subject to updates on a minute-by-minute basis, and largely stale in an hour or so. Further, Twitter is often seen as a great source for "breaking news" even though most will concede the information is often inaccurate and almost always unverified. As Paul Crawley said during our interview, and it bears repeating, "No one wants to wait for the news anymore."

The simple fact is that many law enforcement officers do not understand, like, or trust the media. I discussed earlier how they view many news stories as inaccurate based upon their personal experiences. However, unfortunately, many officers gain a distrust of the media because they do not understand the news cycle. I will discuss the news cycle more in Chapter Seven. I believe that once most officers understand the reasons why news reports often contain inaccurate information and what seems more like opinion than facts, they will at least understand that the journalists are not intentionally attempting to lie or deceive the public. As we discussed in the previous chapter, any effort to intentionally report what they know to be inaccurate information or to deceive the public would be a violation of the ethical standards of their profession.[103]

I see law enforcement agencies make rookie mistakes every day, especially following critical incidents. Although some agencies nail it and get it right every time, most are caught like a deer in the headlights when a critical incident puts them into the spotlight. As discussed earlier, some of the mistakes stem from the rigidity of the chain of command. However, some of them show the utter naïveté of those in command. Unfortunately, their errors and the failure of city managers, county officials, attorneys for the law enforcement agencies, and elected leaders to make decisions often lead to a paucity of information being transmitted to the public. It also provides an open invitation for others to supply the narrative that rightly belongs to and should be supplied by the law enforcement agency.

The Top-Ten Mistakes Law Enforcement Officers and Agencies Make Following a Critical Incident

This list reflects the information I have seen provided by law enforcement agencies following a critical incident from across the United States. Some of the information involves critical incidents in which I have been involved representing officers who found themselves at the center of the media inquiries. Not all of these situations involve an officer-involved shooting. It is important to remember that even a widely publicized complaint of rude behavior by an officer can occupy the headlines for days or months. Going forward in this book, I will no longer separate the informal media from other professional sources. It does not matter where the negative news stories appear; they all have the potential to damage the reputations and careers of individual officers as well as the relationship between the law enforcement agency and the public, including journalists. So, here is my top-ten list in no particular order.

1. Failing to respond to negative stories in the press
2. Failing to anticipate negative media attention
3. Failing to use resources to push back against negative media attention
4. Waiting for negative news stories to "blow over" or "go away"

5. Putting the wrong person in charge of disseminating information and responding to media requests

6. Failing to have a policy in effect to handle negative media attention

7. Releasing facts that have not been vetted and cannot be supported

8. Failing to immediately correct negative or inaccurate information promulgated in the media or other sources

9. Failing to properly monitor news stories to allow the agency to be proactive, responsive, and follow through until the end of the life of the story

10. Failing to follow up when all of the information is known and the underlying investigation can no longer be compromised

As you look through this list, you may see some statements that describe your agency and, perhaps, your own mistakes being driven by policies. Take a deep breath and keep thinking through it. Most importantly, keep reading. There is nothing wrong with having made mistakes. The tragedy is repeating them.

Once you have identified errors on this list that apply to your agency or others that you have discovered reading this book, make your own list. Critically ask yourself these three questions:

1. What did we do wrong in handling the media attention surrounding the last critical incident?
2. What changes can we make to avoid mistakes in the future?
3. What individuals and training are necessary to make the changes needed to improve our policies, our practices, and our self-assessment?

These are often difficult questions. Further, if you do not identify at the outset the names, titles, and required training of the individuals you need to assemble to fix the problem, your efforts may be for naught. For example, an overpowering city manager or city attorney can overrule the decisions of the chief of police and may have a tendency to do so in times of high stress. Therefore, you should have them involved in this critique and planning process. You should also consider involving a media relations expert or attorney who practices in this area who can provide input into the three questions posed above as well as how you can make changes that will truly make an impact in the future.

Let's review the top-ten mistakes in detail and explore why they can have such a devastating effect.

1. Failing to respond to negative stories in the press

By now, you have the distinct understanding that I do not believe in sitting idle in the face of negative news stories, especially those that disseminate inaccurate or false information. Such a strategy not only makes it difficult to climb the curve when attempting to correct the negative images and opinions created by the negative stories, but the damage to individual officers may be irreversible. Consider that Darren Wilson was cleared of wrongdoing by every public entity that investigated his actions, yet his law enforcement career is over.

Second, and this is even more basic and undeniable, during this time of negative press, journalists want to hear from you. They will give you opportunities to respond, and you will not be forced to chase them down to get a sound bite on the air. Think about how to respond, take the time to develop a strategy, and be prepared to answer tough questions. When the interview is over, release your own statement in the form of a press release, recorded statement, video, or message via social media or your agency website. This will prevent any journalist from misquoting you, make the statement and information more readily available to the media and the public, and discourage journalists with an improper agenda from unfairly editing your words.

2. **Failing to anticipate negative media attention**

This is unforgivable. I bet if we closed the doors and sat around a table, a dozen law enforcement officers and agency heads could create a list of twenty events that are likely or highly likely to bring negative media attention upon a law enforcement agency. For your reading pleasure, I will include my own list. Here goes:

a. An officer-involved shooting

b. A law enforcement officer getting arrested for anything, especially a DUI or an assault

c. The death of a child, pregnant female, or elderly person during an encounter with a law enforcement officer

d. The use of force by a law enforcement officer that results in the death of a family pet

e. The execution of a search warrant that results in an officer-involved shooting or use of deadly force

f. An allegation of racial profiling

g. An allegation of misuse of public funds

h. A lawsuit filed against the law enforcement agency or the government entity alleging improper use of force, violation of any law, or discrimination against employees or citizens

i. A hostage situation wherein anyone is injured

j. A serious car crash involving a law enforcement officer on duty that results in an injury or a death— even if the decedent was attempting to elude the officer

k. A chase that results in a car crash involving an injury to anyone other than the driver of the fleeing vehicle

l. An allegation of excessive force

m. An investigation by federal authorities into the law enforcement agency or any law enforcement officer for any reason

n. Any civil disturbance that results in a clash between law enforcement officers and protestors or rioters

o. Any protest that is not completely peaceful

p. The escape of an inmate from custody

q. The inadvertent and improper release of an inmate

r. Any public clash between your law enforcement agency and another law enforcement agency, public safety entity, or government entity

s. Any allegation of false arrest

t. An allegation of a delayed response that led to an injury or severe property damage

u. An allegation of a tactical entry into the wrong business or residence

v. The death of a prisoner in custody

w. A high-profile crime that captures widespread media attention due to the number of people killed, the types of injuries, the method(s) of death, or the motivation of the perpetrator

I'm quite certain you will have others on your list that would only make me revise this one! So, if it is this easy to come up with a list, why don't agencies have a plan to respond to every one of these events?

Take the time to draft a model press release. This process will cause you to think about some valid questions: What information will the journalists want? What information are we likely to have in the first hours and days? What information is not likely to be available? What information do you anticipate that you will be required to withhold to protect the integrity of the investigation? What units are likely to be involved in such an investigation? Is it appropriate to tailor the story to a spokesperson other than the assigned PIO or command staff? These are all legitimate inquiries that will force you to consider details that are typically left to chance or evaluated on the fly at the last minute.

3. **Failing to use resources to push back against negative media attention**

You have a relationship with journalists, and some are stronger than others. During a wave of negative press, you must rely upon your connections for assistance in getting out your message. Local journalists know that long after the national media leaves your parking lot, they will be at your door seeking information on a homicide that affects the community but has not captured the attention of the media outside your city or county. This, along with your personal relationship, will be a motivating force in securing their assistance.

You can also use social media as described in Chapter Four. Also do not forget about the most powerful tool you have in your arsenal—the press conference. If you hold a press conference, you must properly announce it, provide packets for attendees, and make arrangements for parking and seating for photographers as well as journalists. They will come to you, and you can in a very real sense control the message. I will discuss press conferences in more detail in Chapter Eight.

4. **Waiting for negative news stories to "blow over" or "go away"**

This has been the subject of much debate in the past several years. Let me help you with your analysis—they will not "blow over" or "go away." Perhaps this was the case years ago, but especially after the events listed above, the media attention will not go away. If you do not fill in the blanks in the facts being reported, someone else will. If you do not correct the misinformation being reported, it will become "established" by the sheer force of being reported over and over again and being inserted into the whirlwind of the internet. At some point, it is nearly impossible to reverse that tide, at least not entirely.

You do not need to put out an encyclopedia of information, but releasing general information as well as statistics and the progress of the investigation is ALWAYS a better option than remaining silent. Suspects have that right; law enforcement agencies do not. Put simply: avoid the information vacuum!

5. **Putting the wrong person in charge of disseminating information and responding to media requests**

I discuss the general considerations about this in Chapter Six, but to summarize those points, don't put someone who hates the media in front of a camera, on a phone, or in the presence of journalists. It will not end well. For this point I want to dig deeper.

Every agency has PIOs and command staff with different backgrounds, work histories, and ages. Perhaps in the case about an officer-involved shooting in a low-income apartment complex, you should allow a PIO who grew up in a similar environment to make a plea for cell phone footage of the incident. I will never be convinced that there was no cell phone footage of the encounter between Officer Darren Wilson and Michael Brown. However, the police department was not asking for it and, as I said on CNN live a few days after the event, anyone who possessed such footage might be fearful of coming forward. I spoke with an officer who attended one of my classes. He grew up in a very rough area in inner-city Detroit. He is also convinced that cell phone footage exists, or at least it did at one time. In an area where officers were not welcome, their actions were certainly filmed on a regular basis. Perhaps a plea for such footage by an officer who can state publicly and from personal experience how hard it would be to provide it, would make a difference.

Make certain that the person in charge of receiving and responding to requests has appropriate training in the laws of your state. In preparation for writing this book, I surveyed the open-record laws, which are known by various names, in all fifty states in the United States and Washington, DC. The laws vary a great deal, as expected. However, they all have a few things in common. First, they tend to be complex and reference other state statutes. Second, they have been interpreted by case law that may alter the common and apparent meaning of the statute. Finally, case law places agencies on notice as to what information must be released, the acceptable format for requests, and what records are exempt from disclosure. It would be quite the extraordinary law enforcement officer or civilian who is able to become and remain up to date on these decisions. Whoever is placed in charge of receiving and responding to requests *must* have access to an attorney to assist without the need or formality of going through the chain of command. The failure to put these measures in place is equivalent to placing a competent person behind the wheel of a patrol car, ordering them to travel through crowded traffic while driving lights and siren, and then blindfolding them.

6. Failing to have a policy in effect to handle negative media attention

Whether or not your agency is certified on a national or state level, once you anticipate or experience an event for which your law enforcement agency was not prepared, you should begin assembling a team to draft a policy to address it.[104] Policies reflect the collective wisdom of the agency and provide a guideline for action. Policies do NOT provide a blueprint with rigid details and specific steps. Like a use of force policy that recognizes that officers will need to use force at some point in the course of their duties, there are laws surrounding the use of force, and the use of force must be regulated. The use-of-force policy does not proscribe specific steps and would be unworkable if it did. The same is true of a policy developed to respond to negative media attention. Create guidelines to assist in responding to the event, and leave sufficient room for the imposition of reasoned judgment.

You must begin with a recognition that the policy will be a public record. Second, I would not be shy about sharing it. The policy should state that the agency will promptly respond to all media inquiries and disseminate any and all facts that can be shared without compromising an active criminal or administrative investigation. Third, recognize that having a policy on this topic may be above the national standards, but having a media policy is certainly not.[105]

7. Releasing facts that have not been vetted and cannot be supported

Police officials initially reported that Ferguson Police Officer Darren Wilson was not aware of a recent strong-arm robbery in the area that video footage confirmed was perpetrated in part by Michael Brown. This information proved false, and Officer Wilson was aware of the strong-arm robbery as well as the description.[106] I recall hearing the statement by Ferguson Police officials that Officer Darren Wilson was not aware of the strong-arm robbery. I remember because I was certain that, absent a serious fluke, that statement was likely inaccurate. The strong-arm robbery occurred close enough to the area of the shooting that Michael Brown and Dorian Johnson were able to walk there in a few minutes. Therefore, if a lookout or the dispatch to the crime were put out on the radio or via mobile data terminal, Officer Darren Wilson would have been aware of it. Unfortunately, when the inaccurate statement was corrected, it only fed the fire of a cover-up and conspiracy.

8. Failing to immediately correct negative information promulgated in the media

It will happen. The law enforcement agency, sometimes due in part to the extreme pressure to release information, will make an error. When that occurs, correct it immediately. Doing so not only avoids having the misinformation in the news cycle for a long period of time, it also allows the law enforcement agency to minimize any potential damages in a civil action. A basic concept of punitive damages, for example, is the goal of punishing a bad actor for acts that are wanton, reckless, or done with the intent of causing harm.[107] Swift efforts to correct misinformation can effectively limit or even extinguish a claim based upon the release of improper information. State laws vary, so you should check with counsel who is licensed in your state.

Be swift, be concise, and if possible explain the reason for the error. People will understand an error made in good faith. While the media coverage may still be less than forgiving, the story of the misinformation will eventually be replaced by the law enforcement agency's efforts to correct the error. If the information concerns an individual or an entity, contact the appropriate representative, or attorney, as soon as possible and in every case before the correction is released. Do not delay in the release, but make every effort to have the person or entity at issue learn of the error from you first. This will avoid a surprised person being placed in front of a camera answering a journalist's question with the words no one wants to speak, especially under those circumstances: "I don't know what you're talking about."

After the event and pressure from the critical incident is over and the pace at the agency returns to the normal chaotic fervor, find out how the misinformation rose to the level of being released. I do not recommend a full-scale and public internal investigation unless the circumstances warrant such. Normally, such releases are the result of inexperience, an inadvertent statement to the media, or a simple misunderstanding, such as the failure to properly mark a document as a draft.

One final thought: this can be a very embarrassing and tense time for an agency and the corresponding government entity. Have the courage to admit the cause of the mistake, and do not turn your PIO or public affairs commander into a scapegoat.

9. **Failing to properly monitor news stories to allow the agency to be proactive, responsive, and follow through until the end of the life of the story**

Every law enforcement agency should have a person assigned to monitor social media sites and news sites for stories involving the agency. This can be done easily by setting up a Google alert for terms that will capture and report stories about your agency. I use this feature to monitor the quotes that I provide to media sources. You can control the frequency from immediate and frequent alerts to daily summary updates, and the results will reach you via email with a link to the actual mention. You can also search Google, Yahoo, or other search engines to discover mentions of the law enforcement agency.

Learning that your law enforcement agency is in the news is critical. It will alert you to pending media attention and allow you to direct and manage resources. You will be prepared for requests for information and therefore respond in a timely manner, and you are able to predict the degree of media attention the story will receive. Remember that the news stories will often involve a search for information, and you can use the stories to locate witnesses and people with information and formulate any responses or proactive measures.

The coverage serves as a valuable training tool for command staff, politicians, management, and PIOs. Finally, the stories should be preserved as evidence in the event someone brings a lawsuit against the law enforcement agency or an individual officer, or if an individual officer seeks to bring a defamation action related to the coverage. My firm routinely monitors news stories for this purpose among others mentioned here.

10. Failing to follow up when all of the information is known and the underlying investigation can no longer be compromised

Perhaps the main reason that the civil unrest in Ferguson ceased was the release of the transcript of the grand jury proceedings. Although the United States Department of Justice released a full report on March 4, 2015,[108] the transcript of the grand jury proceedings allowed the public, the media, and others to see for themselves the number of witnesses interviewed, the amount of evidence examined, and to hear the words of all of the witnesses, including Dorian Johnson and Officer Darren Wilson. The transcript, nearly five thousand pages long, gave an insight into the process but also to the conflicting statements and the problems with the witnesses who had been paraded before the media and whose statements had defined the narrative that Michael Brown was shot in the back while his hands were in the air. The transcript also demonstrated the lengths the investigators went to in an effort to learn the truth.

Too often, the agency moves on and forgets that journalists and the public want the complete story. Sometimes, the agency simply believes that their efforts to follow up will revive or keep the story alive longer. Nothing could be further from the truth. You must tell your story until it is complete. Let journalists and the public know when the information is available and the costs of procuring a copy.

There may some second-guessing about why some information was not released by the agency while the investigation was pending, but making the effort to either answer questions or make the full investigation available — minus, of course, any information privileged from release under law — will create an atmosphere of cooperation and a recognition that the journalists have a job to do.

This practice also allows journalists to see the thoroughness of the investigation and the degree to which the agency went to learn the truth. You have a real chance that the stories following the release will be positive and will further spark productive dialogue and relationships between your agency and the media. It may also serve to discredit those who inappropriately and prematurely condemned the agency or an individual officer. As most public disclosure laws allow the agency to charge for the preparation and release of these items, the costs to do so should not be a burden to law enforcement or any government agency.

Finally, this practice provides some credibility for the agency. At the outset of the next critical incident, journalists will know that they will eventually have everything. It is ironic that the demands of the news cycle and the journalists' profession may make it nearly impossible to look through the investigation and difficult to convince their customers that the story is newsworthy at that time. However, they will no longer be able to deny having the full record, and neither will the public and critics.

Agency Polices Often Favor
a Spirit of Openness with Journalists

In researching this book, we solicited media policies from several large law enforcement agencies. While some of our requests were caught in the whirlpool of bureaucracy,[109] we did receive several that were very helpful and instructive, and I appreciate the assistance of the agencies that responded.

The policies we received all contained position statements in the preambles or at the start of the policy itself stating unequivocally that the official policy of the law enforcement agency is to cooperate and work with journalists. Here are some examples:

> The Atlanta Police Department will assist news media personnel and the public by releasing impartial information and will cooperate with the media at the scene of crimes, accidents, and other public safety incidents.[110]

> CMPD (Charlotte Mecklenburg Police Department) recognizes that a spirit of cooperation and openness is an essential component in fostering the trust and support of the community it serves. It is generally appropriate to release information unless it would be detrimental to the investigation or prosecution of a crime, or is of a confidential nature according to personnel and public records laws.[111]

> It is the policy of this department to provide relevant and timely information to the media and the public. Release of information shall not violate privacy rights or jeopardize ongoing investigations or prosecutions. Access to information, scenes, and events will be balanced with the safety of victims, citizens, and department members. Release of information shall be governed by the Pennsylvania Right-To-Know Law.[112]

> The purpose of this General Order is to establish policy and procedures for the distribution of information regarding the activities and performance of the Department to the general public through the facilities of print, broadcast and electronic media inquiries. This Department recognizes that protecting the constitutional guarantees of both fair trial and free press is a responsibility of the police.[113]

> The Portland Police Bureau believes in fostering positive press/media relations. As such, public information will

be provided to the press/media in an accurate, timely, and detailed manner consistent with the law and public safety considerations.[114]

While far from a scientific survey, readers can see not only the words but also the spirit of these policies. Law enforcement as a profession is encouraged nationally to seek input from media sources to ensure that efforts are being made to foster positive relationships. The Atlanta Police Department's media policy references a national standard for law enforcement agencies that seek or acquire accreditation from the Commission on Accreditation of Law Enforcement Agencies, Inc., commonly known as CALEA.

At least annually the PAU will solicit input from the media as it relates to the public information function (CALEA 5th ed. standard 54.1.2).[115]

CALEA is a credentialing authority comprised of the efforts of the International Association of Chiefs of Police (IACP), the National Organization of Black Law Enforcement Executives (NOBLE), the National Sheriffs' Association (NSA), and the Police Executive Research Forum (PERF).116 According to the CALEA website, the credentialing process promotes and serves the following goals:

- ❖ Strengthen crime prevention and control capabilities,
- ❖ Formalize essential management procedures,
- ❖ Establish fair and nondiscriminatory personnel practices,
- ❖ Improve service delivery,
- ❖ Solidify interagency cooperation and coordination, and
- ❖ Increase community and staff confidence in the agency.[117]

CALEA promulgates standards on every aspect of law enforcement activities and updates those criteria in an effort to keep pace with the evolving standards of law enforcement and changes in the law. At the time of this writing, the authority is reviewing and in discussion on the sixth edition of standards. The accreditation process involves a period of self-assessment, on-site assessments by commission assessors, and a final evaluation process.[118] Over six hundred law enforcement agencies in the United States are accredited through CALEA, and at the time of this writing, more than a hundred more are in the self-assessment phase working toward accreditation.[119] It is important to note that many states have accreditation programs as well.

The point of all of this is to note that on a national level, the policy of cooperating with media is instilled into law enforcement agencies and law enforcement executives. Therefore, if journalists are not receiving the cooperation they desire or believe they do not have a good working, professional relationship with an agency, they should reach out, schedule a meeting, share a meal, and work toward a resolution of such issues.

How the Stratification of
Law Enforcement Agencies Provides for Media Inquiries

All of the policies I reviewed provided specific instructions to law enforcement officers of all ranks when faced with media inquiries. In addition, the policies contained references to CALEA standards intended to ensure accurate and timely responses to media inquiries consistent with the law. In most cases, in a manner that should come as no surprise to journalists, the agencies created divisions or units that are charged with receiving and responding to inquiries. Further, as has become the norm, the law enforcement officers serving on these units are tasked with preparing for critical events and the media attention that will accompany them by responding to the scene. It is not uncommon for the PIO or a member of the Public Affairs Unit 120 to be notified about every high-profile or critical incident, just as any member of the command staff.

The name of the unit or members may vary, however, the message delivered through the policy is clear: Ensure that law enforcement officers who are trained in media response will be available to field requests for information and that information will be forthcoming within the guidelines of the law and departmental policy.

While this may provide a level of frustration for the journalist who arrives at the scene of a critical incident and wants to speak with the first officer they meet, that is the trade-off for having access to an individual, such as a PIO, who will be briefed and be able to provide more details from both a street and operational level than a responding law enforcement officer. Although this may lead to delays, journalists will receive information from officers who are not tasked with handling a critical incident. Further, the PIO actually wants to speak with journalists and will have the ability to seek out and provide follow-up information in response to questions. In most instances, the officer on the scene will leave at the end of her shift and will have neither the time nor the authority to provide information at a later time.

I have been on the scene of officer-involved shootings when journalists were attempting to obtain quotes from or interview officers who were arriving on the scene or securing the perimeter. Not only will this usually prove fruitless, as those law enforcement officers are not likely to have as much information as the journalist may think, it also leads to bad relations between the journalist and the law enforcement agency. Many officers are private people who do not want to be quoted or have their faces shown on television. It may seem counterintuitive, but many law enforcement officers would rather face a dangerous, wanted felon than speak in public or stand in front of a television camera answering questions. Forcing them to do so is not a good idea, and the law enforcement agency is walking a fine line. They do not want officers on the scene to respond to every journalists' request with "no comment," and they also cannot force reluctant members of the agency to provide information. The compromise is that the officers designated as liaisons to journalists are tasked with that function. Journalists can improve their relationships with agencies by working within that framework and pushing for follow-up information as necessary.

Opportunities Wasted by
Law Enforcement Officers and Law Enforcement Agencies

Every hour of every day, law enforcement officers in the United States distinguish themselves through acts of bravery, self-sacrifice, and service that demonstrate they are worthy of the public trust. Although some actions seem trivial, I submit to you that nothing could be farther from the truth. To demonstrate this point, I will call on a personal experience and encourage you to reflect on your own experiences.

In 1997, I drove by a pet-grooming location on my regular beat. While I was passing the business, I saw a skinny German shepherd chained to a post. He was next to a dumpster, and the doors to the top of the dumpster were hanging down in front of him. I saw the dog try to run up the doors to get into the dumpster, presumably to get something to eat. Based upon the length of the chain, it appeared that if the dog reached his goal, he would hang himself when he fell into the dumpster. I pulled to the side of the road and went into the business just to let the owner know that the dog could be in trouble shortly. When I entered the business, I was nearly knocked over by the stench. Eventually, we discovered that the pet-grooming location was actually a puppy mill, and about twenty-two German shepherds were suffering in squalid conditions, living in cages that they never left, and were essentially starving to death. The story garnered the attention of several news stations for weeks. The owner was arrested and prosecuted, and her business license was revoked. At every turn, the story seemed to resurface. I tell you this to prove a point. I also shut down an illegal child daycare facility on my beat. However, the latter did not, to my knowledge, ever receive a minute of media attention.

I was in law school at the time of both events. I was stopped and thanked when I walked into convenience stores in my jurisdiction, stopped by law students and faculty members who had similar messages and kind words, and received an award from the Atlanta Humane Society that hangs in my office for my efforts to shut down the puppy mill. It seemed that the people could not get enough of the story. In my mind, the fact that parents were dropping their children off in a house to have them cared for in a windowless basement without a toilet or running water, much less fire-detection equipment and an exterior door, was far more newsworthy and important, and I am a dog lover! Nonetheless, the public and the media were interested in the efforts of a local law enforcement officer because it captured the attention of their customers.

Now think to your own memories. All of the law enforcement officers reading this book have had this experience. You are at an event, perhaps a family gathering, a Fourth of July cookout, or a birthday party, and you begin relating a story about a traffic stop—not a felony stop during which you apprehended one of the FBI's most wanted fugitives, mind you, just a normal traffic stop that resulted in an unusual interaction between you and a citizen. Perhaps it was the person who was speeding because they had diarrhea, the person weaving in rush-hour traffic because they were putting on makeup in the fast lane of the interstate, or the constitutional scholar who dissected your actions using legal terminology from the time of the Revolutionary War.[1] Irrespective of the facts, watch the interest and undivided attention afforded your story. An outside observer could believe you were relating the winning lottery numbers to those assembled around you. It is a simple truth; the general public is fascinated by the work of law enforcement officers. Although they may remain attentive for many reasons, they will, nonetheless, be engaged.

---

[1] Yes. I have experienced all three . . . and many more.

All law enforcement officers know this to be true. Why, then, do law enforcement agencies allow opportunities to pass during which they can captivate the public they serve by relating these events? The beauty of social media is that the law enforcement agency and the individual law enforcement officers are not dependent upon formal media sources to spread the word of your good deeds. A simple snippet of video of City of Gainesville Police Officer Bobby White playing basketball with some children in a neighborhood not only spawned national news stories, it also led to a celebrity visit and a gathering of more children who also had great interactions with the law enforcement officers in the area.[121] The celebrity Shaquille O'Neal has served as a reserve law enforcement officer in the past in California, Arizona, and Florida.[122] The story was captivating and entertaining. It also struck at the heart of a lie being told by hate groups across the United States at the time: law enforcement officers do not care about young black males. That narrative is false and pernicious.

Your law enforcement officers—irrespective of the number of calls you answer, the population of your jurisdiction, or the number of arrests you made last year—engage in interactions with citizens that would not only interest the public, but would also serve to highlight the true dedication to public service inside every officer. All that is necessary is to use the resources you have, including relationships with journalists, to disseminate those stories to the public.

I have heard, from law enforcement officers and agency heads, some of the most absurd reasons for not getting these stories out. Some think that it is pandering to the public. Others believe that if they keep coming out with "fluff" stories, no one will take them seriously. The most amazing excuse was that if the agency keeps the spotlight on the agency and their law enforcement officers, it will encourage journalists to dig harder to find something bad. Talk about overthinking a concept! The journalists who are antipolice would take a story of your law enforcement officers giving away kittens and hundred-dollar bills and put a negative spin on it. However, as I state many times in this book, those folks are, as one appellate judge stated, "rare as hen's teeth."[123]

I think, deep down, law enforcement agencies are bitten—or more appropriately, infected—with a principle that is rampant among many command staff: "We don't reward people for doing their jobs." Okay, I get that. However, you must admit that doing the job of a law enforcement officer, especially today, is worthy of some recognition. Part of this philosophy is driven by the humble nature of most public servants. How many times have you heard law enforcement officers who were recognized for bravery say, "I was only doing my job"? Yes, you were, but you did it well; you did it even when doing so put your life in jeopardy, and we probably couldn't pay some people enough to get them to do it. In short, it's okay to crow about the efforts of your law enforcement officers.

Take a moment to review your law enforcement agency files for the events of the last thirty days. How many officers changed tires for motorists? How many spoke with kids at a youth center or a school? How many shot a perfect score at the range?[124] How many traveled to take the best training offered in the United States on a topic? Do you have a peer counseling program? How many of your officers serve in the United States Armed Forces as reservists? How many officers in your agency were recognized for public service outside of the workplace? How many officers in your agency are pastors, coaches, or volunteers for various charities? Did a particular unit in your agency solve a tough case, get specialized equipment, or receive recognition? I bet that in twenty minutes, you could put together a social media story, YouTube video, or press release on the officers in your agency that would drive more internet traffic to your agency website, give insight into the fine men and women you employ, and garner the attention of at least one local journalist.

Law enforcement officers make 11 million to 12 million arrests per year.[125] Obviously, officers do not arrest every citizen they meet. Law enforcement officers encounter complainants, victims, witnesses, traffic offenders, people involved in traffic collisions, store employees and other customers getting gas when they pick up a cup of coffee, wait staff and other diners when they eat a meal on duty, court staff, people who ask for directions, store owners they visit during their shifts, stranded motorists, and many others. From my own experience, even when working overnight from roughly 10:30 p.m. to 6:30 a.m., arrests are likely a ratio of ten citizen contacts to every arrest and likely as high as twenty to one. Even when looking at law enforcement units that make more frequent arrests than patrol units, such as a warrant unit, those officers still make dozens of citizen contacts each day in addition to the wanted people they are seeking. This data is not currently being gathered. However, if law enforcement officers and agencies were to do so, I believe the results would be staggering.[126] You have more than enough material. As the old managerial texts once said, "Catch your people doing something right."[127] Don't forget your 911 operators as well. They handle more crises over the phone in one shift than the average person ever dreams of encountering in a lifetime.

As you can tell by now, I like lists. They help facilitate discussions and give busy people a head start. Here is my list of the top-ten media opportunities wasted and overlooked by most law enforcement agencies. There are many others, and they may vary depending upon your community, your region of the United States, or your agency mission.

1. New hires, retirements, and promotions
2. Membership in organizations made up of law enforcement professionals, especially when your law enforcement officers hold leadership positions
3. Interagency cooperation of any type and on any level
4. Law enforcement officers who took an opportunity to help a citizen with a problem like changing a tire, finding a pet, teaching a class on personal safety, or giving someone a ride home after a collision

5. Law enforcement officers locating a lost child or an elderly person
6. Law enforcement officers performing first aid, CPR, administering Naloxone, or using an automated electronic defibrillator (AED)
7. Law enforcement officers winning awards or receiving recognition from civic groups
8. Law enforcement officers hitting milestones in physical fitness
9. Graduations from citizen police academies, Police Explorer programs, basic police training, or advanced and specialized training like the FBI National Academy, the Southern Police Institute, Northwestern University's management programs, or completing the Traffic Accident Reconstruction Specialist or Master Instructor certifications
10. The deployment and return of law enforcement officers who serve as reservists

Folks, this is like shooting fish in a barrel with a hand grenade! It's easy because your officers are doing the right thing every day. If you follow this formula, you will soon fill your social media platforms with positive stories about your law enforcement agency and officers. The next time a critical incident drives national attention to your agency, interested citizens and journalists will read every one of those stories and walk into town with a different picture of your law enforcement agency and officers in their minds. Further, you will find them reporting on the critical incident with the stories you put out. It is part of their DNA. They want to have as much information as possible to make their stories more engaging than the competition. The first time there is a lull in the fury of reporting on the critical incident, you will find some of those positive stories or even the fact that you have them posted for people to see making the news.

What Is Your Agency Story?

Every law enforcement agency has a story. This is more than just the mission of the agency. It's a good thing too, because most of the mission statements sound like they were written by the same person battling intractable insomnia.

This is more of what the law enforcement agency does on a daily basis. It is their focus, the work in which they take pride and to which they devote the most resources. It attracts your recruits and encourages your senior officers to stay until retirement. It is your story, and you should be telling it.

Are you the DUI seekers, the fugitive hunters, or the city department that is a part of the small town you patrol? Are you a small agency that patrols a large geographical area? You can also separate the law enforcement agency by unit. The domestic violence unit prevents domestic situations from progressing down the spiral of increasing violence shown in studies and protects children caught in the middle. Your elder abuse unit looks out for scams targeting the elderly, and your computer-based crimes-against-children unit searches for and apprehends child predators who use the internet to lure children. If you need to get the story to tell, ask the law enforcement officers serving in the unit for a one-paragraph description of the work of which they are most proud.

Keep in mind that the law enforcement agency story might be very different from the one the public has in mind. The state patrol is known for working on the highways, arresting DUI drivers, chasing perpetrators, and working crashes. City police are seen directing traffic, working parades, and being present on street corners. Sheriff deputies are seen on television and print media working in courtrooms, chasing fugitives, and serving warrants. But we all know they do more than that. We let the video and the pictures people see on the news and in print media control the perception of the public. They do not see the deputy working as a school resource officer, the trooper speaking about DUI dangers in high schools before the prom, or the city cop teaching a firearms-safety class. They do not see it because law enforcement agencies do not make them see it by putting that information out at every opportunity.

Once you have the law enforcement agency story defined, use it to the fill the narrative you want to promote using your social media resources and your contacts with journalists. Some will say that the agency will make itself vulnerable by showing a propensity to be too focused upon one area of criminal activity, or that journalists will be confused by the effort to focus attention on one aspect of the agency's mission. However, you should recognize that news agencies do this very same thing. Watch a few days of their programming and you will see a propensity to focus on certain types of stories, sometimes giving other stories short shrift, and a tendency to use the same commentators for special stories such as those with legal or financial angles. As you read that sentence, you probably began thinking about a media outlet or media personality that you know. If you have an opinion right now about their slant on topics, you'll feel confident that you could tell their story for them. The difference between law enforcement agencies and the media is that the latter will never let you or anyone else get the chance to tell their story. Law enforcement agencies allow it to happen all the time.

Once you have the story nailed down, look around at the work of your law enforcement officers, the statistics at your fingertips, the statistics you have the ability to gather but currently do not track, and the community you serve. How popular do you believe a story will be that focuses on your law enforcement officers who serve as reservists? Well, if you have a Veterans of Foreign Wars post, an American Legion post, and a military base in the area, you can bet it will be very popular. How active is the local Mothers Against Drunk Driving chapter? You can bet they will be willing to celebrate your record of detecting and apprehending DUI drivers. When groups become interested in the stories that you put forward, they will promote those stories on their own social media sites. They will also advance those stories by bragging about your department, and their members will tell your law enforcement agency story to their friends, coworkers, and neighbors. The story you allowed a PIO to tell that took about thirty minutes and little, if any, financial resources is now the talk of the town, and thanks to the internet, it will be around forever.

During and following the media focus on Ferguson, Missouri, I was involved in dozens of interviews on television, radio, and in print media. I answered one question that was posed many different ways, and it stemmed from a statement by then Attorney General Eric Holder to the effect that law enforcement agencies need to be more in touch with their communities. Frankly, I was incensed at his comments and believe that it further showed him to be out of touch with America's law enforcement officers. However, as I received and answered the question over and over again by pointing out the plethora of programs in place and that have been in place for over thirty years, it occurred to me that law enforcement agencies do not brag enough on what they do. If those programs and efforts, whether coordinated and funded or not, were brought to the forefront by the law enforcement agencies themselves, the public and the media could not deny their existence. As to why those programs were not front and center of every law enforcement agency, the answer, I believe, is that the agencies were not encouraged to do so, were not aware of how easy it is to accomplish with limited resources, or, more than likely, they were too busy doing their jobs. However, law enforcement agencies cannot afford to remain quiet any longer.

The premise here is to remember a basic fact that you know because you work in a law enforcement agency: an agency is not an entity nor a building. A law enforcement agency is the officers and support personnel who do the work of serving and protecting the public. It is not enough to have photographs of the front of your new building on your agency website or a huge picture of the chief with a link to her bio. Show the officers doing their best every day. You would not tell your family's story by showing pictures of homes. You would show family reunions, graduations, weddings, and other examples of the events that typify your family. The same is true of your agency. Want further proof? Go to the websites and watch the commercials and advertisements for media outlets. You will see their journalists in the field meeting with people and smiling. You will see them traveling to the news, reporting the news, working to obtain information to report, and suffering hardships to do so, such as wind, rain, and other threats. That is a lesson that every law enforcement agency should learn.

Chapter Six

Who Should Be
the Face in Front of the Camera

*I find television very educating. Every time somebody turns on
the set, I go into the other room and read a book.*

Groucho Marks

I would venture a guess that nearly every law enforcement
officer reading this book has taken a class, or several, about
interviewing and interrogating people. There are many points
conveyed in every one of those classes. The three principles are
(1) be prepared, (2) look and act like a professional, and (3)
remember that the majority of communication is nonverbal. As
you will see, they apply for our purposes whenever a law
enforcement officer is on the receiving end of the questions and
the scrutiny.

Preparation

I have been interviewed hundreds of times. Whether the
interviews involved a client who was involved in an officer-
involved shooting or accused of wrongdoing, an informational
exercise placing me in the role of a subject matter expert, or
speaking about my books, all of them required preparation. That
preparation varies based upon the topic, the information
available, how many times I have been interviewed about the
topic or issue, the audience, and the type of media.

Sometimes, the preparation phase is hours long for a ten-
minute interview. This is especially the case when I expect specific
questions related to the law and I must perform research and
analysis prior to the interview. I may also spend a lot of time on
the internet reading about current events and specific law
enforcement officer-related incidents in the area of the country

that comprises the audience. This can be a challenge, as I recently did a radio interview with a host that is syndicated on 250 stations around the United States.[128] It is even more challenging when appearing live on CNN or Fox. In those environments, every word is broadcast internationally. Do not let this intimidate you, though. As nearly every media outlet has a website, the same can be said of your local newspaper, and every quote you provide is subject to going viral.

The fact that your words could be broadcast around the globe, and really never leave the internet once they are there, should also tell you something. You cannot be aware of every critical incident in every city in every state. Therefore, you must be prepared to handle inquiries about critical incidents that you have never heard of before. That is not an easy task, especially if the person interviewing you does not want to play well with others in the sandbox or is looking to catch someone on camera or on the air by surprise.

Let's take a moment to examine the background, experience, training, and motivation of most people who provide interviews on behalf of law enforcement officers and agencies. I am often surprised that most officers who do so do not have training in working with the media. I am also surprised that most law enforcement academies do not spend any time telling recruits how to act if they are confronted or approached by journalists, even though the least senior officer on the scene is often asked to stand at the crime scene tape. This exposes them to being the first officer questioned by journalists. While there is no need to place a forty-hour block of instruction into every law enforcement academy curriculum, a few simple points would not hurt. I will provide some basics for street law enforcement officers and supervisors later in the chapter.

In most law enforcement agencies, the direct contact for media inquiries is the head of the agency, a member of command staff, or a person designated to be a liaison with the media. In larger agencies, and increasingly in smaller agencies, the designated person has a title of Public Information Officer, or PIO. While not always the case, many times the PIO is a sworn law enforcement officer in that department. However, I have seen instances wherein the PIO was a civilian with a great deal of media experience. These situations deserve some mention.

The Civilian PIO

There has been a trend in the past ten years for law enforcement agencies to hire a former or retired journalist to serve as the PIO. This has generally worked well, but I've seen it fail too. The theory is that if you hire a person with a great deal of experience working with the media, like a former or retired journalist, they "speak the language" of the media sources and will be able to provide a solid, informed, and professional presence and contact. The hope is that they will be able to tame and manage what many law enforcement agencies feel is a disorderly and disruptive process.

Many times this works. Like any hiring decision, it often depends upon three factors. First and foremost is the skill level and experience of the person hired, second is the expectations of the law enforcement agency and the new hire herself, and finally the degree to which the people outside the law enforcement agency will accept and respect the new hire. In my experience, here are some landmines to watch for and that explain why some civilian PIOs have not fared well. Their failure can be catastrophic for the law enforcement agency and the journalist who often cannot go home again.

Journalists and people who work in the media hand in their resumes to a law enforcement agency with a vast spectrum of experience. The problem is that most law enforcement agencies and most public human resources departments do not know what to look for in their resumes. The difficulty is that most people do not understand the true job and training of a journalist. I discuss more of this in Chapter Three, but suffice it to say that just because a person was able to go to a location, gather facts, speak with sources, and write a story does not mean that they will be a good fit as a PIO for a law enforcement agency. Think of it from this perspective. When you see the resume of a career officer, you know what it means to see that they increased in rank, worked in several high-risk assignments, completed several schools, or obtained certain certifications. However, you do not know if the former journalist who spent "eight years reporting crime stories for WWTF" knows anything about law enforcement. They could have merely passed on the information they received from their sources, and while they may be excellent at doing so, the role of a PIO answering those questions from journalists is very different. To the law enforcement agency, the applicant works in a nearly secretive and unknown world, and any person who claims to have insight into that world is too often and too quickly labeled a subject matter expert. Every law enforcement officer experiences a version of this phenomenon when they are at a wedding, party, or backyard barbeque and someone finds out they are a law enforcement officer. People immediately begin asking questions about every area of law enforcement assuming you can answer every one, and you become the expert. Do not fall into this trap.

There is a difference between being behind the camera, radio microphone, or recorder asking questions and being peppered with questions on the side of the road in the cold during an impromptu press conference following an officer-involved shooting. Journalists are rarely caught without answers because they are the ones asking the questions. You must screen applicants to ensure that the person you hire can catch the arrows and not just throw them.

If you have a former or retired journalist applying for a job as your PIO, trust your interview skills and create some type of assessment that will allow you to gauge how well they think on their feet, how much they know about law enforcement officers and law enforcement in general, and their personal feelings about critical incidents as well as agency priorities. If you ask the person a few mock questions and they keep telling you they would need to research that and get back to you, you may have struck at the heart of their knowledge base. If they are not even familiar with the basics of search and seizure or use of force, you may be in for a long training period before you could trust them to answer tough questions or provide background knowledge without a sworn law enforcement officer next to them to catch tough and more detailed questions. Do they support the agency's efforts to teach firearms safety to civilians? Do they agree with undercover operations? Many journalists believe that undercover efforts, especially in journalism, are unethical.[129] Do they understand and support the use of SWAT teams and "no-knock" warrants? These are critical issues for any PIO. It is best to sort them out before you put them in front of a camera.

The next issue is the mutual expectations of the agency and the new hire. Will this person become the face of the law enforcement agency, or will they simply advise those who are? Will they perform research to hand to a PIO or the chief prior to a news conference? Will they be tasked with gathering any media coverage of the law enforcement agency and keeping a record and library to not only defend the law enforcement agency, but also to critique performances? Will they be provided a set of facts and be asked to draft news releases? Are you planning to use them as a resource to help train individuals within the agency through a coaching program and watching out for landmines on individual stories and critical incidents? If so, it may be that you need formal training and an experienced attorney for critical incidents and not a full-time person on your payroll. Irrespective of the expectations, they must be set out clearly. I have seen situations involving former media personalities who were brought into a law enforcement agency, and they left within a short period of time because either no one knew how to maximize their skills and talents, or the job was not what they expected.

The last factor to consider is the degree to which the public and the media will accept and respond to the former journalist working in your agency. Recent surveys[130] have shown that not everyone has a favorable opinion of people in the media. That typically means journalists, as the average person has no idea about the meaning of the term "media" except for the journalist's name on the news article, the voice on the radio, or the face on television or the internet. So do not automatically assume that having a former or retired journalist will shield you from criticism. In fact, you may draw complaints that the law enforcement agency is employing a professional to spin the facts.

A PIO who is a law enforcement officer always brings a large degree of credibility to the table. They are trained and have performed the job of a law enforcement officer, even if they are not presently assigned to those functions. The sworn PIO also has the knowledge base necessary to answer questions about procedure and the law, in most cases, without putting the journalist off and asking for more time to respond to a question. Finally, the sworn PIO is wearing the uniform of the law enforcement agency. While this may, in limited circumstances in my experience, expose them to allegations of being biased, remember that a PIO is not expected to be objective. They are putting out the facts, or expressing the law enforcement agency's side of an issue. It is okay to "advocate" for your side. Most journalists are unaccustomed to having someone advocating for law enforcement officers, but even an average sworn PIO will fall naturally into that role.

I have seen law enforcement agencies use retired or former journalists as civilian liaisons with the media. I have also seen them use civilians with a tremendous amount of experience with the media in other settings such as political campaigns, chambers of commerce, or in a corporate environment. Some have degrees in journalism as well. Oftentimes, the people in this role fill in for the sworn PIO or the agency head when necessary, but the majority of their work is done behind the scenes. They write press releases, set up news conferences, call journalists with information the agency needs to get out such as significant arrests, information about wanted persons, and information about changes in the law. They also act as a primary contact for the agency to avoid the journalists getting the head of the law enforcement agency on the phone every time they have a question.

Training for PIOs and
Law Enforcement Officers Who Work with the Media

I have seen an extremely wide spectrum when it comes to the training of law enforcement officers who work with the media. Most states offer media training to officers as elective courses, and in every state there is a process to create a course if one does not exist. Further, there are specialized schools available for officers that provide training in this area. In addition, several private, corporate entities are now offering classes.[131] The list provided in the reference section is by no means all-inclusive. The point is, there are formal training classes available. This means that there is no excuse or justification to place an untrained and ill-prepared person in front of a journalist. This is especially true of agency heads who, for some reason, resist training in this area. When I see a law enforcement agency head on the news, read their quotes, or hear their sound bites, I can tell instantly if they have been trained. With appropriate training, they get their points across, do not appear flustered, and put their agency in a better position than it was before the story.

The same is true of law enforcement agency heads who are not well trained—you can spot them instantly. They are easily taken off message, appear nervous, get frustrated with questions, and do not have answers. Just as the trained law enforcement agency head furthers the work and message of her law enforcement agency, the untrained and ill-prepared law enforcement agency head can destroy not only the credibility of the agency, but also the trust of the community and the morale of the law enforcement officers working within the agency. Their responses can also encourage journalists to push further for information and answers.

Look and Act Like a Professional

We all know a person who could put on a freshly pressed thousand-dollar suit and look like a rumpled mess in five minutes. We also know someone who can take a uniform out of the dry-cleaning bag, put it on, then look like it was slept in for a weekend. I do not know what it is, but some folks do not wear their clothes well.

It's not just clothes, mind you. Do you know someone who has a nervous habit when they speak that makes you want to scream? Perhaps they fidget, play with their change, rock back and forth on their heels, blink constantly, or adjust their clothing. Many times, they are not aware of it. In law school, a friend of mine was giving a closing argument in a mock-trial class. He had a habit of grabbing the bottom of his suit jacket below the pocket on the left side. He apparently wanted to make certain that no one stole his suit while he was addressing the jury. I counted at least thirty times that he did it during a ten-minute closing argument. When I brought it to his attention, he had no clue he was doing it. However, it was one of the most distracting habits I had ever seen. Once I pointed it out to him, he was able to eliminate the behavior. It's difficult enough having people pick up conflicting messages from your nonverbal communication. Distracting habits will cause people to completely ignore your words because they are focused elsewhere.

Obviously, the person representing the law enforcement agency should be articulate, but I have heard my share of "ums" and "ahs" and other overused words such as "well" and "you know." It is also important that the person speaking use words correctly. Misused words not only confuse people, but they reduce the credibility of your law enforcement agency. Here are some examples from my observations: "Pacific" is an ocean, not a word that modifies like "specific." It is even more damaging when the misused words relate to law enforcement. For example, a Taser is not a "stun gun." It is a conducted energy weapon. AR-15 does not stand for "assault rifle," and there is a huge difference between an automatic weapon and a semiautomatic weapon. Law enforcement officers use hard hand strikes, not punches. Every statement to the media, any media, is an opportunity to educate the media and the public. If the person speaking does not understand or use correct terminology, that opportunity is lost.

Law enforcement officers speaking to the media should be in freshly pressed suits, sports coats, or uniforms whenever possible. There are exceptions when the interview must be done on the fly or on the scene of an incident. However, you should keep a fresh set of clothes on the back of your office door or in your assigned vehicle. It may be hard to find a phone booth to change in these days, but the PIO who looks fresh and resembles a recruiting poster at 0300 hours carries more credibility with the public than you can imagine. You only get one opportunity to make a first impression.

You should also prepare to get caught off guard, blindsided, challenged, set up, misquoted, angered, asked confusing questions, accused of wrongdoing, compared to bad law enforcement officers and bad law enforcement agencies, and amused by the ignorance of the questions you receive. If you do this long enough, you will experience all of these events. Why? Well, even though journalists are overwhelmingly professional, there is always one in the bunch who may be ignorant and ask a question that sounds condescending or rude, who really does not like law enforcement officers, or who is trying to link the critical incident at your law enforcement agency with others around the United States. You may also face amateur journalists who listen to law enforcement scanners and respond to the scene of critical incidents and press conferences. You must prepare for all of these possibilities and be happy if they never come your way. I will share a few from my personal experience.

I had a radio host, during a live broadcast, accuse me of being an "apologist for law enforcement." This was at the end of a long interview during which the host proved he was an anatomical oddity—he did not have a ratio of two ears and one mouth, or at least he never learned to use them in the correct proportion. He used words like "blow someone away" when referring to an officer-involved shooting and, one of my favorite statements, "You and I both know . . ." In fact, I have no idea what he knew, and as the interview went on, I was convinced he knew less and less. In response to his accusation, "Aren't you just an apologist for law enforcement," I simply said, "No." I was silent at that point. I knew he could not stand it. He *had* to speak. "How can you say that, Mr. LoRusso?" "Well," I responded, "law enforcement has nothing to apologize for." He thanked me for coming on his show and ended the interview.

I was on Fox News live with Neil Cavuto when there was much talk about "demilitarizing" law enforcement, and the United States Congress was considering removing armored vehicles from law enforcement agencies around the United States. As you know, this eventually occurred in several jurisdictions. Neil Cavuto was a gracious host and asked me why a law enforcement agency would need armored vehicles. The week prior, law enforcement officers responded to a massive street brawl in Texas involving a whole passel of outlaw bikers. Perhaps it was a gaggle or a herd, but in any event, there were a bunch of them. Several shots were fired, several folks were shot and stabbed, and many people were arrested. In addition, many people were wanted for their participation in the melee. I used this recent event to answer his question. I asked him, if he were a law enforcement officer who was asked to drive up to the safe house where the wanted bikers lived, and if there were video cameras on the outside of that safe house—as has become common—would he want to drive up in a shiny marked patrol car or an armored vehicle? He paused and said he never quite thought about it that way. The interview was a great experience, and I will always respect him for being curious to hear another perspective and admitting that he had not considered the day-to-day work of law enforcement officers when looking at the story. He also admitted that the person he had as a guest knew more about the topic than he did. As I watch newscasts, I realize that trait is becoming increasingly rare. My preparation for that interview made all the difference.

Finally, I have had interviewers misstate the law, sometimes innocently and sometimes deliberately. When that occurs, you cannot speak without correcting the error. First, you are a source of authority. Second, if you answer the question without correcting the journalist, you are agreeing to their statement. For example, I want to follow up on a conversation I had with a journalist that I mentioned earlier. While on camera, she said, "Well, I want to talk about the clearly unlawful officer-involved shootings." Now, if I said "okay" or "we can do that," I would have been accepting her premise. It was important to understand exactly what she meant by a "clearly unlawful officer-involved shooting," so I asked her this question: "What makes an officer-involved shooting clearly unlawful?" She stated, and I quote, "Like when they shoot someone in the back." Her response gave me an opportunity to educate her and the audience about *Garner v. Tennessee*,[132] the science of action and reaction, and the fact that it is not automatically illegal to shoot someone in the back. We had a nice discussion and I gave her a copy of *Garner v. Tennessee*[133] before she left. She also told me, "Well, just because it is legal doesn't mean they should do it." *Baby steps, Lance*, I thought. *Baby steps*. Showing my frustration would have been quite unproductive, in part because I would have lost an excellent opportunity to educate.

Don't Try to Be the Smiling Dog

If you have ever approached a stray dog, or answered an alarm call and encountered a family pet who was not amused at your unannounced presence, you know that dogs cannot hide their feelings. They also are hardwired not to make any effort to do so.

We see their reactions, suspicions, insecurities, and sometimes anger displayed in three dimensions for all to see—and hear. You will never see an angry dog, full of suspicions and fear about your presence, suddenly "smile" by wagging his tail as he bares his teeth. If he did, who would believe him? In the interests of giving equal time, I will say that cats may have perfected the trait of hiding their feelings, or perhaps they just do not care if you know how they really feel. Even so, the first time you encounter a truly angry cat, you will have no second thoughts about where they stand.

Just watch a few newscasts on television and you will see the many moods of the people interviewed and captured by the camera. You will see the person who is enamored with the media. They are so flattered that they have been selected for an interview that they can barely sit still. This is true irrespective of the topic of the interview. Whether they are discussing their quiet neighbor who "always kept to himself" or providing analogies between rail-bound conveyances and weather phenomena, they have a bright effect, they keep their heads up, they display a relaxed posture, and everything about them signals that they are enjoying the experience. They are, to follow through with my analogy, wagging furiously. On the other side of the scale are the people, and we have all seen them, who are being chased down the street by journalists, microphone in hand and cameraman in tow, while questions are hurled one after another as if the first ten were ignored due to syntax or grammatical errors. There are people representing every point in between these two extremes. You need only take a look at YouTube for specific examples.

Where do the law enforcement officers and civilian PIOs, as well as your agency leadership, fall on this spectrum? I love to hear people tell me at lectures, on the phone, and in casual conversations that they hate the media, but they "know how to handle them." Here's a little secret—they are not fooling anyone. Although your reactions and body language may change during any one interview, you cannot be the smiling dog. We will explore this further, but here is perhaps the best advice you will receive from this book: don't talk to journalists if you hate the media.

"Hate" is a strong word. "Hate and mistrust are the children of blindness."[134] Now, let's move beyond the Sunday school analysis. There are folks who do not care to watch or read the news, there are folks who could take or leave it, there are those who follow stories for professional reasons, and there are those who truly despise anyone in the media. Like any other absolute, hating or distrusting anyone just because he works in the media industry is silly. However, along the spectrum described in this paragraph, there are plenty of folks who hold contempt for or distrust the media. In my experience, many law enforcement officers fall into this category for the reasons stated earlier.

The important thing here is that I am not trying to get you to change your mind. I explain in this book how journalists are trained, why they do their jobs the way they do, their ethics and how they drive their actions, and how their ethics and training affect their beliefs. I've also explained how vital the press is to a free society. However, you are free to believe what you want. You must also be honest and determine where you fall on the spectrum before you stand in front of a camera.

Some law enforcement officers have a legitimate reason for having negative impressions and deeply held beliefs about the media. I know several who are convinced that the actions of a journalist made their jobs more difficult, aided a criminal, or interfered with the relationship between the law enforcement agency and the public. Others have been the subject of media stories and felt like they were unable to defend themselves due to departmental policies. They may also have committed a minor policy violation and received a more serious punishment due to negative media coverage of the incident. I have represented a couple of public servants who fell into that category. One lost a career spanning nearly thirty years due to this phenomenon. Finally, some have been the subject of media "investigations" that were wrong, misguided, and potentially damaging to the officer's career. It happened to me with a journalist who was duped by some convincing folks. If you fit into these categories, there's nothing to be ashamed of. I was able to move on, and eventually had a sit-down with that journalist, but some are not. My advice here is to just be candid with yourself and your agency. If you cannot put your personal feelings aside, even your apathy toward the media, you should not represent the agency. Let's discuss why.

The Majority of Communication Is Nonverbal

Although the percentages vary depending upon where you took your classes on interviews and interrogation, and perhaps the name and skill level of your instructor, every law enforcement officer understands that some portion of communication is nonverbal. Dr. Albert Mehrabian began researching nonverbal communication in the 1960s. His books explore concepts of how information is conveyed through words, tone, and nonverbal communication, and his research and models have been applied to many industries including sales, advertising, and law enforcement.[135] Many of the law enforcement classes regarding communications, whether involving citizen encounters or strictly focused on interviews and interrogations, include this general principle: more communication takes place through nonverbal cues than through tone or the words we use. Several private corporations teach classes to law enforcement officers and others training them to recognize these nonverbal communications and other transfers of information. This is commonly known as kinesic interview techniques. Kinesics is the study of nonverbal communication, or more specifically, "a systematic study of the relationship between nonlinguistic body motions (as blushes, shrugs or eye movement) and communication."[136] The techniques are successful and the science is undeniable. Irrespective of the percentages you were taught, you believe, or you have experienced, there can be no dispute that an enormous percentage of communication takes place without a word being spoken.

So, it is time to think, and I mean truly consider carefully who will be the "face" of your law enforcement agency. This is not a decision that should be made based solely on rank. This will encourage law enforcement officers to speak freely and disclose any personal bias or bad experiences during the selection process. This may also require a change in policy. If your agency automatically lists a few people by title or rank who will liaise with the media, perhaps that list should be expanded. Allow a designated group of individuals to "self-select" for specific news stories. They will make good decisions if you give them the authority to make those decisions.

There must also be flexibility based upon the type of news story. For example, an officer who was a victim of child abuse probably should not be in front of the camera discussing the arrest or search for a child molester. Likewise, a story about campus safety may be more effective using a younger law enforcement officer if you are targeting students. You must have flexibility, because it works. If you watch carefully, media outlets make these types of decisions all the time. I recall one station sending a young, approachable, female journalist to interview female college students about accepting rides home from parties.

So who should be on that list of people? Look for law enforcement officers who understand the role of the media in society and within your agency. Select those who can get along with anyone, and every agency has several of those folks. In my opinion, the chief or the sheriff should not normally be the face of the agency. This is especially true if they do not have any formal training in this area, or if they do not meet the other criteria set out in this chapter. Chiefs and sheriffs are not immune from gaffs in front of the camera. Sometimes, they are too willing to be political when the circumstances simply call for a factual answer. The head of the law enforcement agency can always follow up and provide a follow-up quote or statement, but in most cases, it is best to allow lower-level ranks to handle the initial media inquiries. Not only does this prevent the chief or sheriff from being pulled away from other duties, it also gives the person in front of the media an "out" for time to answer a difficult question or a decision about releasing documents. The chief or sheriff cannot claim that they need to check with a higher authority prior to answering a question or making a statement. A side benefit of this practice is that when the chief or sheriff does appear, the media will see the situation as serious.

There are a few exceptions to this rule, however. The first is the serious injury or line-of-duty death of an officer. That situation always requires a personal statement from the head of the agency. Next is a significant arrest involving public corruption. In those instances, the law enforcement agency head must be seen as putting himself on the front lines of the fight. The same is true of any instance involving multidisciplinary task forces, the combined efforts of law enforcement agencies, or controversial decisions made by the agency, especially those regarding policy. Finally, in the unfortunate event that a law enforcement officer is arrested, at some point the head of the agency will probably be required to speak. This can be done through a press release or recorded statement that is emailed to the media. Journalists will understand that the head of the agency likely cannot answer specific questions due to the pending and continuing investigation. However, you can expect them to ask anyway. That is why a "one-way communication" event like a press conference may be best. You can also post a video on your law enforcement agency's YouTube channel, social media platforms, or website.

Once you select the folks who will speak, the next step is setting up a system to monitor the officers or civilians who are speaking with the media. As discussed elsewhere in this book in more detail, most law enforcement officers and agencies see the media as a distraction, especially during and immediately after critical incidents. All too often, the intense media scrutiny is seen as an isolated event, and the law enforcement agency quickly moves past it. However, all performance benefits from feedback, and media interviews are no exception. Due to the time demands of the agency, it may be necessary to hire an outside entity to perform this review or a "spot check" of selective media interactions. Over the course of several instances and reviews, the agency will find itself staffed with an experienced, polished, and effective cadre of media liaisons.

One final thought on this topic: do not underestimate the impact of a retired law enforcement officer appearing on camera as a representative of an organization like the Fraternal Order of Police. Paul Crawley had some interesting insight on this issue.

> Many times, retired officers can provide valuable insight into use of force or other topics. This is an opportunity for the Fraternal Order of Police to educate journalists and the public and perhaps give background and context when the law enforcement agency may not be able to release details in order to protect the investigation. Those retired officers have a great deal of credibility.

Chapter Seven

Zero-Time News Cycle

Everything is being compressed into tiny tablets. You take a little pill of news every day—twenty-three minutes—and that's supposed to be enough.

Walter Cronkite

At one time, media sources operated according to a predictable cycle. This is traditionally known as the news cycle, which is defined as the time gap between the release of one story and the follow-up story.[137] While the cycle depended to a large extent upon the type of media, there was a pattern to their main functions: gather facts, develop a story, and publish the story. For example, a daily newspaper would work on a twenty-four-hour cycle with hard deadlines to get stories out in the one edition of the paper that customers expected every day. Breaking news was incorporated through the work of very talented folks who were able to change the layout of the paper on the fly. The saying "Stop the presses!" comes from the notion that if a story was important enough to warrant inclusion in the edition being printed, the printing presses would actually be stopped and the type reset to include the information or the story.[138] The failure of the print media to react quickly, due to a new printing system, is partly responsible for the famous headline in the *Chicago Daily Tribune* on November 3, 1948, announcing that Thomas E. Dewey defeated Harry S. Truman in his reelection bid to retain the office of president of the United States. Truman famously held up the paper after he won reelection.[139]

Radio always had the ability to "rewrite copy," or the information read by news personalities to allow for breaking news or developing facts.[140] The nature of the radio format allowed for interruptions of regularly scheduled programming to broadcast live. This was further facilitated by the fact that, unlike print media, news was broadcast more than once each day.[141] As a matter of course, developing stories could be handled more efficiently. However, there was still an understanding that the news ran in cycles, likely due to the fact that no one wanted to listen to a radio show that played news all the time.[142] After all, who would want that? How wrong they were, as our appetite for constant news has proven to be insatiable.

Television began broadcasting news in 1941 with two fifteen-minute broadcasts on the Columbia Broadcasting System, now known as CBS. Even as the format developed, television was dominated by theater-type shows and sports competitions.[143] Even later in the 1940s, when there was a desire to have more news programs, presumably to increase advertising revenue, the news was short and news events were covered by showing news reels, many of which had already been shown in movie theaters.[144] Politics formed perhaps the biggest push to cover live events after the live broadcast of the 1952 presidential nominating conventions and Walter Cronkite was dubbed the first "anchorman."[145]

The Korean and Vietnam Wars pushed the major networks to bring the news of the war to the public through television. In 1968, Walter Cronkite went to Vietnam to cover the Tet Offensive.[146] In 1980, the Cable News Network, CNN, began broadcasting, and CNN Headline News followed with a twenty-four-hour-per-day news show in thirty-minute cycles.[147] During the Gulf War in 1991, CNN Headline News was a source for people around the world to tune in, often live, to briefings and developing stories about the war.[148] Soon after, other cable news outlets like Fox News, MSNBC, BBC, and Bloomberg began broadcasting news around the clock, and in 2011, CNN and CNN Headline News became available twenty-four hours per day through live streaming over the internet.[149] Several radio stations began broadcasting news on a twenty-four-hour basis as well, and oddly enough, they also stream live over the internet, thereby attaining a global reach. Even small radio stations have this capability.

The effect of continuous news outlets has been tremendous. While people still think in terms of news cycles, the term is really a misnomer. There is no time between broadcasts anymore. This leads to a rapid effort to keep newscasts fresh and interesting to satisfy customers. No one wants to see and hear the same news broadcast over and over again. So the stations switch anchors, change the order of the stories, and highlight the one story that always changes, the weather, which is predictably broadcast at the same time after the top and bottom of the hour to keep customers tuned in.

Finally, internet news sources provide a mixture of all news cycles and tend to update stories depending upon the interest level of their audiences. For example, because people pick and choose the stories that interest them when they are connected to the internet, internet sources can afford to provide several "menu items." The fact that the selection of one story does not preclude the viewing of another, and the fact that, for the most part, the consumer pays nothing to view and read means there is no harm in updating some stories on a daily basis while others are expected to be revised on a minute-to-minute basis, especially when new information becomes available. Internet sources also have the luxury of pulling their stories from a variety of sources, from the traditional like the AP and websites of mainstream, professional sources as well as what I have termed the "informal media."[150] As I discuss in Chapter Four, this consists of blogs and social media sites like Facebook, Instagram, Twitter, LinkedIn, Snapchat, and others as well as the comment sections of legitimate, professional news sites which are, for the most part, unregulated. Internet news sources pull stories from hybrid sites like regional online-only publications and independent publishing sources.

Faced with dependence upon and competition with internet news sources and around-the-clock television and news-only radio shows, print journalists are looking for ways to keep their stories fresh, updated, and attractive to consumers. So, while the rule once was true that a newspaper journalist would only be calling you for an update one or two times each day, that is often no longer the case. The most obvious reason is that the newspapers, facing declining readership[151] of the print versions of their paper products, long ago launched their own internet-based news sources consisting of online versions of the newspaper and online-only articles and stories. This enables the traditional news source to update stories, have a constant presence, and better serve their customers.

So what is the effect on law enforcement agencies and law enforcement officers? What I have termed the "Zero-Time News Cycle" has had a profound effect on law enforcement agencies and officers. Perhaps the best example was the broadcast of the arrest of Rodney King on March 3, 1991. Rodney King was a convicted felon with a significant criminal history and an alcohol problem. He led police on a one-hundred-mile-per-hour chase in Los Angeles, California, because he was on parole and did not want to return to prison.[152] A video of his arrest provided to the news by George Holliday sparked not only controversy, but bloody riots, resulting in the deployment of US Army troops and Marines and the mobilization of the California National Guard.[153] The riots followed a trial in state court, in which a jury returned a verdict of not guilty. During a second trial, Sergeant Stacy Koon and Officer Laurence Powell were convicted in a federal case of violating the constitutional rights of Rodney King. Two other law enforcement officers, Wind and Briseno, were acquitted.[154] I was working as a street officer on March 3, 1991. I distinctly recall that the video of the arrest was available for viewing around the clock. It played during every segment of news, and a CNN executive reportedly called it "wallpaper" because the network played it so often. President George H. W. Bush even felt compelled to comment on it.[155]

The George Holliday video changed the game for law enforcement agencies and law enforcement officers. I was policing across the United States, about three thousand miles away, and people on my shift were accused of racism and excessive force. People began carrying video cameras or videotaping law enforcement officers when we showed up at calls. This was no small effort then, as video recorders were not digital, they were large, and often were quite heavy. What we saw across the United States, perhaps for the first time, was the effect of a full-scale media focus on a single law enforcement agency by media outlets of all types and sizes using twenty-four-hour television coverage. Law enforcement agencies and officers learned, or should have learned, valuable lessons from that coverage. Once the coverage of a critical incident turned into a juggernaut of nonstop stories, there was little anyone could do to steer the story in a different direction, even when lives were at stake. More than sixty people were killed during the riots in Los Angeles after the first trial.[156]

How the News Cycle Functions

I have lectured about this topic on many occasions, and after thinking about the concept for hours, I finally came up with a way to illustrate the inner workings of the news cycle generally and how it applies to law enforcement specifically. You will not find this analogy in a textbook, and perhaps it is appealing only to my warped sense of humor, but it is intended to bring to mind a visual and a concept that will keep law enforcement agencies and officers on their best game when forming strategies to work through intense media coverage following a critical incident.

Imagine the news cycle like a washing machine full of white socks. In the center of a top-load washing machine sits a device called an agitator. We've all watched the action of a washing machine and observed how the agitator not only moves the socks back and forth, but also allows the socks to move from the top of the machine to the bottom and back. This is a continuous cycle that moves the socks through the wash tub. Now, imagine looking into that washing machine. You will see a seemingly endless parade of white socks moving around in the water and coming up to the top, only to disappear back to the bottom. The news cycle is similar.

News stories are everywhere. Journalists find them in many ways, and many are called into the news desk. While some have the luxury of receiving calls to notify them of upcoming events or breaking news, most journalists rely upon their contacts in the community and their own efforts to monitor what is going on around them.[157] The world of the journalist often consists of checking with contacts, meeting with people about events, speaking with sources who are in the know about various topics, and then following up on those efforts to determine if there is a story available that will interest customers. When a news event occurs, like an officer-involved shooting, the journalists start looking for something to use for their story. Enter the washing machine analogy.

As the journalists look around for information on the critical incident, what they see resembles the washing machine filled with white socks. All of the white socks represent information about the officer-involved shooting such as the date, the location, the name of the person shot, the name of the law enforcement agency, and perhaps the type of event that led to the officer-involved shooting. The journalists will keep looking for information that is different than what the other journalists have for one simple reason: they are in competition with those folks. So they will keep staring into the washing machine and examining the white socks as they come up to see if they can learn something new. However, when their story deadline approaches, they will write the story with what they have to fulfill their job duties. Remember, though, when it comes to critical incidents, especially an officer-involved shooting, journalists know there is more information available, so after they report on what they learned, they will return to the washing machine to continue scanning and examining socks.

Often after the first twenty-four hours following an officer-involved shooting, there is nothing new coming from the law enforcement agency. The agency has released the information they believe they can release without compromising the investigation or interfering with the ability of the investigators to vet potential witnesses. So the journalists will diligently begin to search for more information to fulfill their duties and do their jobs while keeping the stories engaging. Where will they look? Anywhere they can, and the degree of their diligence depends upon a few factors. The first is the individual journalist. Like any other profession, there are some journalists who will dig extremely hard and others who will make a few calls and hope something turns up. Second is the pressure placed upon them by their superiors. If there is not a lot of other news breaking, if the officer-involved shooting occurs in a small town or in an area where tensions between law enforcement officers and citizens are high, the journalists will likely feel pressured to find more information. This may include looking for witnesses, going to the scene and looking for any markings on the ground that may indicate more precisely where the shooting occurred—like paint marking the location of a patrol car—or asking people in the area if they know anyone who took pictures or video of the shooting. Third, and perhaps most important, is the degree to which the story has garnered widespread attention. If the story in the journalist's backyard captures the attention of the national press, you can bet the journalist will kick her efforts into overdrive. New information from a local associate that is passed onto a national news outlet can help the journalist's career by providing a platform to move to a larger news market and on to promotions and larger salaries. Journalists want to succeed and advance in their fields just like anyone else.

No matter what their efforts entail, the journalists will keep checking that washing machine to see if there is anything new popping up. They do not want to be the last news outlet reporting the name and assignment of the law enforcement officer involved in the officer-involved shooting, the number of shots fired, the location of the person's injuries, or any other important facts. So they will keep an eye out on those white socks. When a new fact goes into the swirl of the washing machine, it may just be another white sock. This may be another witness who pops up who really has nothing new to say. However, when the law enforcement agency or someone else throws a brightly colored sock into the washing machine, all of the journalists scramble to look at it. They will examine it, see if this is truly new information, and see if it provides insights that clarify information released in the past. They will also determine if this new information can lead them to new sources. Simply put, that new, brightly colored sock will capture the attention of the journalists. As you will see in the next paragraph, this is true irrespective of who throws that sock into the washing machine or how accurate that information is. This is especially true in the case of an officer-involved shooting when the law enforcement agency may not be able to verify or refute the information when asked.

If the brightly colored sock is thrown into the washing machine at a time when the journalists are not receiving any new information, they are more likely to take action before they are able to fully verify the veracity of the information. Now, do not confuse this with a journalist blindly publishing whatever they hear. They will make a reasonable attempt to vet the information. Normally the first source they consult will be the law enforcement agency, but, as stated above, they may not be able to reach anyone, or they may get an equivocal but appropriate answer such as: "We are still investigating and cannot release more details at this time." At this point, the journalist will predictably go to the source of the information, or brightly colored sock, and interview them. If this is a TV or radio news journalist, they will want to get someone on camera or tape. Once this information is out there, it will be uploaded to the internet, and for all practical purposes it is there forever. As an example, here is an interview done by CNN on August 15, 2014, or six days after Michael Brown was shot and killed. Here is the headline:

What We Know about Michael Brown's Shooting[158]

After that shot, Brown broke free from the officer's grasp, both women told CNN, and started running, but he only got about 20 feet from the squad car by [Piaget] Crenshaw's estimate.

"The cop gets out of his vehicle shooting," [Tiffany] Mitchell said. "[Brown's] body jerked as if he was hit from behind, and he turned around and he put his hands up. . . . The cop continued to fire until he just dropped down to the ground, and his face just smacked the concrete."

This was an example of a professional journalist looking for information during a time when the law enforcement agency was putting out very little. The story was published under the name of Elliott McLaughlin, who was a news editor at the time. He is a well-educated and experienced journalist who obviously believed the two women had information to add to the story.[159] The story also contains the statements of Dorian Johnson, who was with Michael Brown during the strong-arm robbery at the store a few moments earlier and was walking with Michael Brown when Officer Darren Wilson encountered them.[160] The information in this article was disproved by forensic evidence and the testimony of other witnesses.[161] I truly wish Ms. Mitchell was able to record on her cell phone what she reportedly saw. At one point, it seemed the entire world wanted to see it.

The News Cycle Meets the Investigative "Cycle"

I often hear law enforcement officers complain about the media and their coverage of a homicide, especially an officer-involved shooting. One of the most common criticisms is that journalists often report facts that are inaccurate or fail to verify facts before they release them in a story. Although these complaints may be well founded in certain instances, often the journalists are not analysis should not start and end with the accuracy of the facts reported. This is unfair. Even law enforcement officers may operate under a set of facts that are disproved after a time. The reporting of inaccurate facts, or facts that are *later shown to be inaccurate*, which is far more common, is a function of the divergent goals between law enforcement officers and journalists, especially following an officer-involved shooting.

Whenever you compare the actions of one profession to another, it is important to start with their goals. If their goals align, then there is more of an opportunity for their actions to mirror each other. However, divergent goals will logically lead to a fundamental difference in the definition of success and a commensurate disparity in methods.

Journalists are bound by ethical rules discussed in Chapter Three. However, they are also part of a network of private corporations that thrive on reporting news in a timely manner. Make no mistake about the world of the journalist and news agencies. They live in a highly competitive environment. In a way, law enforcement officers live in a competitive world as well. Journalists compete for ratings, being the first to report breaking news, market share, and popularity among customers. Law enforcement officers compete against each other regarding many issues simply because they are typically hard-charging, driven people who do not like to lose—especially when lives are on the line. However, law enforcement officers investigating an officer-involved shooting compete against two major opponents that are both relentless, powerful, and ubiquitous: the clock and the criminal element of society.

There is a difference, however, between the way both professions fight against the clock. For journalists, the clock represents a sort of taskmaster run by their customers. They expect that the news will always be fresh, engaging, sometimes entertaining, but *always* on time. For law enforcement officers, the clock represents a dual-edged sword. On one side is the ticking of time that has the potential to allow bad guys to escape, recollections to fade, and evidence to be lost. On the other side is the relentless power of persistence. Once the evidence is gathered, the witnesses located and debriefed, and the arrest made, the world will have forever to pick apart the work of the law enforcement agency and the investigator. This reality gives rise to the mantra of the homicide investigator: "Remember: do it right the first time—you only get one chance."[162] This is especially true in the modern environment regarding officer-involved shootings. Once a law enforcement officer starts on a case, they must remember at all times that getting the facts right and arresting the correct person or determining that a homicide was justified is worth taking the time to do properly.

The following chart demonstrates the divergent goals of journalists and law enforcement officers following a critical incident. I believe that if law enforcement officers keep this chart in mind, they will understand the motivations of journalists. The same is true for journalists who will read this book and learn more about the law enforcement officers they follow and seek to interview as they navigate through the investigation of a critical incident. If both sides understand each other, perhaps there will be more acceptance and less acrimony. You may even find some common ground.

News Cycle	Officer-Involved Shooting Investigation
Fact-gathering process	Fact-gathering process
Driven by journalist's instincts	Driven by law enforcement officer's instincts
Stories are handled by novice and veteran journalists	Investigations are handled by seasoned veterans
Driven by journalist's bosses	Driven by law enforcement officer's bosses (in part)
Driven by customers' appetite for the topic	Driven by prosecutors (in part)
Driven by competition with other news agencies and journalists	Driven by a search for evidence
Deadlines rule	Deadlines external to the investigative process are irrelevant
Journalists and their staff are in control of the mechanisms and processes required to produce their stories	Law enforcement officers are dependent upon outside entities and timelines, i.e., crime labs, search warrant results, and other information sources to continue and close the investigation
Operates well while in possession of limited facts	Operates in search of and best when in possession of all available facts
Process follows a search for stories that will attract and maintain the attention of customers	Process follows the evidence to answers
Looking for inconsistencies in facts, statements from law enforcement agencies, and other sources	Tracking down all details
Little time to vet "witnesses"	Diligent effort to verify every statement made and every fact provided by every witness
Competitive	Methodical
3–5 days (usually), but months for high-profile stories	As long as it takes to get it right

News Cycle	Officer-Involved Shooting Investigation
Get facts to "press" as soon as they can verify them to the best of their abilities or to the industry standard	Withhold facts to vet "witnesses"
Resources vary depending upon the scope of the story, the size of the media outlet, and the potential to increase ratings and the customer base	Resource dependent with the ability to seek assistance with complex or difficult cases, but media attention does not drive the allocation of resources
Puts pressure on law enforcement officers and agencies for answers and information	Frustrated by media pressure on law enforcement officers and law enforcement agencies for answers and information
Moves onto the next story when the news cycle drives stories in another direction	Stays with the investigation until it is done
Inaccurate or "what we know right now" reports, while not ideal, are expected	The release of inaccurate information can jeopardize the ability to locate witnesses, secure evidence, and reach an accurate conclusion
Recognizes the opportunity for follow-up reports to correct inaccurate statements	One shot to get right
May face limited liability for inaccurate reporting	The release of inaccurate information may result in the loss of careers, discipline, permanent damage to the reputations of people improperly identified as suspects, and the investigation as a whole

Chapter Eight

The Mechanics of Media Relations

When it comes to friction between law enforcement agencies and journalists, the biggest enemy is speculation. Journalists and media outlets need information to keep their customers informed and to fill the space of their medium. During and after a critical incident, they want information from law enforcement officers and agencies. When they do not have information, many begin to speculate about what is happening and why. This can lead to strained relations between the law enforcement agency and the journalists. When the law enforcement agency provides information to journalists, even if that comes in the form of knowledgeable spokespersons, the reports will be more accurate. From a journalistic perspective, they will also be more timely and engaging.
That is a win for everyone.

Pete Combs
Forty-year veteran of print and radio media outlets

You have three options when asked questions by journalists. You can reply "no comment" and risk suspicion and angry news media, you can decline to comment and give a reason, or you can say something but make it innocuous if necessary. Always give a reason if you are not able to provide information.

Paul Crawley
Veteran television journalist

I've represented many law enforcement officers in the age of social media and nonstop news coverage. One of the last things I tell them when I leave them after the scene has been secured and they are released is this: "Do not watch the media, stay off social media, and ignore the comments to news stories. You were there and you know what happened; you will not learn anything from following the media coverage." While I hope all my clients listen and heed my advice, some unfortunately have ignored this admonition. Worse, in some cases, is the fact that spouses have ignored this advice. The resulting devastation can take years to repair.

A few years ago, I represented a law enforcement officer who lawfully used deadly force, killing a man. He had school-aged children. After nearly a year of reading the barrage of foul and hateful statements based upon a cavernous lack of knowledge of the facts, the law enforcement officer left the state and moved his family. When he told me he had enough, he added that he got tired of his kids being told their dad was a murderer. I specifically recall the conversation regarding his wife's desire to personally contact the media sources and tell them the truth. I strongly advised against that plan, and based upon her level of frustration and emotion, several news organizations in Atlanta owe me a debt of gratitude. He was eventually cleared of any wrongdoing.

Every news source, whether professional, mainstream, print, television, radio, formal, or informal, shares information on the internet. The use of the internet not only allows them to reach a larger audience, it also allows them to create a relatively free "archive" of their efforts. The benefit of this is that a search for terms and select words will bring those stories back to the forefront for people searching, as well as other journalists who are refreshing their stories or doing research on a new story. The internet is somewhat akin to a "whirlpool file cabinet" of information, a great deal of which is false, that never goes away. It is populated by anyone with a computer, and the information is not vetted as a whole, and rarely by website. This gives rise to one of my favorite quotes about the internet:

Everything you read on the internet is true—every word of it.
Abraham Lincoln

The information on the internet is also supplied by companies that gather data from a myriad of sources. For example, paid services "sweep" online public record sources to "populate" the myriad of websites that boast the ability of a person to perform a public record search online, usually for a fee. Once this information is gathered and placed on the internet, it is extremely hard to remove. After being hired to help a client remove inaccurate, and reportedly sealed, court information from the internet, I worked for over a year and was successful. However, there is no guarantee that a future sweep of public records will not repopulate this information onto the internet.

This background information is necessary to fully understand the devastating and long-lasting effect of negative or inaccurate news stories. As explained previously, journalists are always working off deadlines. Law enforcement officers and agencies, must accept that news stories will, as a result, contain some inaccuracies, even if the journalist is doing her best to be as accurate as possible. For example, in the hour following an officer-involved shooting, many facts—and certainly many details—are simply not known. For this reason, it is important for law enforcement officers and agencies to understand the details, or mechanics if you will, of working with the media.

It's Not All Unicorns and Rainbows

Working with any group outside of your organization will involve periods of blissful relations and events that would make even the most patient person want to scream. Often the conflicts are the result of competing goals, differences in culture, and miscommunication. However, with some preparation, under-standing, and diligence, I hope you can turn the pleasant periods into the marathons and the unpleasant into short sprints.

There is a famous quote about the legislative process: "If you like laws and sausages, you should never watch either one being made."[163] The same can be said about the relationship between law enforcement agencies and journalists. It is, at times, a relationship more akin to sometimes-feuding neighbors and relatives than anything else. However, there is a reason for this. Behind the scenes—and I've been fortunate to spend a great deal of time in news studios, radio stations, and newspapers to a lesser extent—both law enforcement agencies and the journalists share a commitment to their mission in the face of uncertainty and pressure. For the law enforcement agency, there is the unknown of how their efforts will be viewed by politicians, the public, and journalists; the need to make decisions using the chain of command; and a recognition that every decision will be reviewed and may have civil and criminal ramifications. For the media, there are deadlines, competing stories, chain of command issues, processing and editing functions that affect when a story is ready for release, and the intense time and space demands inherent in the media itself. In short, the calm, cool, and collected news anchor appearing on your television most often does not accurately reflect the fervor of the news station that led to that broadcast.

During the peaceful times—for example, when the media journalists are covering a story of an awards presentation at a local law enforcement agency—everyone will get along well, no one will seem tasked or impatient, and aside from some logistics such as camera placement or parking, the likelihood of a confrontation or even harsh words is remote. To the contrary, following a critical incident, everyone is in a hurry, unknown facts lead to unanswered questions and frustration, and the pace of the events alone can lead to conflict. There is a simple reason for this: there are people on both sides of the microphones and cameras. When people are under pressure, they often become "task focused" and are prone to impatience, suspicion, and second-guessing the motives of people whom they perceive are working against them. Remembering this may help you defuse a toxic situation before either side builds a wall.

Disseminating Information to Journalists

Every law enforcement agency should have a mission to be open with information that is deemed public. The determination of what information is public and what information may be held confidential is often set out in state law, federal law, and case law on many levels. However, many agencies go beyond those parameters. For example, in the past several years many agencies have learned that it is not enough to wait until a person requests crime statistics. Many have started publishing the information on their agency websites, through social media, and via internet portals. As I have discussed, a modern law enforcement agency must have someone dedicated to keeping the public and journalists informed.

Many times, journalists will use the vehicles available to the general public to obtain information. Although the names and the language of the statutes vary, the concept is the same: state law provides that information must be released to people upon request unless there is a reason to withhold the information. As professionals, you should use the correct terminology within your state. Do not ask someone to file a "FOIA" request if your state does not use that term. FOIA is a federal statute, and the acronym stands for Freedom of Information Act, referring to the federal law by the same name codified at 5 U.S.C. § 552 signed by Lyndon Johnson in 1966.

I did a survey of all fifty states and the District of Columbia to determine the similarities and differences among and between the state laws directed at the disclosure of information held and or generated by a public entity. As expected—and mainly due to the political differences between state legislatures—the language, requirements, and procedures vary greatly. I will include a list of the statutes for your convenience in Appendix A, but the details of each would likely increase the length of this text by one third! Oddly enough, often the longest sections of the statutes involve the exceptions to disclosure requirements. You can use this list to begin your research and training programs to ensure compliance with your state laws.

The survey of these statutes produced some interesting results. First, the list of what constitutes a public document varies greatly. Some statutes spell this out in detail while others make blanket statements indicating that all documents and records are public unless a specific provision classifies them as exempt from disclosure. The time required for a government entity to respond to a request for disclosure also varies from a few days to as long as thirty days. Several states' statutes do not specify a time frame for production, and many have two time frames. The first is to acknowledge the request or the existence of materials responsive to the request, and the second is for production of the materials. Many states also provide for the public entity to request an extension of the time required to produce the documents, when necessary, due to issues regarding the retrieval of archived documents or complying with requests that will result in the production of voluminous materials.

Very few states require the request to be in a particular format. I have personally seen confusion with this provision and was once told by a records clerk that my signed request, written on letterhead from my law firm, was legally insufficient, and I was required to fill out the form provided by her law enforcement agency. We had a nice chat, and although she never agreed with me or researched the law, she did consent to calling the county attorney for advice within the three days required for a response. That was a wise decision and saved her sheriff some legal fees.

The exemptions contained in the statutes are, quite frankly, a mess. Depending upon the state, the exemptions range from a few sentences to entire paragraphs. It is critical to keep the person in charge of this function at your law enforcement agency up to date with the law. I can assure you that the attorneys on call for the media outlets you encounter will be well versed and current in their knowledge. I once saw a journalist who was denied access to a courthouse obtain a signed order from a judge within thirty minutes. There is no reason to get into a dispute due to a lack of education or training.

Surprisingly, not every state protects the home address and family information of law enforcement officers. This is becoming more common, but it is not standard. While I would expect journalists to exercise sound judgment with this information, especially following a critical incident, one journalist famously released Darren Wilson's home address following the death of Michael Brown. Consider that the life of the law enforcement officer and his family is placed in danger, real danger, when his home address is released following a critical incident.

The other point of variance is the amount that can be charged for responding to the request. Some states allow a charge for researching the request and gathering the responsive materials, and others do not. Some statutes contain specific schedules of charges by the page, by the hour for production, and for certification of the materials produced. I have seen some law enforcement agencies charge for a DVD upon which the materials are copied for production when I ask for the materials in electronic format. I have never objected to this. However, I have had law enforcement agencies and government entities refuse to produce the material in electronic format, even when the materials are in that format before production. Essentially, they want to charge for printing an electronic document into paper form when I request the materials in their original form. That is just silly. Both sides need to work together.

Finally, the statutes vary as to the remedy for the failure to produce the documents requested. Some statutes set out specific remedies such as judicial review of documents withheld under exemptions or when the exemptions are not clear. Others merely state that the records must be produced. However, law enforcement officers and agencies should understand that there is a general right to force a public entity to comply with the law. It is called a writ of mandamus. You should also know that judges usually have the discretion to award attorney fees and expenses to a person who prevails in a suit specified in a statute or through a writ of mandamus. These suits lead to bad publicity for the law enforcement agency, bad relationships between the law enforcement agency and journalists, and an air of distrust between the law enforcement agency and the public, and the fees and expenses can become quite costly. If the exemption is not clear, I recommend that a law enforcement agency consult with the person requesting records if the law enforcement agency believes the records are subject to an exemption. If you cannot come to an agreement, you can jointly request a ruling from a court. This procedure is more likely to avoid battle lines being drawn and fees and expenses being assessed against the loser. Of course, you should involve an attorney in this process.

Remember that these statutes are remedial and meant to foster disclosure and openness. When a court is faced with interpreting these laws, the court, and appellate courts, will likely err on the side of disclosure. Therefore, law enforcement agencies should pick their battles carefully and avoid the battlefield completely when possible.

Press Conferences

A press conference, also called a news conference, is a formal event during which a person, company, or other entity gathers journalists for the purpose of disseminating information to a group of journalists at one setting.[164] We have all seen press conferences on television and seen photographs taken during press conferences in newspapers. They follow a predictable format wherein the person disseminating information speaks and then addresses questions from the journalists assembled in the room. Sometimes the questions are supplied in advance in writing, and sometimes they are posed spontaneously from the floor. In rare circumstances, the speaker will not entertain any questions following the conclusion of her prepared remarks. If you have never watched one from start to finish, do not rely upon the snippets and edited footage you may see on the news. Go to YouTube and watch several. You will learn a great deal.

A press conference can be used to provide new information to journalists, to provide a briefing on news that is developing, such as a critical incident or natural disaster, and to provide follow-up information for a news story that has been in the news cycle for some time. The key to holding a press conference is that there is first and foremost new information to provide to journalists and the public. A press conference should never be used to dress down a journalist or media outlet, to air political feuds, or to transmit primarily negative information about an individual or group. Journalists reasonably expect that the announcement of a press conference will afford them the opportunity to obtain a great deal of information in a short period of time and that they will be allowed to ask follow-up questions. If your press conference does not afford those opportunities, you may damage your credibility as a law enforcement officer or agency.

The advantage of a press conference is the degree of control afforded the law enforcement agency using this format. Typically, the agency can select the spokesperson in advance and avoid impromptu questions being posed to random law enforcement officers in the agency. Further, the agency can avoid the piecemeal dissemination of information and ensure that the information provided is accurate, cohesive, presented in a logical order, and complete.

The format of a press conference, which will be followed nearly universally unless the law enforcement agency has a reputation for failing to respond to questions, provides an opportunity for the spokesperson to speak first prior to responding to questions. It is also possible to request written questions in advance of the press conference. Although all journalists invited to attend may not provide any written questions, the questions the agency does receive will help prepare the spokesperson for the conference. If the agency has a reputation for failing to answer questions, journalists may begin by asking questions before the spokesperson has an opportunity to start or finish her remarks. There is a definite etiquette to conducting a press conference. Learn it and stick to it, and you will advance your professional relationship with the journalists who attend.

Press conferences can be informal as well. For example, at the scene of a critical incident or mass casualty event, you can expect that numerous journalists from all available media outlets will assemble waiting for official word of the incident and to ask questions to inform their customers. Unlike a traditional press conference that may be announced hours or even days in advance, an informal press conference can be set up close to the scene in a safe area and take place a few minutes after the announcement. The announcement can be done via cell phone, text, Twitter, Facebook, Instagram, or in person by having a PIO advise the assembled journalists where to gather and when. At the appointed time, the spokesperson can provide information the journalists need to create their stories, advise them of the progress being made, any procedures in place for their safety, and perhaps most important, the time and location of the next press conference. Done correctly, a law enforcement agency may turn a potentially chaotic forty-eight hours typically filled with disorganized and constant media inquiries into an orderly process.

Whenever there is time to do so, which is all but the most extreme and emergent circumstances, the agency should announce the press conference via facsimile, email, all agency social media channels, the law enforcement agency website, personal phone calls, email, and any other method available. The goal is to gather all of the interested journalists—those who support you and the few who will not. Provide the date, time, location, and topic of the press conference. If there are special instructions regarding parking, security screening, limitations on seating, or other issues, provide that information in the announcement of the press conference. You want to allow all interested journalists adequate time to arrive, set up, and be seated, if possible, before you begin.

The law enforcement agency should also prepare a press packet and have enough available for every anticipated attendee. I also recommend putting multimedia such as video and audio clips onto DVDs for the attendees to take with them. You must respect the fact that all media outlets use video and audio. You must also anticipate that if you show or reference a video or audio recording you will be inundated with requests for those items immediately following the press conference. Avoid overloading your records and PIO staff and provide it before the press conference in the packet. If you are unable to do so, provide a reason why during your statement. Here is an example following a hypothetical critical incident in which a driver struck a deputy and two drivers while the deputy was investigating a car crash on the side of the roadway:

> This afternoon, I will reference a video that has assisted our investigators with their understanding of the events that we are here to discuss. Unfortunately, we are unable to show the video or provide copies at this time because the video contains victims that have not been identified and we have not yet been able to notify the next of kin. We are working to identify these victims and make appropriate notifications. Working in cooperation with the district attorney and the county legal department, we will release the video as soon as we are able to do so. Please note that when you receive the video, you will hear some blanks on the audio. The deputy involved in this situation asked two victims for their dates of birth and social security numbers before the driver struck the deputy's marked vehicle. As you are aware, that information cannot be released under state law.

This statement accomplishes several goals. First, it advises the journalists attending and the public that there is video available of the incident. The public will watch the video of the press conference that your law enforcement agency will stream live and upload to your agency YouTube channel. Second, you have advised why the video is not being released at this time. Third, you have clearly stated what must happen prior to the release of the video. Finally, you have prepared anyone who receives the video that the audio will be partially redacted to comply with state law.

As stated previously, the agency maintains control over many aspects of the press conference. However, it is important to remember that the journalists are guests in your department. Be considerate. If the press conference takes place in August in Atlanta and you know the journalists and camera operators will be walking one hundred yards from the designated parking area, have cold water available. The same is true, but the beverage will change, for a press conference in January in Minneapolis. A large pot of hot coffee will do wonders for your media relations.

It is important to arrange the room properly for a press conference. Do not attempt to squeeze thirty journalists, their support staff, and their equipment into a conference room designed for ten people to sit comfortably around a large table unless you can remove the table. No one wants to be uncomfortable, and all of the journalists in attendance want to be able to sit with sufficient room to write. They all want to ensure that their support staff, such as camera operators, have clear views of the spokesperson. While power is generally not an issue, as a good host you should consider having a set of power strips available plugged into available power outlets.

Before the first journalist attends, law enforcement officers and the spokesperson must arrange the room and determine the location of microphones, cameras, and journalists. You should also place and monitor your own video and audio recording equipment. It is vitally important that you have a record of everything you said, every question asked, and your responses. You should also upload the video to your law enforcement agency

YouTube channel. You can also live stream the press conference to your Facebook page using the live video option.

Remember that many journalists use programs such as Periscope or simply use their smartphones to record video. One video I found shows a camera view, likely from a smartphone, looking straight up the spokesperson's nose and up at their face. Do not allow your spokesperson or your law enforcement agency to be portrayed in a less than professional manner because you failed to set parameters. Cameras, microphones, and journalists sitting too close can be very intimidating to your spokesperson. Advertising and channel identifiers on microphones can block the spokesperson's face, particularly if they are short in relationship to the lectern. You should take all reasonable steps to put your spokesperson at ease. Sometimes this means designating a location for all cameras. Given the size and footprint of most tripods, you should probably designate more than one.

I have seen some horrific blunders at press conferences, and you can find them by searching the internet. Just search for "press conference fails" and you will see your fair share. I received 2.3 million hits when I ran that search. What makes a press conference fail? Well, let's create a list.

- ❖ Failing to introduce yourself as the spokesperson
- ❖ Failing to have every person who speaks for the agency introduce themselves
- ❖ Bad lighting in the room
- ❖ Poorly positioned cameras that place your spokesperson in a bad light
- ❖ Microphones covering the face of the spokesperson
- ❖ Background noise from the hallways, parking lots, or overhead such as airplanes
- ❖ A poorly dressed spokesperson
- ❖ A statement that goes on for too long

- ❖ A spokesperson who interrupts when journalists ask questions
- ❖ Failing to allow sufficient time for questions and answers
- ❖ Failing to direct questions to the press packet, when appropriate, to be consistent
- ❖ Failing to remain calm when questioned repeatedly about the same topic or when faced with an inappropriate or rude question
- ❖ Failing to ask for clarification if the spokesperson did not hear or understand the question
- ❖ Failing to begin on time, although it is appropriate to wait if weather or traffic will delay several journalists
- ❖ Failing to end the press conference when the questions become repetitive
- ❖ Failing to call on one journalist at a time to avoid confusing questions and having people talk over each other
- ❖ Failing to designate who will respond to specific questions if there is more than one person present from the law enforcement agency or other entities
- ❖ If there is more than one person present for the law enforcement agency, they should never interrupt each other
- ❖ Failing to keep the press conference focused on the topic at hand and the dissemination of information
- ❖ Allowing one journalist to monopolize the question period
- ❖ Failing to state, in the opening statement, what information will not be available, what questions cannot be answered at that time, why, and when that information may become available
- ❖ Failing to advise when the next press conference, release of information, or other communication on the topic at hand will take place and in what format, and provide contact information for the person in charge of that effort

This list may seem exhaustive, but I assure you, it is not. Watch some of the disasters available for viewing and you will see what can go wrong. Many appear hilarious and would be unless you were involved.

Another thing that can cause difficulties is if the journalists leave the press conference and seek out the law enforcement officers who are mentioned or involved in the incident that is the focus of the press release. While you cannot prevent journalists from finding and speaking with civilians, you must advise officers and their private counsel prior to the press release that they should be prepared for this scenario. Nothing could be worse than having an officer blindsided by several journalists while she is leaving the precinct or arriving home after picking up groceries.

It is important to determine who will act as the spokesperson. While this may seem intuitive, it is not. Sometimes, it is best not to have the chief or sheriff act as the spokesperson to avoid a challenge that the decision to release information rests with him or her. A spokesperson may need the ability to defer to the decision of the chief or sheriff on a question. That is not possible if the head of the law enforcement agency is behind the microphone.

Select a person with some experience and training in handling media questions and a person with a professional public speaking demeanor. As stated earlier, you should prepare for these events by running drills and allowing PIOs from other jurisdictions to act as journalists asking tough or just persistent questions. While there are many classes available for law enforcement officers to attend prior to acting as the agency spokesperson during a press conference, here are several tips:

❖ Dress in a clean and pressed uniform or a suit in similar condition.

❖ Introduce yourself at the start of your remarks, including your name, rank or position, and agency. Do not assume that the journalists in attendance will understand rank insignia or recognize the chief or sheriff.

❖ Do not lean on the lectern when speaking.

❖ Do not read the entire time, even if it is important to recite some facts with specificity. Look up and make eye contact.

❖ Do not rush the opening statement, and take a reasonable time to answer questions.

❖ If you do not have some facts available, offer to obtain that information and put it out to the group within a reasonable time period. State when that information will be available and how you will disseminate it.

❖ Be honest, always.

❖ Do not fidget.

❖ Stand up straight, make eye contact with the person who is asking a question, and answer yes or no when possible. You can explain your answer after you have done so.

❖ Do not respond to a question that you did not hear or understand. Ask the journalist to repeat or clarify the question.

❖ Incorporate the question into your answer so that your statements are complete for listeners who may not be able to hear a particular journalist's question, such as "No, we are not able to release the victim's name yet as their next of kin has not been notified. We expect to release this information at the next press conference tomorrow morning."

❖ Thank the journalists for attending, always.

❖ Obtain contact information for everyone who attends the press conference to allow you to document who attended, facilitate future contact, and verify the contact information you have on file.

Holding a press conference can be nerve-racking and create very tense situations. You are inviting journalists of all opinions, personalities, and experience levels into a room together. It is not an exercise for the faint of heart or the unprepared. Remember the advice I provided earlier in this book: journalists will read your body language and determine when you are nervous, evasive, frustrated, or angry. If you cannot keep your composure, you should not be behind the microphones. If you cannot hide your personal frustrations and play poker, stick to the slot machines.

When the press conference is concluded, you should expect that the journalists in attendance will seek private interviews with the spokesperson or others to pose follow-up questions. Remember from earlier in this book that the journalists are in competition to provide their customers with unique perspectives. The one downside of press conferences for journalists is they all receive the same information at the same time.

If the spokesperson will not be available for follow-up questions, let the journalists know this in advance and provide a statement in the press packet. If the agency PIOs will be available for follow-up questions, you should let the journalists know. If the spokesperson is the chief or sheriff, it is a good idea to announce this at the end of the opening remarks to avoid one journalist believing he was slighted because he did not receive a follow-up interview. If you make a statement that you will not be providing follow-up interviews and that you have released all the information that is available at this time, do not grant interviews to some journalists and not others. This will understandably cause friction and a loss of credibility for your law enforcement agency.

You should schedule your press conference at a time that will allow the journalists in attendance sufficient time to meet publication deadlines. If you are unsure of these parameters, call a trusted journalist in each media type and ask. Sometimes, this is not possible. That is why you should always provide a location for radio and television journalists to record or perform live feeds. This can be an area of the parking lot that provides a backdrop of some law enforcement vehicles or the agency building. Direct the journalists to these locations at the end of the press conference to avoid having them stay in the room longer than you desire. Concerns for security, privacy, and the ability to avoid the intentional or inadvertent recording of conversations within the law enforcement agency can be alleviated through this process.

As soon as you release information concerning a press release, you must expect that people may try to impersonate journalists and attend. While a gathering at the agency is generally open to the public and you may be prohibited by law from excluding anyone, you can limit questions to bona fide journalists. This will require two activities on your part. First, you should place someone at the door to greet the journalists as they arrive, hand them a press packet, and keep a list of the media outlets that attend. Second, you can ask for press credentials to verify a person's status.

The issuing of press credentials is a thorny subject. In my research for this book, I learned that some law enforcement agencies issue press credentials to assist journalists in accessing events and the locations of incidents where officers are controlling access.[165] Of course, press credentials should not allow a journalist access to a crime scene or other restricted area, but it may be appropriate to allow a journalist and a film crew to drive through an area struck by a tornado with a law enforcement escort. I also learned that some law enforcement agencies do not issue press credentials and that many journalists have no desire to "register" with a law enforcement agency to perform their jobs. Irrespective of the practice in your law enforcement agency and community, the media outlet employing the journalists will usually issue an identification card that is typically worn around the neck. The question as to how to treat and what access to grant to "self-proclaimed" journalists who host blogs or simply write about current events on social media is unsettled. My thought is if they handle themselves in a professional manner, the law enforcement agencies would do well to treat them as journalists. Be prepared, however, for some resistance from traditional journalists who may not hold such individuals in high regard.

Press conferences are valuable tools for the law enforcement agency and journalists. You can avoid much of the feeding frenzy described in Chapter Two by providing a predictable method for journalists to obtain information and updates. Some events, such as an officer-involved shooting, civil unrest, manhunts, and natural disasters may lend themselves to regular daily press conferences. Be sure to be punctual and schedule the press conferences at a minimum in the morning and evening to allow sufficient time to meet journalist deadlines.

Press Releases

A press release is a written statement that provides information to journalists and the public concerning an event. It should be direct, pithy, grammatically correct, and well written. Consider the famous words of two professionals in this vein:

> *I didn't have time to write a short letter, so I wrote a long one instead.*
>
> Mark Twain

> *There is no great writing, only great rewriting.*
> United States Supreme Court Justice Louis Brandeis

Well-written press releases take three things: a list of facts, more than one person to review and edit the draft, and time. The last ingredient is nonnegotiable. No one can write their best work in the first draft. No one can edit their own work to reach a professional quality. I can assure you every book you have read, including this one, has been pored over and corrected by professional editors. Finally, no one can edit documents properly when they are under pressure to get the facts absolutely correct, meet a timed deadline, and are left without the ability to step away then come back to review the document.

This is usually not a problem in the law enforcement agency because press releases typically must be drafted, reviewed by the chain of command, reviewed by the department's legal advisor or government attorney, and in some cases reviewed by the prosecutor's office. Given these requirements and the fact that the press release will be in the public realm forever, here are some recommendations:

❖ Start the process early.

❖ Determine who must approve the press release and put them on notice that it is coming.

❖ Consider a meeting of the involved parties and get their input before the first draft is started.

❖ Give clear deadlines as to when the press release must be edited and returned to the person responsible for releasing it.

❖ Designate the task of circulating and editing the draft press release to one person.

❖ Use the "track changes" feature in Word or some other method to have a record of who added or deleted information from the draft press release.

❖ Remember that your drafts are likely subject to release as public records. Therefore, you may choose to meet in person to review drafts.

❖ Verify every fact in the press release and be prepared to "show your work" in the event of a challenge or follow-up interview.

❖ Explain any legalese or law enforcement jargon and provide references to statutes and case law when possible. Consider directing readers to your agency website, blogs, or specific statutes to avoid making the press release too long or cumbersome.

❖ Provide references to sources outside the law enforcement agency when appropriate, such as case numbers and files in a clerk's office, reports of other law enforcement agencies, or public documents such as property records or warrants.

Every press release should inform journalists and the public. It should also build credibility for the law enforcement agency. Be honest, be objective when necessary, and admit when information is not available, cannot be released, or will be released at a later time.

Below you will find an excellent press release concerning an officer-involved shooting involving two law enforcement officers. You will see this press release is short, to the point, provides the information journalists would need to prepare a story, and advises on follow-up information. This is an actual press release and is available on the internet from several sources.

Arizona Department of Public Safety Investigating Officer-Involved Shooting in Morenci
Tuesday, January 27, 2015

Morenci—Department of Public Safety (DPS) is conducting the criminal investigation of a shooting involving two law enforcement officers and a suspect in Morenci, Arizona.

The Greenlee County Sheriff's Office received two 911 calls before midnight regarding a disturbance involving a male suspect. A Greenlee County Deputy and a Clifton Police Officer responded to the disturbance and observed the suspect driving in the area. The officers initiated a traffic stop with the suspect when shots were fired by the suspect and both officers. The suspect, a 29-year-old man, was deceased a short time later and both officers sustained multiple gunshot wounds. The officers were transported from the scene with serious injuries and are currently in stable condition.

The press release, which is still available on the department's website, has a hot button to contact the PIO concerning this press release.

I particularly like this press release and use it when teaching classes because it contains the information that I believe is essential to a press release involving an officer-involved shooting. To be clear, a law enforcement agency should always put out a press release within a few hours of an officer-involved shooting. You can accurately predict the information journalists will need, so provide it through a press release. Here are, in my humble opinion, the essential elements:

❖ What brought the law enforcement officer(s) to the location of the officer-involved shooting? Was it a call for service, self-initiated activity such as a traffic stop or stopping a suspicious person, a request for assistance from another law enforcement officer or agency, or a crime in progress?

❖ How many law enforcement officers were on the scene at the time of the officer-involved shooting?

❖ What law enforcement agencies were involved in the call, the officer-involved shooting, and the situation that led to the officer-involved shooting?

❖ How many suspects were on the scene of the officer-involved shooting?

❖ What is the condition of the person who was shot?

❖ What is the condition of the law enforcement officer(s)?

❖ Who is investigating the officer-involved shooting?

❖ When did the officer-involved shooting occur?

❖ Where did the officer-involved shooting occur?

❖ Who should be contacted for further information?

You will notice that these points are available within a few minutes and certainly within a few hours of the vast majority of officer-involved shootings. The information need not be specific, as in the press release above, specifying the number of shots fired, by whom, the location of injuries, or other information that must be withheld to properly vet witnesses. However, by putting some information out to journalists and the public, the law enforcement agency will build some trust and allow the journalists to communicate information to their customers.

Every law enforcement agency must have a person on staff who can write and edit a press release. There are classes available to train officers how to do so all over the United States. Further, there are plenty of online resources available. My search of "how to write a press release" yielded tens of millions of results.

If there is a reason to request that the media outlet hold off on reporting the information until a time certain, you can request an embargo. This request is printed at the top of the press release along with the time when the information can be released. You will note that most press releases are marked "for immediate release," and the media outlet is free to use the information at any time. Embargos are used with announcements but generally do not work well in the law enforcement agency context. For example, a law enforcement agency could request an embargo for twenty-four hours until the last remaining next of kin is notified. However, it is probably best to delay the press release until the information can be used immediately. You can, however, satisfy anxious journalists by letting them know that you will be sending a press release shortly, especially if you advise the reason for any delay. This will, providing you have been true to your word in the past, typically prevent the journalists from contacting you asking for information ahead of the anticipated release of the information.

One final note: any law enforcement officer mentioned in the press release, or who is the subject of the action addressed in the press release, should be notified prior to its release. When possible, they should be provided a copy, and if they have private counsel, or if the law enforcement agency has retained counsel, that attorney should receive a copy in advance of journalists. This is your press release, and although you may entertain input from counsel for the agency or an individual law enforcement officer, you must make the final decision about what to include.

Reviewing News Stories, Insisting on Corrections, and Responding to Inappropriate Editing or Unprofessional Behavior

It is essential to have someone in your law enforcement agency review the news stories concerning your officers and agency. You should have a repository of those stories and use them to demonstrate your law enforcement agency's openness with the media. Inevitably, you will take issue with something in a story that you believe is inaccurate—or worse, untrue. You should always reach out to the journalist first. However, keep in mind that often the issues that you believe are egregious may simply be a matter of miscommunication or degrees of efforts by journalists to avoid seeming one-sided. In the event that the journalist has breached a professional duty—or worse, intentionally set out to do harm—it is important to know how to respond.

I first want to address retractions. This issue has occupied many courts over the years. If a statement is incorrect, you can usually request a retraction or correction. In most cases, if the journalist and her chain of command agree that the information as reported is incorrect, they will issue a retraction or correction. The difficulty begins when the parties do not agree that the information is incorrect or inaccurate.

Many states have "retraction statutes" that require a party to seek a retraction prior to filing suit. Some of the statutes are very specific regarding the time frame within which a person must demand a retraction. In other states, the failure to seek a retraction will limit the type of damages sought if you bring suit. If you have not figured this out by now, you should get an attorney involved if you believe you have been damaged by an inaccurate news story. Pursuing a defamation suit against a journalist or media outlet is very difficult, and in many instances, the burden is higher if a law enforcement officer is bringing the suit, as you may be considered a public figure. Do not try to drive this road alone. Find an experienced attorney, act quickly, and even then, proceed with caution.

Most journalists are taught to verify their sources, and most media outlets are run by experienced managers and editors who ensure that the stories they publish have been vetted. More common is the concern over improper editing of quotes. Short of recording every interview, and in some states both parties must consent to this, there must be a level of trust between the law enforcement officer and the journalist. As I have stated in this book, you must work to develop that trust over time. If you find yourself incapable or unwilling to trust any journalist, I recommend that you move out of the role of interacting with journalists. Such distrust will only foster animosity that can have far-reaching ramifications for your agency.

I believe the biggest risk to the reputations of law enforcement officers and agencies is the informal media and untrained "journalists" who report and publish in that space. It can be very difficult to find some of the people involved in hate and defamation campaigns on the internet, and even harder to find a jurisdiction in which to bring suit against them. However, aside from the advice you should seek from an attorney licensed in your state, I encourage you to do everything possible to preserve the offensive post, blog, photo, comment, or other publication as quickly as possible. Do not assume that it will be available tomorrow. Take a photograph or a screenshot of it as soon as you see it. It is easy to shut down web pages and social media pages. While you may be able to obtain the information with a subpoena, you will likely be required to show proof of the offending post prior. Do not get caught without your evidence.

How to Respond When Journalists Attack

Just as there are different personalities in every law enforcement agency, so there are different personalities in every newsroom. I have very good relationships with many journalists, and I am proud that we can disagree but still be cordial. At the same time, I recently had lunch with a lawyer after we spent four years litigating a contentious case against each other. Perhaps I am unique, but I do not believe that is the case.

I will admit that there are a few journalists whom I do not care to spend much time with beyond our professional interactions. In some cases, it is a personality clash, and we both recognize it. In others, I simply do not care for the way they treat my law enforcement officer clients. As you can imagine, I am neither shy nor reserved about my feelings in this regard, and to their credit, neither are they. However, we come together when necessary, and typically I have information they need for their stories. They quote me accurately for two reasons. First, they are professionals. Second, they know I will never help them again if they are unfair to me or my clients. I will reiterate that these situations are rare.

Through the course of many interviews I have, on rare occasions, run into journalists, or more accurately people who portrayed themselves as journalists, who were, in a word, abrasive. Perhaps caustic is a more accurate term. Many times their attacks were planned, albeit poorly, and designed to get me to lose my composure. No matter how tempting that is, do not do it. I have confirmed what I long suspected: those folks are few and far between because they do not last long. In fact, in time they end up speaking to themselves, and their commercial viability in a fiercely competitive market evaporates. In every sense, such interviews and interviewers are rare.

Some of these folks were attracted to me because of my books. I say that because most law enforcement officers will not encounter this level of idiocy. However, I will provide you with a list of warning signs to let you know that the interviewer has an agenda and you may be set up to fail at the outset.

❖ If there are two interviewers involved, are they seemingly on opposite sides of the issue? This is a technique to get you to agree with one on an extreme position so they both can pounce.

❖ Are they spending more time talking to themselves than asking you questions? This is especially important on controversial subjects when the host may attempt to use one or two of the words you manage to get out to further pontificate.

❖ Are they asking questions aimed at the facts of a case or the law, or are they asking you to comment about the feelings or perspectives of people you never met? Let me give you a hint: it is impossible to do so without stepping into a hole.

❖ Do they change the subject when you have a clear, rational, and evidence-based response to a question?

❖ Has the interview strayed at the outset from the stated topic and purpose?

To be clear, I do not have a boss or a chain of command. I can afford to respond to inappropriate behavior as I see fit. Law enforcement officers, at every rank and position, do not have that luxury. You must be prepared to gracefully exit such interviews quickly. Trust me on this, they will not get better as time goes on. Politely thank the interviewer for their time and advise that you have another appointment. If you are a PIO, report the situation to your chain of command in the event that the person files a complaint. Keep a list of the name, the station, the name of the show, and the name of the producer to avoid stepping into that trap again. I have a few such folks on a list.

If you find yourself under attack during an interview and you cannot extricate yourself, slow the pace of the conversation. You can do this in many ways. First, slow down the pace of your statements and answers. Sometimes, the person on the receiving end will mirror your pace. Most of the time, however, they will begin speaking more quickly in an effort to keep you off balance. Ask them to repeat a question. This breaks up their pace and can throw them off balance. There is nothing wrong with saying, "I would like to respond, but you are speaking so quickly I'm having a hard time understanding you, and I want to make sure I am clear on your question." You can also ask the person to break their question down into a few questions by stating, "There was a lot in that last statement. I prefer to answer one question at a time." Finally, do not accept the premise of a question if it is false, and reject it as soon as the person finishes speaking. For example, I have had several people ask questions like, "If all a cop has to say is 'I was in fear of my life,' how can you ever expect people to have faith in the criminal justice system in the United States?" My response would be, "In order to be found to have used deadly force in an appropriate manner, a law enforcement officer must say far more than 'I was in fear for my life,' so I'm not sure how to respond to your question."

If you find yourself in a situation where the interviewer has changed the topic of the interview or strayed into topics that he agreed to avoid before the interview, do not be caught off guard or dragged down that rabbit hole. Simply state, in response to their question, "Your question surprises me, as we agreed that we would be speaking about another topic." You can also state, "When we spoke prior to this interview, I advised that I was not able to answer questions about that particular matter at this time." In my experience, these techniques typically bring the interview back around to the realm of fairness. If not, it is a sign that things will only get worse.

Do not expect to have perfect responses come out of your mouth without practice. Have your fellow PIOs and those from neighboring jurisdictions grill you. Practice what you would say in response to the worst anti-law enforcement officer statement possible. Remember, the more you practice, the more you will be able to control your emotions, facial expressions, and body language. Videotape your responses and reactions to questions, and work to maintain your composure. Finally, take some time to review people placed into the barrel on YouTube or other sites and learn from their mistakes. Like range time and defensive tactics, the time you spend practicing now will make you more effective under the stress of the moment.

How to Handle Impromptu Interviews

Although they never bothered me, I know many people—law enforcement officers, politicians, and public relations professionals alike—who dislike unplanned interviews. For many people, they feel like they are not permitted to prepare, put their best foot forward, or represent their law enforcement agency in the most professional light possible. Aside from my consistent advice to prepare for this through training and practice, I will say that you can respond in a way that strongly encourages the journalists to schedule the next interview.

Not all impromptu interviews are intended to make you look bad. Some are merely based upon an opportunity. Others are created because you have not been returning calls from the journalist. This should never happen. If you find yourself caught off guard, ask what the journalist wants to discuss. While it is preferable to ask this off camera, sometimes it is not possible. Do your best to look professional and calm when you ask. If that question appears on camera, it will be a signal to viewers that the journalist surprised you, and people will empathize with you.

Refer the journalist to other sources within the law enforcement agency, and answer the question with an invitation to conduct the interview at your office so that you can have the facts, statistics, or other information readily available. If the interview gets out of control because you are completely unprepared and caught off guard, thank the journalist and advise that you look forward to meeting with them later. You can even throw out a time certain. Most journalists will not try to ambush people, as it makes for bad relations. However, if you employ these techniques, a journalist is not likely to attempt this technique with you twice.

Why Do So Many Law Enforcement Officers Distrust the Media, and How Does That Affect the Relationship between the Law Enforcement Agency and the Media in General?

I have been speaking with law enforcement officers and agency heads for many years about this topic since I first started working with journalists as a crime prevention officer in 1992. I have also had a lot of great discussions with journalists about this topic before and after interviews. In preparation for writing this book, I increased those efforts. While this is far from a double-blind, peer-reviewed scientific survey, I believe it would be helpful for the journalists reading this book to read what I learned.

Law enforcement officers generally recognize the importance and role of the media. Like most people, they are consumers of news. They have their favorite news sites, newspapers, radio stations, and television stations. They also do not care for some journalists, and for the most part, it is not due to personal experience. These feelings, good and bad, are formed in the same manner and for the same reasons as the rest of your customers; they like the people with whom they most identify. So what gets the law enforcement officers upset at a particular media outlet or journalist? Here is a list from the comments and conversations I've heard:

❖ The journalist reported a version of events from someone that seemed unbelievable.

❖ The journalist seemed biased against law enforcement officers based upon the way he kept pushing someone to say something negative.

❖ The journalist should know that proper police procedure was followed because they have the report. Why are they reporting someone's version that doesn't match the statements of the people, both law enforcement and civilians, who were there?

❖ The story got so many facts wrong, and I know what happened because I was there.

❖ The media outlet devoted so much time to the allegations of wrongdoing on the part of the law enforcement officer, but when the law enforcement officer was cleared, they barely mentioned it.

Some of these comments can be chalked up to a lack of experience with journalists. For example, journalists will likely report what a purported witness said even if it is contrary to the police report. However, some of these comments should be cause for reflection.

In an age of electronic media, speed is king, and sometimes the journalists either do not have the time or do not wish to spend the time to dig deeper into the relatively minor stories, like a car wreck that backed up traffic for hours prior to publishing what they learned from speaking with people on the street. Journalists operate in a world of limited resources like everyone else, and perhaps the most limited commodity is time. However, consider the perspective of the law enforcement officer in our traffic scenario. She was standing in traffic, surrounded by people texting, or likely otherwise impaired, directing traffic in the poor weather conditions that caused the wreck and working to clear the roadway. All the while, calls are backing up in her beat, supervisors are pushing to have the roadway cleared, impatient drivers are honking and yelling, and the law enforcement officer is working to get enough information from the vehicles, the drivers, the passengers, and the roadway to write a report that she may have to defend in court. So as a journalist, you can understand why inaccuracies in reporting how that law enforcement officer spent a few hours on the interstate, or the statement of a frustrated driver complaining about the officer, might rub a law enforcement officer the wrong way.

As to the issue of spending equal time reporting a law enforcement officer being cleared as media outlets spend examining the critical incident and the controversy surrounding it, that one has everyone scratching their heads, including me.

I know and explain to law enforcement officers that those decisions are made above the pay grade of most journalists. I also know that by the time the officer is cleared, the public and the journalist have usually moved onto another high-profile story. However, all law enforcement officers, not just the ones involved, feel the effects of the suppositions and allegations following an officer-involved shooting. They are attacked, most often verbally but in some cases physically, for the alleged actions of another officer simply because they wear the same uniform.

Even when the attacks are not direct, the constant barrage of negativity toward the law enforcement agency causes a disconnect between officers and the public. For example, one law enforcement officer friend of mine asked a woman for her driver's license, and she was unable to find it. He wrote her a speeding ticket and a ticket for not having her license on her while she was driving. He verified that her driver's license was valid, so it was more of a formality that she is required to have her license in her possession to allow the officer to verify that she is the one driving. When he approached the car the second time, she handed him her driver's license that she found while he was in his patrol car checking her tag and license status on the computer. When he asked her why she did not hold it out the window and honk or wave to get his attention, she said, "Well, I thought if I did any of that, you would shoot me." A month or two before this traffic stop, an officer in another jurisdiction shot and killed someone who reached for what the officer believed was a weapon after repeated warnings to put his hands up. News coverage of the incident had scared this woman to a loss of common sense.

Consider this fact: the law enforcement officer, the officer's spouse, friends, neighbors, relatives, church family, little league or other group parents, college alumni friends, high school buddies, and coworkers are all customers of media outlets. They all share these frustrations. Wouldn't it make sense to show fairness in these situations to gain and retain customers? If a journalist was accused of professional impropriety, what level of coverage would you desire when she was eventually exonerated?

Create a List of Information You Will Release as Soon as Possible Following a Critical Incident

Some pieces of information simply cannot be released immediately following a critical incident. For example, toxicology reports, exact wound paths, the number of shots fired, ballistic reports, and other information will likely not be available for weeks. However, a great deal of information is known to the law enforcement agency immediately following the incident and is available for release.

I have seen a great deal of confusion on this point. Law enforcement agencies will cite the open-records law in their state and use the time limit for responding to a request as the reason for a period of delay they feel they must employ. This is inaccurate. When information is in the hands of the agency, they can release it whenever they deem appropriate if it is not privileged, such as social security numbers, and they receive approval from the district attorney and their internal chain of command. Often, the release of this information can defuse tense situations and create an air of openness.

For example, releasing the names of the departments involved in an officer-involved shooting will not harm anything. This information will not change and will be subject to open-record requests eventually. Other facts, such as the reason for the officer's presence on the scene, will also be known and will shed light on the encounter. Once you decide what information you will release, absent exigent circumstances, pass that information on to the journalists who typically report on critical incidents involving your agency as soon as possible, even before they ask for it.

In certain circumstances, it may be necessary to expand this list of information. For example, if there is controversy surrounding whether or not the decedent was shot in the back and the medical examiner can clearly testify that was not the case, put that information out to journalists and the public as soon as possible. This not only has the effect of quelling rumors; it also exposes any false witnesses who are seeking media attention.

It is important to remember that once information is made public, you can no longer cite an exemption such as "the matter is under investigation." Once the information or materials are made public, you cannot withhold them in response to further requests.

What to Do When Your
Law Enforcement Agency or Officers Were Wrong

I've spoken with chiefs and sheriffs as well as line officers when the facts are undeniable that an officer or agency acted inappropriately. It is heartbreaking to many, and they know it will have a lasting effect on the law enforcement agency and their relationship with the community. It can take years to rebuild that trust, and it may never again exist for some.

The best thing an agency can do is act swiftly and with candor. Put out a press release with the information and promptly respond to requests for information. Normally, a press conference is not necessary, but it could be depending upon the severity of the event.

> *The public and the media must be told as soon as possible, as soon as you know, if something improper occurred. The agency must reach out to the person who was injured or the family and explain what happened as best as they can. They must also provide information as soon as it becomes available and provide a clear line of communication. It is the right thing to do.*
>
> Dan Flynn, forty-year veteran of law enforcement

The law enforcement agency must inform journalists and the public of the status of the investigation, the next steps, and who is conducting the investigation. If an outside agency is brought in by the chief or sheriff, state that fact emphatically and provide the appropriate contact information for that agency. Confirm that your agency is cooperating with the investigation, and advise the status of the law enforcement officer.

Finally, advise what is being done to discover any other wrongdoing as well as to prevent similar situations from occurring in the future. You can discuss the eventual process review and administrative investigation that will be focused inward to get to the facts about what happened and how to prevent it. Many law enforcement agencies have rebounded from such events. However, it will take increased efforts by individual officers as well as senior members of the command staff to meet with community members to reassure them. When it appears something is wrong inside your agency, the only cure is to open the doors and windows and let journalists see for themselves whether it is an isolated incident or pervasive. Perhaps the worst strategy possible is to close ranks and shut down the flow of information.

Chapter Nine

How the Chain of Command Can Be Toxic to a Good Media Strategy

What you cannot enforce, do not command!
Sophocles

Following a 911 call, an ambulance pulls into the parking lot of the mall. The driver, who is likely an emergency medical technician, maneuvers through parked cars, pedestrians, and traffic to the man who is down. Security officers stand by at the entrance to guide them through the crowd.

When they find the man, he is unconscious. A couple of people, including a relative, are holding him and trying to speak with him. The paramedic begins examining the man while the EMT speaks with the relative. Upon examination, the paramedic finds a medic alert necklace indicating that the man is a diabetic. The paramedic immediately obtains a kit, pricks the man's skin, and tests his blood sugar. When the test reveals a level of forty, the paramedic removes a small tube of glucose from his kit and puts a small amount of the gel from the tube onto the man's tongue. In about one minute, the man opens his eyes and begins trying to speak.

The scenario above shows the reality and importance of standing orders. I represent a lot of medical personnel, including nearly one thousand doctors, physician assistants, thousands of nurses, and other licensed or certificated professionals. Standing orders proliferate their daily efforts to treat, revive, and save people.

A standing order is a set of commands or instructions provided to professionals to allow them to act in a set of prescribed circumstances without the need to obtain approval from a physician or a specialist.[166] Standing orders are intended to facilitate the mission of healthcare under circumstances that are anticipated and for which a plan has been developed.

Many standing orders are routine, such as the start of an intravenous line in the emergency department or the taking of vital signs in a doctor's office. However, others are used in emergent circumstances, such as the insertion of esophageal airways in trauma patients, the administration of fast-acting and powerful drugs in the case of an overdose, or the use of four-point restraints in the case of a violent patient. Standing orders are critical in that they save time, and routine in that they are the result of consultation amongst medical professionals to determine what must be done in a set of circumstances to improve patient outcomes and avoid delay.

Law enforcement in the United States also employs this model of standing orders. For example, in the case of a bomb threat, officers will clear an area around the suspected device. In the case of a bank robbery, they will try to let the suspect exit to avoid a hostage situation. However, these standing orders, like those in the medical arena, evolve over time. Years ago, officers were taught to hold a perimeter and call for SWAT personnel in the case of an active shooter. Today, they are trained and expected to enter the building or facility to seek out the assailant.

The concept of standing orders has crossed professions between law enforcement and the medical realm as well. Officers throughout the United States now carry Naloxone and are taught to administer the drug to suspected overdose victims. They are expected to administer this drug without instruction from a physician or input from a paramedic. The process is credited with saving lives everywhere it has been implemented. Only a few years ago, the notion that law enforcement officers would carry and administer a drug in the field was the subject of humor as well as Chicken Little—like cries of crushing liability.

Despite the existence of standing orders in the law enforcement context, there are times when no such orders exist. When faced with an event that occupies resources across more than one group or division of the agency, law enforcement efforts will be coordinated by people higher and higher in the chain of command. This is a function of the rank structure in every law enforcement agency and typically works well to bring resources to resolve the crisis at hand. However, this process is not conducive to the free flow of information, especially to those outside of the agency.

This process has been in place for many years. Inside of the agency, it facilitates the work of the agency and nearly always benefits the public. For example, there may be a need to provide uniformed officers to control traffic flow and entry into the area of a hostage situation. The hostage negotiators are typically detectives; the officers maintaining the inner perimeter around the hostage taker's location are likely tactical or SWAT-trained officers; and the decisions such as shutting off the water and electricity are likely being made by an on-scene commander in coordination with a mobile command center that may be blocks away. The direction to uniformed officers to hold an outer perimeter blocks away is also facilitated through this process. As complicated as this process may appear on an organizational chart or in a policy, it is a fluid and two-way exchange of large amounts of information in the backdrop of a life-threatening and rapidly evolving situation.

In the midst of all of this organization, the presence of highly trained and experienced officers and the resulting ability to make split-second decisions, one question can seemingly stop the process cold: "What should we release to the media?"

In many law enforcement agencies, this question sparks more questions than answers. There are many valid considerations, such as:

❖ Has the victim been identified?

❖ Is the name of the perpetrator known?

❖ Are suspects at large?

- ❖ Will the release of information hamper the ability to properly vet witnesses?
- ❖ Is there video of the incident or subsequent events?
- ❖ Is there an active search for evidence?
- ❖ Is the crime scene ill-defined, or is there more than one?[167]
- ❖ Has the family of the victim been notified?
- ❖ Is the suspect involved in other crimes, and will the release of his name compromise other investigations or put other victims at risk?
- ❖ Has the collection of evidence been hampered by crowds, traffic, weather conditions, or resources such as the need to search a body of water?

Obviously, this list is not exhaustive. One of the critical questions for the law enforcement agency may be, quite simply, "Do we know what happened yet?" Journalists should be aware of this.

On the other side of the crime scene tape, so to speak, are journalists eager to obtain sufficient information to complete their stories on time. They may hear of the situation by monitoring law enforcement radios, phone calls from citizens who call their favorite news source, or Twitter messages such as "lots of cops in front of the Bags of Money Bank." You will recall that the raid to kill Osama bin Laden was exposed by a neighbor who posted a message on the internet wondering aloud about the helicopter activity in the area.[168] Once they are aware of the situation, journalists are bound by their ethics to investigate and provide information to their customers.

When journalists seek information and the law enforcement agency does not respond quickly, there is an understandable level of frustration in the news trucks and at news desks in the community. Depending upon the magnitude of the event, that frustration could extend to media sources around the United

States or around the world within a matter of hours. During and after the trial of George Zimmerman in 2013, I was interviewed about the use of force, neighborhood watch programs, and legal procedures by international sources, including Radio Russia. Every source was on a search for information. The frustration is due to the need to report something to their respective audiences. It is also due to a simple fact of life: journalists have bosses too.

This frustration and the law enforcement agency's response through layers of organization is further complicated by another process that is beyond the control of anyone in this familiar scenario: the news cycle. I discussed the news cycle in more detail in Chapter Seven.

So here is where the wheels can come off the bus. I believe the overwhelming majority of law enforcement agencies and media sources enjoy good working relationships. There is a free exchange of information on a regular basis regarding crime statistics, staffing, new training tactics, and crime prevention and awareness stories. These types of stories fall into the public interest realm. They allow the law enforcement agency to get messages out to the communities they serve and help the media sources provide a service to their consumers as well as fill their reporting space. This is especially true on slow news days.

However, when a critical incident is unfolding, especially an officer-involved shooting, law enforcement agencies often find themselves on the receiving end of an onslaught of media inquiries. Often, these inquiries are not brought forth by the same journalists who covered the purchase of your last canine officer. To the contrary, the coverage of these types of stories is on a different schedule, managed by different producers and editors, and written by a different set of journalists who may be strangers to the command staff and public information officers at the law enforcement agency. This leads to a tremendous amount of friction when information is not forthcoming from the law enforcement agency.

Media requests following critical incidents take many forms. The journalists may call the main line of the department if they are from out of the area. However, the majority of the requests will come from the personal relationships built up through years of interaction and communication between *individual journalists* and *individual law enforcement officers*. There will be calls to the direct line of the law enforcement officer without going through the main switchboard, and cell phone calls will be the norm. Text messages and email will also dominate the inquiries, as will social media communications in the form of private or public messages. There is never a shortage of requests, but the reasons behind the typically slow response is more complicated.

In many situations, the short answer as to why it takes so long for law enforcement agencies to respond to media inquiries is quite simple: they are busy being a law enforcement agency. Unless the mission of the agency requires assistance from the media, such as to warn citizens of road closures, hazards, or to aid in the search for suspects, the primary missions of law enforcement are to protect the public, investigate criminal activity, and make arrests. So it is important for journalists to remember that a law enforcement officer who is not returning your calls may truly be busy being a law enforcement officer.

The reality of this situation is that behind each journalist is a team of producers, editors, and bosses who are driven not by the patience of the journalist on the ground who may truly see the complexity of the situation and the reasons why no information is flowing from the law enforcement agency, but by the clock on the wall. Their advertisers expect a venue that will captivate consumers and potential clients. Stale news stories that have already been reported by other outlets hardly keep a news source front of mind with the public. So the pushed journalists become more insistent, and the already tasked law enforcement officers become even more impatient. Friction is inevitable.

Largely, this tension, which has led to near full-scale battles between law enforcement agencies and media sources, is unnecessary. Law enforcement agencies plan for natural disasters, terrorist attacks, hostage standoffs, and active shooters, but do they have a policy and drills on media onslaughts? "Onslaughts" is used here in the traditional dictionary-defined sense as "a large quantity of people or things that is difficult to cope with."[169] I have attended and seen large-scale law enforcement drills involving dozens of agencies and hundreds of law enforcement officers, but rarely do those drills include mock media inquiries, releases, and press conferences. I believe that is a lost opportunity, and I know plenty of journalists who would be happy to participate to help the agency work through their processes, train their law enforcement officers, and refine their policies. Besides, the entire drill, especially the involvement of the media, provides another story to fill their respective spaces. It is interesting, compelling, and "good PR" for all involved.

What is the agency policy on the release of information during a critical incident? Is the agency ready to implement the policy with less than one hour of advanced warning? Following the August 9, 2014, shooting of Michael Brown by City of Ferguson Missouri Police Officer Darren Wilson, it was clear that the City of Ferguson Police Department was unprepared for the local, national, and international media attention. This was the beginning of a seemingly endless and perfect storm. Media sources were left without information to report; nearly every media source in the world was either focused on Ferguson or present in the area. International time differences further complicated the news cycle factor, and the public was intently focused on the events, waiting, quite impatiently, for information and answers. When those answers did not come from official sources, journalists did what they are trained to do. They began looking for information sources in the community. As expected, much of what they found was inaccurate and damaging, but it was repeated every time the news cycle began anew until new information became available. An example, cited in Chapter Seven, is a CNN report from days following the incident. Based upon the physical evidence, the sworn grand jury testimony of dozens of witnesses, and the official report of the United States Department of Justice, we know that this information is completely inaccurate. However, it fed a narrative that led to massive property destruction, civil unrest, and innumerable injuries to private citizens and law enforcement officers alike.

So how does a law enforcement agency work to prevent this friction, frustration, and the damage therefrom? The answer is clear: standing orders. Just as the hospital provides standing orders for professional caregivers, law enforcement agencies should create and implement standing orders for the release of information. Just like the hospital model, the stakeholders, including media sources, should be consulted. There are certain facts in every critical incident, especially an officer-involved shooting, that will not change. Journalists need the information their consumers demand, and those consumers are the people served by the law enforcement agency. Therefore, everyone wins when appropriate information is released in a timely manner.

These standing orders for the release of information must include not only the information to be released, but the timing of the release, how it will be released, and perhaps most important, especially following an officer-involved shooting, from whom the information should flow.

This should not be a controversial topic. There is information that will never change that will shed light on critical incidents and will not affect criminal cases or civil litigation in the future. The release of any information will help keep the media sources focused on the incident and not on the fight over information requests.

We can divide the facts surrounding the critical incident into three categories. The first is what you know and what will never change—like the experience, training, work history, and prior use of deadly force, including cases cleared by a grand jury— regarding the law enforcement officers involved. This also includes the location of injuries to the suspect and law enforcement officers as well as the history of the suspect with law enforcement and the criminal justice system.

The second is comprised of facts you do not know now but are capable of determination later, like toxicology, the number of shots fired, and the number of shots that struck or injured the suspect and law enforcement officers or bystanders. In the third category are the facts that are likely incapable of determination, like the motivation of the suspect. While we may discover such information later or assemble sufficient information to create a likely motivation, unless the suspect tells us the "why" and actually tells us the truth, we all recognize that some questions will remain forever unanswered.

Preparing ahead, putting standing orders in place, training, and participating in drills will avoid the need for every release of information to flow through the chain of command. Every law enforcement agency trusts its law enforcement officers, supervisors, and command staff to make split-second decisions with lives hanging in the balance. Avoid creating situations wherein those same officers lack the direction, confidence, or authority to properly respond to requests for information from journalists. Even patient journalists will grow frustrated when the release of routine information is slowed to glacial speed by going through the chain of command.

Chapter Ten

Plan, Brief, Execute, Debrief—Every Time

Let our advance worrying become advance thinking and planning.

Winston Churchill

Never look back unless you are planning to go that way.

Henry David Thoreau

I've been fortunate to meet and work with many people who served honorably and with distinction in our armed forces. All of them made a difference, and many of them served in high-risk units executing missions that involved high levels of planning and technical precision. From them, I learned a pattern of planning and review that, in their worlds, was far more important than checking boxes on a form. They followed this process to save lives.

Law enforcement agencies follow these steps with regard to special operation activities such as SWAT, search and rescue, civil unrest, and other high-liability activities. However, how many agencies follow these steps regarding the dissemination of information and responses to critical incidents? I hope this chapter will convince law enforcement officers and agencies that this process is essential. It will not only improve the agency's response to a critical incident, the time spent on this process will also improve relationships with journalists as you seek their input.

Plan

The process prior to taking the first step toward the goal is perhaps the most important. There is a recognition that the people who will be involved in the mission or project have the basic skills to be successful. However, if they do not, this is the time to evaluate their skills and arrange for training. This is also the time to ensure that the people involved have the tools and equipment they need.

The planning phase is the time to bring together the subject matter experts, the trainers, and the people in charge of the mission with the people charged with obtaining the result. Each person brings to the table a specific set of skills and information, forming a unique perspective that will be added to the discussion of how to accomplish the mission or goal.

During this phase, the goal must be defined, broken down into manageable tasks, and clarified for the group. In addition, the plan must be tested—verbally, physically, or on paper—in an attempt to discover any flaws, shortcomings, or obstacles to success. Once the plan is complete, and likely put on paper, this phase of the process is complete.

Brief

The briefing phase is when the plan is communicated to all who will be involved at any level. This will include the people on the front lines who are actually putting hands on the process to complete the mission, those in charge of ensuring resources are brought to bear, the folks involved in the contingency plans, and the commanders who oversee the mission and how that mission fits in with the larger picture or efforts of the agency.

Briefings can be short, long and detailed, verbal, or a combination of verbal and written. However, this is a critical phase and cannot be overlooked or given short shrift. There must be open communication during this process to allow for any last-minute changes that may have arisen as well as any obstacles that may have been missed during the planning phase.

Execute

This is the action phase of the process. This may be the shortest phase in terms of time, or may take place over months. However, this is the culmination of not only the planning and briefing phase, but also the years of training and effort on the part of those involved.

Debrief

A debrief is not as intuitive to many people. It is defined as "a process of gathering stakeholders after the execution of a plan to evaluate and critique not only the outcome, but the process from the planning phase through the execution."[170] The debrief is the time when open and honest discussion is critical to success. It is so important many professions, including physicians, use a "no-rank" environment where critiques are provided in a respectful but candid environment. All those present must understand that the effectiveness of the group, the mission, future operations, and the safety of those involved is more important than egos or feelings.

I have heard comments from many people that debriefs are the most important part of the process. This is certainly the case in the medical profession where a process called "peer review" employs a cause-and-effect review known as a "root-cause analysis" to determine why a patient outcome occurred.[171] However, in the medical profession, in most states, the peer review process is private, protected, and privileged from release by statute.[172] The debrief process in government, specifically in law enforcement agencies, is for the most part a matter of public record. That does not change the importance of the debriefing stage or the reasons for completing it.

So, now that we have described this process that is used by medical staff, many law enforcement agencies for high-liability activities, and elite military units, there is a sad fact that law enforcement agencies must face. In the overwhelming majority of cases, this process is never followed regarding media relations or communications during and after critical incidents.

In my experience, law enforcement agencies are completely reactionary to media attention during and after critical incidents. When the critical incident is over or the fevered pace subsides, most law enforcement officers and agencies quickly move to the next demand for services. I say this not to criticize but in the hope that readers will take a hard look at their own houses. In that vein, let's look at the typical way in which media inquiries are handled during and after critical incidents.

The Crisis Arrives

There is a reason why the phone in my bedroom is on my side of the bed. I am on call for the State of Georgia Fraternal Order of Police and a hospital system with twenty thousand employees. One too many calls at "zero dark thirty" completed the migration of the landline phone from my wife's side of the bed to mine. It seems like the first rule of media attention and critical incidents in general is they happen at inconvenient times when the agency is least prepared to respond. This can be holidays, weekends, and all hours of the night. Murphy, it seems, never owned a watch.

This is where the critical incident response and media response diverge. Law enforcement agencies know how to respond to the former because they happen with some frequency. For example, officers respond to homicides. We know how to respond, how to investigate them, and what resources are needed, and law enforcement officers can probably predict with relative certainty how the minutes, hours, and days following the event will unfold. This is the case as well with an officer-involved shooting. From an investigation perspective, this is a criminal investigation of an aggravated assault or homicide. The only difference is that the victim and the shooter is a law enforcement officer. The investigative process of securing the scene, gathering evidence, interviewing witnesses, and interviewing the shooter and the person shot is the same. To the investigators, they will approach the investigation like any other. However, the media inquiry following a typical homicide is far different from that following an officer-involved shooting.

When the journalists investigate a homicide that does not involve an officer-involved shooting, there is certain information that the journalist will be required to obtain to make her bosses happy and do her job. You can probably list these facts, which include the name of the victim, the time and location of the homicide, the type of weapon used, the motive, any issues of justification such as self-defense, the name of the perpetrator, the relationship of the perpetrator and victim, whether or not an arrest has been made or is imminent, and whether or not the public is in danger.

In a standard homicide investigation, detectives will not have a problem providing this information or knowing, and explaining to journalists, that certain information cannot yet be released. Most journalists will understand that information will be withheld in the normal course of business and will likely go along with this, at least for a little while, in the hope that they will be contacted in the future when the information is available for publication. This is where the relationship between the journalist and the detectives or department's PIO is critical. It is that expectation built upon the strength of past experiences that will convince the journalist there is a benefit to publish what they have without pushing too hard and creating hard feelings.

An officer-involved shooting is a different critter altogether. For the journalist, there are many other questions they must answer, especially in the modern era of heightened scrutiny on officer-involved shootings. I submit that there has always been a heightened level of scrutiny regarding officer-involved shootings. What has changed is a suspicion, and perhaps a presumption, depending upon the journalist and the region of the country, that the use of force was unlawful or constitutes another example of police misconduct. However, to deny the increased vigor with which an officer-involved shooting will be investigated by journalists is to walk into a room of alligators while blindfolded.

When media inquiries develop into an onslaught, even without the presence of national and international media, most law enforcement agencies begin scrambling to determine what information must be released. Most departments have officers who are familiar with public disclosure laws in their respective jurisdictions.[173] Yet time and again, even though some media requests will be directed to one of these trained law enforcement officers, the requests for information typically are directed to individual officers in all areas of the department who may or may not be involved in the investigation. Information is released sporadically, and often incorrectly, despite general orders and policies that prohibit the improper release of information. You simply cannot underestimate the number of informal requests for information via email, texts, phone calls, social media instant messaging, and other avenues.

Unfortunately, law enforcement agencies typically get through those tough situations involving heightened media scrutiny, then move on to the next set of issues facing the agency. Rarely have I seen an agency go through the plan, brief, execute, and debrief progression regarding media response to critical incidents. The reasons are quite understandable, but the effects can be devastating.

There is no time for the planning phase once the critical incident takes place, and sadly, the debrief process is often not a priority once the next crisis or the normal pace of law enforcement activities takes over. The agency ends up more or less surviving the media coverage then waiting for the next critical incident to arise. In this scenario, the best the agency can hope for is that one of the senior leaders who navigated the previous craziness will be available to advise on the next one.

Let's look at this model of plan, brief, execute, and debrief as it can and should be applied to the law enforcement agency's response to media inquiries during and following a critical incident.

Plan

First, gather the people who should be part of this process. This long list should include agency PIOs; PIO supervisors; the agency's records department director or supervisor; the commander of each division including all detective, uniform, and special units; the commander or director of the 911 or emergency communications division; the legal advisor for the agency; and a representative from the office of the agency head. Put simply, when deciding who to involve, use this thought process:

- ❖ Who has a dog in the fight as to how media inquiries are handled during and after a critical incident?
- ❖ Who has experience handling media inquiries during and after a critical incident?
- ❖ Who is expected to receive media inquiries during and after a critical incident?
- ❖ Who is expected to interact with the media during and after a critical incident?
- ❖ Who will be tasked with addressing allegations that the agency improperly withheld information from the media during and after a critical incident?

This may necessitate the inclusion of a trusted media source or retired journalist. The group involved in the planning process should have time to meet, discuss the issues, propose policies and procedures, recommend training, and engage in spirited and meaningful discussion about how these issues will be handled.

The meeting may result in a written policy, general order, or something as simple as a checklist that can be utilized by all people involved in the process. Remember that whatever document is drafted and implemented will likely be requested by journalists either through public disclosure laws or through a lawsuit filed by a media agency if information is withheld or not disclosed in a timely manner.

The planning process must also include some type of testing of the system. This can be done through a "paper-only" exercise using email or a computer-based scenario.

Brief

The briefing process will be quick if the planning process was appropriately extensive. A quick gathering of the key players when the critical incident arises will be enough to set the procedures in order, address any recent developments or unique issues that may interfere with the plan, and designate the specific law enforcement officers and other personnel who will execute the plan.

This is also the time to assess the true scope of the particular media inquiry to be expected. Is this a routine incident like a gas main leak, a natural disaster, a clear officer-involved shooting involving a felony in progress or an officer being injured, or is this a critical incident like a use of force that is going viral on social media? The level of media attention will dictate the resources to be devoted to execute the plan. The presence and attention of national and international media essentially puts your plan into a twenty-four-hour time frame. This will obviously result in calls and inquiries when some unit staff, such as the records unit, may not normally be available.

Execute

Once the media inquiries start, allow the designated individuals to fulfill their functions. Chain-of-command issues should not interfere with responses to the media, as the issues should have been addressed during the planning stage. It is also important to ensure that only the designated individuals respond to the media. There is an advantage in this for the law enforcement agency. The PIO cannot be pushed to provide information she does not have, but the homicide commander who does know more detail may be pushed during a press conference.

Finally, during this process there must be open lines of communications between the media liaisons, the involved unit commanders, and legal counsel if their input is required. Without this type of information exchange, the execution of the plan will go off the rails. This creates a simplified chain of command that obviates the need to "run everything by the chief," which will only slow the process unnecessarily. It is important to remember at all times that all major media outlets have attorneys on retainer, and they will file for injunctions and seek judicial orders with little or no warning.

During my representation of an officer in a particularly high-profile officer-involved shooting, the local sheriff's office prevented a television journalist from using a handheld camera to videotape impromptu interviews in the public areas of the courthouse and the public waiting area of the district attorney's office. When the journalist was told to leave, I saw some minor commotion. About an hour later, the same journalist was back with the "blessings" of the deputies who stood by and watched him engaging in the same activities. I've known the journalist for more than twenty years and asked him what changed. He advised the station's attorney, filed a motion seeking an emergency order from a superior court judge, got the hearing, won the issue, and obtained an injunction preventing the deputies from interfering with the journalist. When it comes to access, the attorneys who work for media sources are experts and are paid well to respond quickly. Do not be caught unarmed in a battle of well-trained and well-prepared attorneys.

Debrief

Once the rapid pace of media attention slows or ends, and in some cases it may never truly end,[174] you must gather the appropriate parties together for a debrief. It is up to the agency when to convene a debrief, but some factors will affect this decision, such as the availability of the relevant personnel.

❖ Are people able to pull away from their duties, or are they still handling the aftermath of the critical incident?

❖ Has the pace slowed enough to truly be able to assess the effectiveness of both the plan and the execution of that plan?

- ❖ Will the pace slow in the near future, or is it important to start the debrief process irrespective of the pace?
- ❖ Is a change of course required, or has a specific incident occurred that requires attention?

Ideally, the debrief will involve at a minimum all of the people involved in the execution of the plan and those involved in creating the plan as well.

The debrief must, in order to be effective, encourage open communication of the facts of the execution and an assessment of what worked and what did not. This can be particularly challenging in a law enforcement agency that operates on a daily basis using an entrenched rank structure. However, if the military, which relies upon a clear rank structure, can engage in open and honest discussions, every law enforcement agency can do so. This is especially true when the reputation of the agency and its relationship with the public and the media is at stake.

The debrief is the time to discuss any changes or additions to policies, general orders, or checklists. It may be appropriate to end the debrief at some point with a date certain to reconvene the planning group.

Finally, the debrief may expose clear instances that require follow-up, intervention, and in some cases apologies. The follow-up may include providing information that was not able to be released previously, but is now available to the public. Intervention may involve meeting with any journalists or news outlets with whom the department or individual law enforcement officers encountered difficulty. Being respectful does not mean the law enforcement agency and individual officers must tolerate mistreatment. It is also important to remember that tensions run high during these scenarios. If a journalist was not treated well, take the time to apologize. It will go a long way to building bridges and increasing the execution of future plans.

The law enforcement agency may want to consider holding an open meeting with local news outlets following or as a separate part of the debriefing process. It is amazing how giving someone a voice will go a long way in building a bridge. While some journalists may never have an open mind about law enforcement officers or agencies, we must play to the larger portion of the journalists who are professionals and the local journalists who live in your community. They have a vested interest in improving the process.

Chapter Eleven

Media Networking—They Need You More Than You Need Them

How did you find America?

John Lennon: Turn left at Greenland.

Do you often see your father?

Paul McCartney: No, actually. We're just good friends.

What do you call that hairstyle that you're wearing?

George Harrison: Arthur.

Do you think these haircuts have come to stay?

Ringo Starr: Well, this one has, you know. It's stuck on good and proper now.

Media questions and responses during the 1964 tour to
America as depicted in *A Hard Day's Night*[175]

It is hard to imagine now just how crazy the media was to get quotes from the Beatles. As much media fervor surrounds the philosopher Kanye West or the fashion icon Kim Kardashian,[176] it is nothing compared to the frenzy created when the Beatles appeared anywhere. The stories are legendary about how the "Fab Four"—John, Paul, George, and Ringo, who must be listed in that order at all times—felt trapped by the press and yet decided to say outrageous things in response to questions.[177]

Journalists were there all the time for one reason—their customers wanted to see, hear, and learn more about the Beatles. This is true whether they loved or hated the band and the individual members, and you can bet both sides of the spectrum boasted large membership. John Lennon, likely at the strong urging of promoters and perhaps his fellow band members, tried to explain one famous comment in a televised interview. I recommend that you watch it. You will see an ill-prepared person attempting to plead for relief without asking for forgiveness. Here is John Lennon's original comment that appeared in a British newspaper as part of an article about his everyday life:

> *We're more popular than Jesus now; I don't know which will go first—rock 'n' roll or Christianity.*[178]

Here are two of John Lennon's statements made during a television interview. He is seated on a couch with the other three members of the band, who look alternatively bored and uncomfortable. Although it is difficult to know for sure, it appears that Lennon is chewing gum while he is answering questions. This was perhaps one of the first disastrous efforts to manage a media crisis.

> *If I'd have said television was more popular than Jesus I might have got away with it.*
>
> . . .
>
> *I'm not saying we're better or greater or comparing us to Jesus Christ as a person or God as a thing, whatever it is, you know. I said what I said and it was wrong or it was taken wrong and now it's all this.*
>
> John Lennon

The comment led to boycotts, protests, and widespread criticism. As popular as the band had become, and as much as the public could not get enough of their music—after all, they were musicians, not philosophers—there was no way to take back the comment and no way to repair the damage. The spin masters and media problem solvers were few in number, if they existed at all in 1964 in the sense we know them now. It is obvious now that no one really knew how to handle the situation.

Despite the controversy, two facts remain undeniably true. First, the Beatles still kept selling records, a lot of records. As of 2014, the group reportedly sold more than 2.3 billion albums, including 585,000 albums and 2.8 billion singles sold on iTunes.[179] To put this into perspective, the Beatles announced the breakup of the band on April 10, 1970[180]—thirty-three years before Apple launched iTunes on April 28, 2003.[181] Second, and critical for our analysis, journalists still wanted interviews and went to great lengths to get them. For many groups and many individuals, John Lennon is not remembered as one of the greatest songwriters who revolutionized music. He will always be the man who insulted Christianity. For journalists, interviews with any of the Beatles was and remains an event that cannot be missed.

Lessons from John, Paul, George, and Of Course, Ringo

There are many lessons to be learned from the Beatles' media mess described above. The first is that not everyone should speak directly with the media. I explored this topic in detail earlier in Chapter Six. It was tough in this case, however, as every Beatle was a celebrity in their own right, and journalists targeted them to appeal to fans and likely, at times, their detractors as well. Second, there is no reason for anyone to speak with the media without some training. This is especially true in a law enforcement agency. There are plenty of schools in the United States, and there are local opportunities to shadow an experienced PIO. The "four lads from Liverpool" clearly had no coaching about handling media questions.

The next lesson is that there are ways to fix a media blunder. While hopefully no one in your law enforcement agency will make a comment that is interpreted as a slight upon the largest religion in the world, I think you can agree that seemingly harmless statements are apparently met with more venom and attacks than Mr. Lennon's unfortunate analogy. Comments about different activist groups, which may be absolutely true, can earn a PIO a spot on the local news and social media for weeks. If you make a mistake, and I mean anything from release of inaccurate information to a true inappropriate comment, correct the information and apologize. Yes, I said apologize. We have become so resistant to anything that means admitting regret or guilt, largely because lawyers are always trying to prevent lawsuits, that we have forgotten how to be human. When you say something that is wrong, apologize. When you misspeak and hurt someone's feelings, apologize. If your poor choice of words is misinterpreted, apologize for the feelings you bruised, albeit inadvertently. Far from a sign of weakness, a genuine apology will garner support.

Do not be afraid to seek the help of a professional to manage a media issue that has gone off the rails. They specialize in messaging and have probably helped people, departments, and governments recover from far worse than your situation, whatever it is. Some of them are attorneys, others are media relations experts who often have backgrounds in marketing or journalism. Sometimes you will need assistance formulating a response to comments or claims made about your law enforcement agency. In the course of representing law enforcement officers, I have been asked for input from my clients and their command staff regarding these types of issues. Often, all it takes is the input of someone who is removed from the situation enough to see a clear and easy solution.

I find it odd that many governments and law enforcement agencies think twice about employing professionals during high-profile cases, especially when agencies recognize the importance of word choice in de-escalation techniques. They also understand the critical nature of nonverbal communication. Given this bank of knowledge, why would a law enforcement agency stubbornly refuse to enlist the assistance of a professional? Attorneys often use them to assist in speaking to juries. It is time for agencies to find the funds and hire someone who can assist in high-profile cases and help put out media fires before they start.

Here is another important lesson: very rarely will the person who made the blunder be able to fix the problem. That is why we discussed at length in Chapter Six whether or not the chief or sheriff should be in front of the camera or be the lead information source with the media. If a PIO makes an error, the chief can jump in and fix it carrying the weight of an authoritative source with a great deal of credibility. What will you do if the head of your law enforcement agency misspeaks? Additionally, as you can see in the video of John Lennon trying to explain his gaff, it rarely works. Almost without exception, such efforts sound like spin, the person's body language is either very defensive or aggressive, and the questions posed by journalists yield responses from the person that deepen the pit in which they stand.

While it may be appropriate for the person to make an apology, either in writing or live, that should end their involvement in that event. Someone else should take over and correct the bad information, respond to criticism, or explain the reason why the bad information was disseminated. If the gaff involved an inappropriate statement, the apology must be enough, and the law enforcement agency must stand firm on how it handles discipline. If you suspend or terminate every law enforcement officer who misspeaks, you may find yourself with a paucity of applicants for PIO positions. You should also remember that the job of a PIO is far less glamorous than you may believe. It is also not easy. Explaining that the PIO will receive additional training is always helpful as well.

One lesson from this incident lies in the video that you can find on YouTube. Although they look uncomfortable and somewhat annoyed, the other Beatles are sitting with John Lennon on a couch when he addresses the media. Who knows how they felt about Lennon's statement, the fuss it caused, or having to sit in front of a bunch of journalists, but that is not important. The key issue is that they supported their "teammate." At the time, people believed that John Lennon was speaking for the group. He and Paul McCartney wrote the Beatles' songs, Lennon was outspoken in other interviews, and he sang lead on several songs. To the media and detractors, Lennon was speaking for the group. However, the presence of the other band members made a statement to the effect that "Our friend may have messed up, but we support him and you should too." Watch the video. Imagine what that scene would have looked like if Lennon were alone and imagine how the journalists would have reacted. Don't abandon your folks. They will make mistakes. Prepare for them and get them through it. Journalists will appreciate your message.

The most important lesson of the case above is that the media kept interviewing the Beatles; they kept showing up at their shows, airport arrivals, and other public events; and they kept printing what they said. I have no doubt that a large portion of the journalists who kept covering the Beatles were Christians and that more than a few were angered by Lennon's comments. However, the reason those journalists, and every other journalist, was present at every opportunity is simple—their customers were interested in the Beatles. That's it. Could you imagine what would have happened if none of the journalists showed up for the interview when Lennon tried to explain his comments? The viewers of television stations, the readers of newspapers, and the listeners of radio stations would have made the phones ring off the desks of the respective company heads. You can attribute it to human nature, but the fact remains that people want to know what is happening. They also want to hear the words of a person explaining a gaff. Perhaps the journalists themselves would have been there even if their bosses had not insisted.

Law Enforcement Agencies and Officers as News Sources

I've been fortunate enough to become friendly with a lot of journalists. Oddly enough, though you must do so with caution, after a relationship begins, you will likely experience two-way conversations that are technically "off the record." When they occur, I never judge, make comments about previous reports that are inconsistent with personal views revealed, or criticize. I welcome it as a learning experience and an opportunity. Most journalists will tell you that they do not discuss politics or their personal views on topics with the public, and to a large extent, this is true. However, people are people and comments slip out.

For example, you may be surprised to learn that some journalists understand and support law enforcement officers being armed with patrol rifles. They may hear about the budget appropriations for the rifles, the new training, and the reasons for the rifles and not think twice about the topic. However, they all recognize that such an event is interesting to some of their customers. They also understand that some people will be in support of the measure and some will think it is a sign that the horsemen of the apocalypse are saddling up. In the end, it doesn't matter because they will want to cover the story. This means that they will work their sources within your law enforcement agency and the government to get information, interview people for quotes, and create a story people will want to read or see. The simple truth is this: whether journalists love law enforcement officers or hate them, officers and agencies do things, take actions, make decisions, and are involved in situations that the public wants to know about. This means that journalists will always need your law enforcement agency and officers as sources. Paul Crawley confirmed this for me when he said, "Invite the media to events like community firearms safety classes and other training events. Let the media fire the weapons. If you offer to educate them, you will find they are willing to learn."

This places law enforcement officers and agencies in a unique position. Despite the ability to get information from public sources, at some point all news articles about law enforcement will need quotes and information directly from law enforcement sources. Many times this is required for accuracy, but in most cases, the journalists are working to get accurate information and, more importantly, information that the general public does not have the access to obtain. How many times have you read about information "from a source close to the investigation" or "officers who spoke to me said" and paid attention to what followed? The general public reacts the same way. Although most people have never requested information under a statute like the Freedom of Information Act[182] on the federal level or similar legislation on a state level, they know they can. What they cannot do, without likely playing phone tag, is get a quote directly from the chief of police or the sheriff about a topic. Although some law enforcement agencies have town hall meetings, and many agency heads have open-access policies for any member of the public, for that level of access, the public must generally rely upon the news media.

The Police-Beat Journalist and Relationships between Law Enforcement Officers, Agencies, and Journalists

The police-beat journalist has been depicted in books, television, and the media. Sometimes they appear as shadowy figures who show up at homicide scenes and always seem to know every cop on the beat. Others are depicted as journalists who, through personal relationships with individual law enforcement officers, could get the "real scoop" before anyone else in the public was "allowed to know." In reality, police-beat journalists are extremely common and it is difficult to operate a news outlet of any kind without one. A lot of journalists begin their careers in the police beat then move onto other roles.[183] In my experience, the majority tend to be very pleasant and interested in the work of law enforcement. While their primary role is to provide information for news stories, that role has evolved. A growing percentage of police-beat journalists see their role as one of oversight with a mission to "police the police."

In his book *Ethics in Journalism*,[184] Ron F. Smith discusses the role of the police-beat journalist and the evolution of that role. "The ethical question is how much cooperation between the news media and law enforcement is acceptable."[185] This concern springs from the perceived "watchdog" role of the journalist. There can be no dispute that journalists have proven effective in this role over government in general. I, along with other law enforcement officers with whom I have discussed this issue, support their efforts.

Currently, it seems that more and more journalists are focusing their attention on law enforcement agencies and law enforcement officers. Therefore, every agency should have well-trained liaisons to the media who can field questions that extend beyond the standard who, what, when, where, why, and how to probing questions about how the investigation into a critical incident will proceed, what policies are in place to guide the investigations, the timing of those investigations, and the level of transparency the media and the public can expect. As Smith states:

> The role of police-beat journalists has changed too. No longer is it their prime job to report on crimes and fires. Both journalists and police agree that another part of the job is policing the police. The media have uncovered police brutality, bribery, and thievery among people who are supposed to enforce the law. On a journalism blog, one person wrote:

> If a journalist just seeks to be a buddy to law enforcement to get better access and quotes for stories, he stands to lose sight of some very troublesome social issues that lurk slightly behind the ordinary veneer of rap sheet "crime and punishment" stories.[186]

This is not an uncommon view and is part of the training of journalists either in the classroom or on the job. I have been interviewed by many journalists who, while they supported the role of law enforcement officers in society, posed some very tough questions to me about specific instances regarding the use of deadly force. Some of the questions were a search for information and others a prelude to a confrontation, or at least an attempt to create one.

You should expect that a well-informed journalist will perform the necessary research to have enough of a basic understanding of the laws and mechanics surrounding the use of deadly force to

257

probe the issue during the interview. You, on the other hand, should be extremely well educated on these topics. You should also be able to point the journalist to other sources to increase their knowledge.

This change in roles has led to two schools of thought regarding police-beat reporting as well as a mix of practices along the spectrum. As you can imagine, as with any other issue, there is a "nonstandard distribution" of journalists falling on the spectrum from being friendly with law enforcement officers and developing strong relationships to those who run from having any rapport with law enforcement officers or agencies and see their relationship as strictly adversarial. This makes for very strange outcomes and advice to journalists from their mentors and supervisors. Ron Smith points to two scenarios that highlight this dichotomy. Here is a view at one end of the spectrum:

> Many editors and police officials would like to develop more relaxed relationships. Editors often urge journalists to ride along with police on their rounds, although some departments have banned the practice because of a Supreme Court decision.[187] The aim of going on ride-alongs was not to get the video appropriate for the *Cops* television show, but to allow the journalists and officers to develop a better understanding of each other's jobs. One veteran journalist urges newcomers to the police beat to be visible, put the time in, constantly be there, show that you actually care, go on ride-alongs, go through reports . . . I would go to the officer-of-the-month luncheons, law enforcement awards banquets . . . just to make yourself visible and to understand more what working as a cop entails.[188]

This is a stark contrast from this position:

Matthew Waite, then a young journalist at Little Rock's *Arkansas Democrat-Gazette*, received a tip that the drug unit was planning a large-scale crackdown on cocaine. Waite arranged to ride along with the police jump teams as they stormed into crack houses ahead of other officers. "Great fun," he said. "High speed chases, deadly force situations, resisting arrests, all within feet of my eyes."

The raids were so successful that police rounded up more suspects than they could handle. They asked Waite to help by moving a truck. He agreed, "Probably because my parents raised me to always be helpful." When he returned to his newsroom, his editors weren't happy. "My bosses weren't against being helpful, but they were concerned about crossing that line between observer and participant and about liability issues." They told him not to do it again, or he would face formal reprimand.

Veteran police-beat journalists were divided on the ethics of his conduct. Robert Short, police journalist at the *Wichita Eagle*, believes Waite was behaving as any citizen might.

If the cop needed you to call 911 or hand him his shotgun to save or defend someone's life, would you do that? Of course you would.

Kathryn Sosbe of the *Colorado Springs Gazette* asked: "What happens when you take a step away from your standards, get caught in the middle, then suddenly try to become a journalist again? You really can't waffle back and forth without causing harder feelings."[189]

Although it may be difficult for many law enforcement officers to understand this example, especially a journalist facing discipline for the actions described above, in my research I found many references to the ethical dilemma facing journalists who become too friendly with law enforcement agencies and officers. However, Pete Combs, a forty-year journalist, dismisses this thought.

> You can and should have a professional relationship with the law enforcement and government officials you encounter. You are both professionals doing a job according to established standards. The professional relationships you build not only lead to better news stories but also increased trust with the community and a more open law enforcement agency.

This thought expresses a principle that law enforcement and journalists must remember: there are real people with real feelings, professional goals, bosses, and egos on both sides of the camera, microphone, and pen.

Another example cited by Smith will, perhaps, resonate with law enforcement officers more easily. When a man held law enforcement officers at bay, he asked to speak with a journalist. Smith describes what happened next and the fallout.

> So, the photographer handed the officer his camera and journalist's notebook. Posing as a journalist, the officer approached the man and took him into custody. The immediate outcome was what everyone wanted: The bad guy was arrested.

> However, the longer-term consequences bothered many in the journalistic community. "Such actions compromise the perceived independence of all journalists and increase the risk they face daily in covering dangerous news stories," Ann Cooper, executive director of the Committee to Protect Journalists, told *News Media and the Law* magazine. A photographer wrote on a Poynter discussion group, "I've

been hit by demonstrators who think my credentials are fake. Now I possibly may face somebody with a shotgun who decides I may not be 'real' media." He also worried that if journalists are seen as an arm of law enforcement, "the credibility of journalists could be eroded."[190]

Just as any other profession wrestles with ethical dilemmas, including law enforcement and attorneys, this case provokes debate. Is the journalist using the goodwill afforded his profession by the public in a manner that will continue to foster a relationship, or will the journalist's actions erode that trust? If the latter is true, what are the ramifications? Will people on the street be less likely to speak with a news crew or an individual journalist because they will suspect the people standing next to them are really law enforcement officers posing as journalists? You can easily find other sources debating this very issue in reference to this same case. Perhaps most telling are the statements from the involved law enforcement officer and the journalist's statement about his actions listed below in their respective order:

> "I think the journalist did a hell of a job," Johnson said. "He put his community before anything else. I consider Andrew to be a hero. He really helped us out. This standoff could have ended with more violence but because of him it didn't have to."
> "I live with these guys," Brosig said. "I see them every day. If something happened to one of them, I would have to live with it. I felt like I had to do something."[191]

In the end, perhaps this is just a matter of the law enforcement officer and the journalist making a judgment call under the stress of the situation and others critiquing those decisions in the light of day without any pressure. Law enforcement officers are accustomed to the "clarity" of such retrospective analysis. I suspect most journalists are not.

I suppose that we can draw a bright line when the life of a person is at stake. However, that has not always been the case. On November 20, 1987, Neva Jane Veitch, an officer in the True Knights of the Ku Klux Klan, reported that her husband and fellow Klan member, Billy Joe Veitch, was shot and killed by "two black men" who kidnapped them in Cobb County, Georgia. Her account of the crime was detailed, and she advised that she barely escaped after being sexually assaulted. Ms. Veitch went so far as to assist a law enforcement sketch artist to help create composite drawings of the perpetrators, and she appeared beaten and bruised when she reported the murder.[192] After exhaustive efforts, including interviews of between fifty to sixty black males who matched the composite drawings, failed to produce a suspect, law enforcement officers were led to Ms. Veitch as a suspect two years after the murder when her lover and fellow Klansman, David Lee Craig, came forward to tell the story of how Ms. Veitch killed her husband. In a twist of fate, Craig came clean when he learned of Ms. Veitch's plan to have him killed. In 1990, a jury convicted Craig of murder, and he was sentenced to two life terms.[193] He hanged himself in prison and sent a letter confessing to Neva Veitch's role in the killing.[194] Neva Veitch pled guilty, was sentenced to life in prison on August 21, 1990, and paroled on July 21, 2010.[195]

Just after her supposed attack, Ms. Veitch went on a virtual speaking tour telling her lies in a demented plan to recruit new members to the Ku Klux Klan, essentially telling her story to any media source who would listen. The footage was important to document her retelling of the story, and it was obvious that law enforcement officers were attending her speaking events to gather information and perhaps obtain their own recordings and footage. I was present for a hearing in Cobb County Magistrate Court involving Ms. Veitch when the lead detective, Roy Rogers, related the facts of the murder. Should media outlets have refused requests and subpoenas for the footage that did not make the cut into news stories? What about the background footage that showed Ms. Veitch and Craig meeting and speaking with others who may have been suspects?

This issue has arisen many times and publicly garnered the ire of the *New York Times* editorialists and the Associated Press (AP) in 2007 when an FBI agent posed as an AP journalist to gain the location and arrest a fifteen-year-old who was terrorizing a school with bomb threats. The ruse consisted entirely of online conversations purporting to be interviews between the suspect and the "journalist," who sent the suspect an email with a draft of the story to allow him to verify the quotes. When he downloaded the file, the FBI located his computer and took him into custody. Then FBI Director Robert Mueller defended the impersonation. However, many in the media were less than amused.[196] A search of the internet will reveal many more of these instances with similar criticisms.

Oddly enough, most law enforcement agencies that I checked with and that I am aware of allow civilians to ride along on patrol with an officer. Typically, the civilian will be placed with a senior officer or a field training officer for safety purposes, and many departments have an informal policy of allowing officers to refuse to ride with a civilian. While some officers might not be thrilled about sharing the front seat of a squad car with a journalist, I am certain that others would be happy to do so. However, journalists must keep in mind that the job of an officer is dangerous in large part because both the level of danger and the timing of critical incidents is largely unknown. Therefore, a journalist riding in a patrol car may find himself working with the officer to ensure that both of them return home at the end of the tour.

Tension between Law Enforcement Officers and Journalists

Even when law enforcement agencies, officers, and police-beat journalists have a good relationship, friction can arise when the demands of the journalists exceed the level of cooperation of the agency. For example, Ron Smith references a lawsuit filed by media sources in Wichita Falls, Texas, to force law enforcement agencies to permit journalists to monitor law enforcement radio transmissions.[197] A similar suit was filed in 2014 against the City of Little Rock, Arkansas, by a pro se litigant.[198]

Media demands for the release of law enforcement records have also led to litigation on more than one occasion. In 2015, a former Ohio college student won a lawsuit against the campus police department that began when she was a journalist for the campus newspaper. The police department refused to turn over some reports, and the student filed suit, which ended in her favor at the Ohio Supreme Court.[199] Lawsuits like these between media sources and law enforcement agencies have been going on for quite a while and will likely continue.

Often the records do not pertain to reports of crimes or investigations. In 2015, the *Virginia-Pilot* won a lawsuit forcing the release of information regarding the employment and training of law enforcement officers in the State of Virginia. The newspaper advised that it was interested in informing the public about problem officers being transferred between departments instead of being fired and tracking the training of law enforcement officers. Although the Virginia attorney general believed the information was not subject to release, the circuit court disagreed. It should be noted that a potential agreement between the parties fell through when the law enforcement agency reportedly refused to turn over the records.[200]

Other suits involve the release of the names of law enforcement officers involved in deadly force decisions,[201] the release of officer personnel files,[202] and the release of tracking information from a Stingray device.[203] The point here is to remember a simple truth. Even though you may have a good relationship with journalists, they will force the issue using the courts if they believe they are entitled to information and will employ the assistance of attorneys to do so. Know the law, think carefully before you deny access to records, and always state a reason when you refuse to produce records, including citations to the law upon which your decision relies.

Working with New Journalists, Old Friends, the Young, and the Restless

I remember distinctly the first time I received a call from a journalist about a situation involving a law enforcement officer that had not hit the news. He called and asked me if anything was going on. I replied, as I nearly always do, "There's always something going on. The question is, does anyone care about it?" We both laughed a bit and he relayed the situation he was researching.

As usual, the issue was not huge, but his customers, and more importantly his bosses, would likely be interested in both the topic and the follow-up. We talked for a bit and played the age-old game: how much information can I learn without telling more than I receive? I do not fault him for this. First, it was his job. Second, we were both doing it. After about twenty minutes, he learned that while the initial reports he received gave the impression the story could have been huge, in reality it would never "grow legs and take off." I pointed him to some resources to verify the information I provided, and he was able to cover the story with an appropriate amount of airtime without spending an inordinate amount of time researching a relatively minor situation.

The most important outcome of that exchange is that we further developed our professional relationship. I've mentioned several times throughout this book that I have relationships with journalists. That is true and I am very proud of that. I do not have a personal relationship with them, but there are some with whom I would gladly contemplate the meaning of life over a beer. Others I would rather keep at a distance. However, as I've pointed out repeatedly, the overwhelming majority of journalists are professionals. As an attorney who represents law enforcement officers, I have a professional relationship with them. You must strive to do so as well. Professional relationships foster mutual respect.

Like most professional relationships, you must remember three basic concepts. First, the other professional is a person. While we hope that professionals will act as such at all times, sometimes that does not occur. They will have good days and bad days, they will have "boss problems" or "family issues," and you will encounter them when they are preoccupied, frustrated, or just in a bad mood. Get over it, just as you would expect them to do if they encountered you on a bad day. Second, professional relationships are built over time. This depends upon how often you interact with an individual or people in that profession. The more you do, the more you will learn their beliefs, what is important to them, their core mission, and what conflicts with their professional goals. Finally, professional relationships generally segregate the person from the professional. It is possible to build and maintain a professional relationship with a person without knowing the name of their spouse, whether or not they have children, where they grew up, and other personal facts. This is especially true in the professional relationships between law enforcement officers and journalists. In general, neither profession likes to part with this information. Therefore, it is good to remember that you need not know a great deal about a journalist to become professional friends and colleagues.

For those who are new to the profession, both law enforcement officers and journalists, it takes some time to seek out and develop relationships. This can be particularly difficult when there is often a degree of suspicion, and sometimes mistrust, on both sides of the equation. However, the journalist cannot be effective without professional relationships with law enforcement officers. This means that at some point, a journalist will make the first call to a new PIO, or a chief or sheriff, and attempt to strike up a conversation. When you learn there is a new journalist in your community, look for an opportunity to introduce yourself, invite them to the law enforcement agency for a tour, and let them know you are accessible. Before you know it, you will have a stress-free conversation, an exchange of contact information, an open line of communication, and perhaps, just maybe, a level of mutual respect and trust. As Rick Blaine famously said, "I think this is the beginning of a beautiful friendship."[204]

You will also run into highly motivated, dedicated journalists who are truly looking for a chance to make a difference in their profession. At times, I have heard law enforcement officers complain about these folks and say they are "too eager" or "just looking for a story." While that may indeed be true in many cases, I ask the officers reading this book to remember when they were rookies, just released from training. You wanted to make a difference, prove your worth, distinguish yourself, and make your peers proud to work with you. You made a difference, and you likely made some mistakes along the way as well. Sound familiar? I believe everyone in every profession feels this way, especially when they begin their careers and probably make the same type of mistakes. However, we learn from those mistakes, receive training, seek out mentors, and grow into the professionals we want to be. That is what separates a profession from a job.

The new, restless, and eager journalist will, like the rookie officer, look for stories that mean something to people in the community. They may seek to educate people about the inner workings of government or answer questions they hear from their young friends and peers who may or may not be journalists. This can lead a new journalist down some strange rabbit holes.

For example, I am honored to lecture occasionally at colleges and universities, typically in criminal justice programs, and I sit on the advisory council of one such program. Over the past few years, I have noticed a palpable change in the questions posed by a small number of these students. Many are spawned by anti-law enforcement rhetoric, others by ignorance, but nonetheless, they are more frequent, and some are downright disturbing. Now, consider that these are students who chose to learn about criminal justice, so they have presumably learned something about the reality of search and seizure. Even so, their questions can be very anti-law enforcement and remarkably ignorant about the laws of the use of deadly force. When these criminal justice students graduate, they form the potential pool of friends and acquaintances for the new journalists in your community. This means that discussions over a beer, at parties, during 5K races, concerts, and festivals will naturally give rise to a desire to delve deep into some of these topics and write stories, and the base of the journalist's story may be something they received from one of these students.

My advice here is to be patient with young journalists. I have watched several grow to become seasoned professionals who fairly and accurately cover stories about law enforcement officers, good and bad. In my role speaking, teaching, writing, and giving interviews, I am currently working with two new journalists who seem to be covering stories about law enforcement officers a lot. They are at different phases in their careers, with one about three to five years ahead of the other. The questions from the younger still tend to be accusatory rather than conversational, and I suspect there is still a great degree of skepticism behind every query. "Will he tell me the truth?" "Will he tell me everything in response to my question, or find a clever way to provide a truthful half answer?" I can hear it in the tone and word choice. The older of the two asks open-ended questions with calculated follow-up. I can generally tell which follow-up questions were planned and which were spontaneous. However, I suspect with time, the younger journalist will become harder to read and hopefully less suspicious.

Just as you evolved and became polished as a law enforcement officer, take the time to extend patience and courtesy to new journalists. Look at it as payback for the supervisors and members of the public who patiently allowed you to grow into your role. In the process, you just might develop a professional relationship that will follow both of you for many years.

How to Handle Bad
Behavior and Broken Promises

I cannot tell you how many law enforcement officers are suspicious any time they learn "someone from the media is on the phone." Please remember these words the next time you hear that—CALM DOWN. Law enforcement agencies receive media inquiries for all sorts of reasons. Many times, the journalist is fact-checking a story. Other times, they are looking for a quote to give some credibility to the information they received, or to appear balanced in their efforts. I understand that there are times when a journalist has completed his research, and more importantly made up his mind about both the facts and the inferences to be drawn from those facts, before the law enforcement agency receives a call. I know law enforcement officers who have received very hostile and terse calls from journalists who will not listen to anything but advise they "just want to verify certain facts before they go with the story." I know what that is like; it has happened to me personally and regarding my clients. However, that is not the norm. In fact, in my experience, it is an anomaly. When it occurs, you must be prepared to handle the call, respond appropriately, and protect the law enforcement agency and the due process of the officers involved in the story.

When I talk about protecting the due process of law enforcement officers who are the subject of a news story, some journalists and community members will bristle at those words. I'm not sure why, really. Law enforcement officers and agencies are required to protect the due process rights of suspects every day. We release information as required, but take care not to discuss active investigations to "protect the innocent," as the famous line goes. When a law enforcement officer is accused of misconduct, don't they deserve the same rights, fair treatment, and a presumption of innocence?

In most cases, if you receive an aggressive or outright hostile call from a journalist as described above, you will not change their minds, and they will likely not listen to anything you say. If they are calling to verify quotes or information, they have likely completed a great deal of research already. However, there is value in speaking with them, and you have a lot to lose by being rude, refusing to answer questions, or hanging up on them.

First, you may be able to determine their sources by the quotes and information they seek to verify. This is critical as some of the information may not make it to the story, and that may be the only way for you to tell if you have a leak within your law enforcement agency or if someone is lying to the journalist. You can point out the falsehoods and put the journalist on notice that they must research the story more before publication. Second, you must learn the issue they are researching, the allegations or concerns they are raising, the law enforcement agencies or officers affected, the extent of community response you can expect, what information upon which the journalist is relying, and the timeline for publication. Third, it is rude not to take a person's call. Finally, there is a difference in a story that reads, "The chief was not available for comment" or "The chief was not able to verify some of the information" and "The chief refused to discuss these allegations." The former conveys that you were busy or following protocol, the latter that you were angry.

While they are rare, if you receive a hostile or terse call like the one described above, take some notes immediately after you finish the call. Write down the time and date of the call, the name of the journalist, as many questions as you can recall, your responses, any facts you refuted and told the journalists were incorrect, and anything the journalist told you about the story, her sources, and when it will be published. This information may prove critical for any internal investigations into leaks and any potential defamation lawsuits. You should also notify your chain of command immediately and consider making a call to an attorney. While contacting the agency's attorney is a good idea, this may be a warning sign that you need to retain your own attorney who will consider your interests first. I have been retained in this role and it is not a position for the inexperienced or fainthearted.

So how do you handle these types of calls, and how do you respond to the inevitable story that will follow? First, as stated above, take the call. Listen more than you speak, learn the scope of the issues, and ask for some time to respond. You may or may not receive some time. If you do not receive additional time, be confident and answer the questions or verify the information you know to be true. For the rest, respond that you will need time to provide information or verify details, and due to the deadline imposed upon you, you will not be able to respond at this time. Second, find out when the story will air or appear in print. Third, get your best and most diligent folks on verifying the facts the journalist relayed to you. You will need answers quickly, and the facts passed on to you must be accurate. Fourth, if the journalist agreed to give you time to respond, stay ahead of that deadline. If you need additional time, call early and request it. If the journalist did not allow time for you to respond, meet with your PIOs, necessary command staff, those who investigated the issue, and anyone you must contact within your chain of command. Once you are all together, draft a response.

Your response may be a press release, a statement on the law enforcement agency website, comments and posts on social media, or, if necessary, a press conference. Except in unusual cases, you should release your statement after the journalist publishes the story. At that time, the public and other media sources will be focused on your law enforcement agency website, social media sites, and any press releases you distribute. You must put your side out in the media. If you are prepared, the follow-up news stories will incorporate your well-thought-out responses and the facts you took the time to assemble. Remember that if you have followed my advice and have a robust social media presence, you can get your facts out through your own media. You can put out a press release, hold a press conference, or post a short YouTube video to respond. As I've preached in this book, your efforts will become the news story, and journalists will be forced to report them.

There are times that you will likely be misquoted. As I was writing this, I heard a quote on the news pertaining to a case in which I was involved. The journalist completely misquoted my client and prefaced the statement with a caveat that the statement was a quote. At this point we have several options, and I suspect that the station would retract or correct the statement if we asked them to do so. However, this would only replay a statement that the client would rather not hear again. This is an excellent example of how such situations can be tricky and why it is important to involve an experienced attorney early in the process.

I have clients call me fairly regularly regarding misquotes. I will share with you the analysis I use during these calls. First, look at or review the report or the statement the journalist made. Did the misquote involve the use of different words, or was the meaning completely different? Language, particularly spoken words, is imperfect. Words are misconstrued or copied down incorrectly during interviews on the phone or in person, accents or phone connections make people difficult to understand, or a journalist listening to law enforcement jargon or terms unique to the profession may misinterpret the words used. All of these examples set out how a law enforcement officer may be misquoted quite innocently.

If the meaning of your words was not altered, and it appears there was a miscommunication, take a deep breath and contact the journalist. Discuss it with them and explain why you believe you were misquoted. If they have a reasonable explanation and apologize, I recommend that you forgive them and chalk it up to experience. It may also provide an opportunity for you to strengthen your professional relationship with the journalist.

If the meaning of your words was clearly changed, the quote changed your words, or after speaking with the journalist you are convinced that the journalist intentionally attributed words to you improperly, take a deep breath and speak with an attorney. The first remedy is likely to write a letter demanding a retraction or correction. If the journalist follows through with a retraction or correction, the law is very difficult to navigate if you go forward with a lawsuit. Remember that you not only bear the burden of proving that the misquote was malicious, you must also prove that you were damaged. The only general exception is if the statement constitutes defamation per se, which is a defamatory statement directly related to one's profession.[205] This is a judgment call that will require the advice and input of an attorney licensed in your state.

I suggest a different approach to a journalist who intentionally misquotes you. Generally, the demand for a retraction or correction will be sufficient to protect the reputation of the law enforcement officer and the agency. This is especially true if the law enforcement officer and agency use the agency website and all social media sites to promulgate the retraction or correction. However, this is a tremendous opportunity for the law enforcement officer and the agency to meet with the journalist and his managers. Be professional and cordial. Offer to host the meeting. Be prepared and have a frank conversation with them, and explain to them that your work with the media is a cooperative effort, that you will always treat them with respect and will expect the same treatment in return. If they refuse to agree to work with you in a more professional manner in the future, explain that they will be left to find quotes and information about the law enforcement agency based upon what is publicly released. Advise that until you are able to come to an agreement, you will not be providing any information to the journalist and their employer on an informal basis and all requests must be in writing. I believe you will find, as stated in the title of this chapter, that they will acquiesce to your requests. Hopefully, this will be a rare occurrence. Remember, they need you more than you need them.

Another complication is when you are misled by a journalist about information known to them, information about an incident, or the focus of their story. As stated previously many times in this book, while it has happened to me and others I've met with, this should be a rare occurrence. As with any other issue with a fellow professional, I recommend that you confront the journalist in a direct but professional manner. Explain that you expect them to remain true to their ethics and you will only work with them if they are honest with you. Listen to their explanations. If you find that they are no longer worthy of your trust, tell them you will only participate in interviews with them in person with a witness present. In response, they will either stop contacting you or submit to your conditions. Either way, you will be able to protect yourself going forward and spend your time conversing freely with the journalists who have earned your trust.

A different situation occurs when a story is printed without input from your law enforcement agency. In my experience, the majority of times this occurs it is a symptom of a lack of a professional relationship between the law enforcement agency and the journalist. Reach out to the journalist and offer to provide information in the future with a statement akin to: "If you had come by the department, we would have been happy to provide you with information that would have added to your story." If they thank you and come by the next time they are doing research, you have made great strides. If they do not, you can address any criticisms of your agency by telling other journalists, the public, and the management of the journalist's employer that you reached out to make yourself and your law enforcement agency available. The journalist will lose credibility if they refuse enough of those offers.

Occasionally, I will see, hear, or read a story that contains inaccurate statements or facts that were easily verifiable. When it occurs regarding one of my clients or friends, it can be maddening. For example, I have witnessed news stories about an officer-involved shooting wherein the journalist completely misstated the law surrounding the issue or gave the impression that the use of force was somehow controversial. An example is emphasizing the words "in the back" when describing the officer-involved shooting even though the shooting was completely justified. Another is repeating facts that have been disproved, such as a situation in Pinellas County, Florida, when social media posts alleged that deputies did nothing to rescue teenagers who drove into a pond during a chase. When the facts are easily verifiable, or the truth is easy for the journalist to obtain, you should call them out on it, but always in a professional manner. As discussed in Chapter Three, some journalists believe it is appropriate to express different points of view even when they do not believe the statements are true. While I understand that some journalists believe this, I believe the majority of people do not. It is inappropriate to include information in a story that the journalist either knows is inaccurate or can easily research and learn is inaccurate. When you contact the journalist, ask if they would accept the same level of fact-checking from your law enforcement agency, especially in public statements. I suspect I know the answer.

All of the information and advice described above works best with established media sources. If the journalist with whom you experience difficulty is a professional blogger without formal education or training or solely based in social media, the issues can be more challenging. I have had a great many dealings with bloggers and online-only news sources. In at least two cases I litigated on behalf of law enforcement officers, the leading journalists who followed the stories the most were bloggers and online-based publications. Some were very polished and professional, and others were neither. While you may think you have less leverage with them, that is probably not the case. Even though you may not be able to contact management of a blog, you can more easily combat the inappropriate behavior described in this chapter in those venues than with traditional television, radio, and print media sources. Think about this for a moment. This is the great equalizing principle I discussed in detail in Chapter Four. You can use your law enforcement agency website, Facebook page, Twitter feed, Instagram posts, YouTube channel, and other social media avenues to combat the information in the same realm. You can even use hashtags to point the readers of the offending blogger to your sites that contain accurate information and rebuttals. The critical points are: do not give up, take action to professionally confront the journalist, and get the accurate information out to the public and other media sources. You might get lucky and find a competing blogger who picks up the controversy and puts out your information.

Lest I end this chapter on a low point, I want you to remember that law enforcement and journalists work well together more often than they face controversy. We have all seen media outlets running stories about wanted fugitives, lost children or adults, wanted persons, and kidnapped children. These stories are proof that there is a working level of cooperation between law enforcement and journalists on a regular basis. Too often, we get stuck in the negative and focus on the last bad experience we've had. Law enforcement officers and agencies must focus on their positive professional relationships with journalists and work to grow them every day.

Chapter Twelve

Putting Theories into Practice

Knowledge is of no value unless you put it into practice.
Anton Chekhov

On March 24, 2015, I was sitting at my desk when I received a call from the wife of a law enforcement officer. I have known him for over twenty years. He is a veteran of the United States Marine Corps, a highly trained SWAT operator, a traffic accident reconstructionist, and on that day, he joined another group—law enforcement officers who have been involved in an officer-involved shooting. I immediately left my office and drove to the scene. I was there in seventeen minutes.

The scene was already indicative of the chaos that was to follow. The shooting took place at a Goodyear store around Cumberland Mall north of Atlanta. The parking lot of the Goodyear was in a shopping complex. I was familiar with the complex, as it was built when I was working in training and public relations, and I had patrolled the area when I was assigned to Precinct Three of the Cobb County Police Department.

At the top of the complex there is a Starbucks with outdoor seating and a Chick-fil-A restaurant with a drive-thru. Behind the Goodyear is the anchor for the complex, a Publix supermarket. Due to the topography, the Publix is at the lowest elevation and the Starbucks is at the top. Therefore, while sound would travel well, the lines of sight from the different locations would vary greatly. In addition, the parking lot where the shooting took place is only partially visible to anyone other than Goodyear employees who may have been behind the building or in the repair bays. It was a nice spring day in Atlanta. I recall walking around in a sport coat and being comfortable. In Atlanta, this means that everyone who could be outside was outside, including the patrons at the locations with outdoor seating. In my experience, this had the potential for a bad combination, and here is the formula of which you should be cautious:

A great number of witnesses

+

Obstructions and impediments to clear lines of sight

+

People focused on tasks like ordering food at a drive-thru

+

People in cars, on foot, and sitting while chatting

+

An area that permits witnesses to leave before investigators arrive

+

An open area that allows people to arrive after the events occurred

+

Businesses that continue helping customers during the investigation

**Difficulty locating and vetting witnesses
and a high potential for conflicting statements**

I also take as a given that the majority of people who were in the area were either speaking to others, on their cell phones talking to people who were not present, texting, sending email, or engaged in social media.

The media story from the officer-involved shooting garnered national attention. You can find stories about the case online by searching for the date, officer-involved shooting, Goodyear, and Smyrna police. At the time of this writing, that search produced nearly three thousand hits, nearly one year after the event.

In the days and weeks following the officer-involved shooting, the media story was at the top of the hour or five minutes past the top of the hour. The law enforcement agency and the involved officer were the subject of a vile and vitriolic social media campaign that contained veiled—barely—threats of violence. Then the media dialogue changed. It happened when I put out a press release.

Here is the entire press release:

For Immediate Release

Contact: Lance LoRusso, Esq.
Phone: 770-644-2378
Email: lance@lorussolawfirm.com

Atlanta, GA – March 31, 2015

On March 24, 2015, City of Smyrna Police Sergeant K. B. Owens was involved in an on-duty incident during which he was forced to use deadly force to protect the life of a fellow uniformed law enforcement officer. Sergeant Owens was the only officer on the scene to use deadly force. The officers were serving a felony warrant.

Prior to beginning his career in law enforcement, Sergeant Owens served four years active duty and four years as a reservist in the United States Marine Corps. He received an Honorable Discharge as a Sergeant. Sergeant Owens has faithfully served the Cobb County community for nearly twenty years. For eleven years, he served in the Smyrna Police Honor Guard attending events and the funerals of fallen law enforcement officers. During that time, he has interacted with thousands of citizens, made hundreds of arrests, contacted numerous armed individuals, including barricaded suspects, and encountered numerous wanted felons. He has been involved in more than thirty-five foot or vehicle pursuits and has made more than one hundred felony arrests. However, he has never before fired a weapon at anyone during the course of his sworn duties.

Sergeant Owens is a highly trained and dedicated law enforcement officer. He has been named the Smyrna Police Department Officer of the Year and Smyrna Public Safety Foundation Officer of the Month. He also received the Cobb County Chamber of Commerce Life Saving Award and two Meritorious Service Awards. He has attended and successfully completed hundreds of hours of training on the proper and lawful use of deadly force. The Cobb County Police Department is currently investigating this officer-involved shooting and the resulting death of Nicholas Taft Thomas. This shooting occurred within the jurisdiction of the Cobb County Police and it is not only appropriate, but also a standard law enforcement procedure throughout the United States for the local agency to investigate any use of deadly force that occurs within its jurisdiction. The Cobb County Police Homicide Unit is comprised of highly trained and decorated officers with many years of experience. It is our understanding that the Georgia Bureau of Investigation will be asked to review the investigation when it is complete. This is also a standard practice throughout the United States.

Nearly every year, according to the Federal Bureau of Investigation, law enforcement officers are killed and assaulted by suspects who choose to use a vehicle as a weapon. A person using a vehicle as a weapon is not "unarmed." Shooting the engine or the tires will not stop the person assaulting the law enforcement officer nor will it stop the vehicle. Such assaults are nearly always fatal due to the mass of the vehicle and the inability of the law enforcement officer to escape injury based upon the speed of the vehicle. The suspect in this case, Nicholas Taft Thomas, pled guilty on May 18, 2014, to Aggravated Assault on a Law Enforcement Officer and other charges. The weapon he used was a vehicle. Those records are available at the Cobb County Superior Court Clerk's Office and through the Kennesaw State University Police Department.

The investigation into this officer-involved shooting will take time and will involve the Cobb County Police Department, the Georgia Bureau of Investigation, and the Cobb County District Attorney's Office. In addition, there will be a separate administrative inquiry into Sergeant Owens's actions likely conducted by the City of Smyrna Police Department. This is again the national standard for these internal or administrative investigations. At the conclusion of these investigations, the results will be available in accordance with the Georgia Open Records Act.

The loss of any life is tragic and four investigations will determine if Sergeant Owens acted lawfully and appropriately. During this time, just like any other person who is the focus of a criminal investigation, Sergeant Owens is entitled to a presumption of innocence. He is also entitled to due process, the right to counsel of his choosing, and other constitutional protections afforded to all citizens under the United States and Georgia Constitutions. Although he was not legally required to do so, Sergeant Owens cooperated with the Cobb County Police Department's investigation. As has become the norm for law enforcement officers involved in deadly force incidents, Sergeant Owens has consulted with an attorney of his choosing. This is his constitutional right.

###

For more information, you may contact counsel for Sergeant K. B. Owens, Lance J. LoRusso, Esq. at 770-644-2378 or at lance@lorussolawfirm.com.

I sent the press release on March 31, 2015. It arrived at the fax machines of numerous media outlets and in the email inboxes of numerous journalists about three hours prior to a rally planned at the headquarters of the law enforcement agency. The rally had been advertised, and reports on the internet boasted hundreds of people attending. I do not know how many people actually attended. My office is a short drive from the law enforcement agency, so several journalists stopped at my office for an interview. They wanted to hear the law enforcement officer's side and to broadcast it when they covered the rally. They wanted to hear another side of the story.

Nearly every outlet wanted to interview my client. We declined because an interview would not have been appropriate. He was the subject of a criminal investigation and would be the subject of an administrative investigation. Further, the district attorney would be examining this case as well as the United States Department of Justice. In short, there was no reason for my client to speak with anyone other than the investigators tasked with examining his use of force on an official level.

As I predicted, to my knowledge every one of the journalists who contacted me pulled the criminal case file I referenced, or at least viewed it online through the clerk's office website. Some had excerpts of the file and asked me questions from the file when they interviewed me a few hours after I sent the press release. They were interested in getting the other side of the story for their newscasts. All of them quoted the press release and used my comments, including the one journalist who entered my office like a bull in a china shop armed with inaccurate facts, which I promptly and professionally corrected on camera. This was an anomaly. The journalists who responded to the press release were genuinely interested in learning and putting out the facts.

So did this effort on my part on behalf of my client have an effect? Well, you can decide for yourself, but here are some facts:

❖ Shortly after the press release, my informal survey by taping newscasts and reading coverage showed that the story moved to fifteen to twenty minutes past the top of the hour and from the front page to the third or fourth page.

❖ Every media outlet that covered the rally quoted the press release.

❖ Media outlets began to discuss the prior criminal history of the decedent.

❖ Media outlets quoted the press release for three months after the release, and I saw a quote from it on the anniversary of the event in March 2016.

❖ When the grand jury cleared my client, the news stories used the press release for background on my client and the decedent.

❖ The dialogue on all social media sites broadened tremendously, and people began defending the law enforcement officer more than they did in the days immediately following the officer-involved shooting.

The law enforcement agency was constrained by a chain of command and legal advice. I do not fault the attorneys. We are paid to be very cautious and calculating when considering next steps. The law enforcement agency did put out a press release when they believed it was appropriate.

I note that the press release above did not make the story disappear, and it would have been unrealistic to expect any such result. However, my press release and the resulting change in coverage and focus illustrates the principles I discussed in this book. It also shows that they work. What began as a one-sided news story quickly became a two-sided story, and the narrative was no longer being controlled by people who did not possess the facts.

In May 2016, approximately fourteen months after the shooting, now Lieutenant K. B. Owens was cleared by the United States Department of Justice. This fact remained quiet for a surprisingly long time until a local journalist with the *Marietta Daily Journal*, Ricky Leroux, published an article on June 2, 2016, about the DOJ closing their investigation.[206] Eight days later, the City of Smyrna Georgia Police Department put out a press release.

MEDIA RELEASE
U.S. DEPARTMENT OF JUSTICE DECISION REACHED IN SMYRNA OFFICER-INVOLVED SHOOTING
Upon conducting a Critical Incident review of the officer-involved shooting that occurred on March 24, 2015, involving Smyrna Police Department Lieutenant Kenneth Owens; the Cobb County Police Department, Georgia Bureau of Investigations, the Cobb County District Attorney's Office, and now the U.S. Department of Justice has determined that the Use of Deadly Force in this incident was legally justified. This case was also presented and cleared before a Grand Jury. This represents the whole of the American justice structure; local, state, and federal. The Smyrna Police Department is satisfied this incident was thoroughly scrutinized, investigated, and evaluated by all levels of the justice system. Moreover, we owe a debt of gratitude to all agencies for their effort, due diligence, and professionalism during this long and tedious process of such an important investigation.
We also continue to offer our heartfelt sympathy to the family of Nicholas Thomas during this period and hope that this decision brings closure for all those involved.
The Smyrna Police Department remains vigilant and committed to providing the highest quality of police services to the City of Smyrna while at the same time maintaining respect for individual rights. The Department recognizes that no law enforcement agency can operate at its maximum potential without supportive input from the citizens it serves, therefore we continue to implore positive relationships with our community and seek out

opportunities to improve upon our services through proactive partnerships with business, civic, and faith-based leaders within our jurisdictional boundaries.
Chief David Lee
Smyrna Police Department

I am printing the entire press release here for two reasons. First, it is important to see the language advising that all agencies with jurisdiction over the incident had completed their investigations and the officer was cleared in every instance. The initial officer-involved shooting and the speculation surrounding it are extremely public. It is only fair that a similar amount of news coverage be devoted to the story when a law enforcement officer is cleared. Several journalists covered this press release.

I speak about these issues and I wrote this book for three main reasons. First, I represent law enforcement officers in critical incidents, and a lot of those incidents are officer-involved shootings. I respond to the scene, and perhaps better than anyone in the law enforcement agency, I see how the cases are handled from the start to the finish and in the years after. I stay in touch with most officers I've represented, especially in officer-involved shootings, so I know how the anniversary of the officer-involved shooting affects them and their families when the news story pops up unexpectedly. Second, I have been consulted by many law enforcement agencies about the handling of media responses to critical incidents. I guess I'm old enough now that many of the young officers I met when I was in the academy and on patrol are now commanders and agency heads. We discuss these issues and I field their questions. Finally, I follow media reports on critical incidents, which are most often officer-involved shootings around the United States and beyond our borders. I see the good and the bad, and I'm often asked to comment on both during media interviews. I've seen large law enforcement agencies that should have the resources to be prepared for such intense media attention be caught flat-footed without a plan of action, and I've seen smaller agencies who respond quickly and competently. Like anything else, it usually comes down to training, policies, and preparation. I have yet to see a law enforcement agency be harmed by a well-thought-out, properly vetted, proactive statement following an officer-involved shooting or from flooding the media, including their own social media sites, with positive stories.

I want to follow up with a comment I made about body-worn cameras. Several quite ignorant people have promulgated body-worn cameras as the sole way to end all controversies surrounding officer-involved shootings. Such statements are naïve. Body-worn cameras have no peripheral vision. They "see" differently in low light and no light conditions—the circumstances surrounding most officer-involved shootings. Body-worn cameras are often misplaced and broken during foot chases and scuffles, and they only record at a fixed number of frames per second, unlike the human brain. In short, body-worn cameras will never provide the point of view of the law enforcement officer using force. One of the people in a class I taught provided an excellent analogy: people think the body-worn camera will provide the same clarity and angles as the cameras that fly by wire over a professional football game. In reality, if the quarterback were wearing a camera, you would not know to whom he threw the ball or if they caught it. All you would see is three large human beings trying to knock him down and take the ball. While body-worn cameras will help in many cases, they are not the answer to every problem, especially those created to increase the controversy.

Imagine how a critical incident in your jurisdiction would be reported if every media outlet could go to your YouTube channel or your social media sites and learn about the extensive training you put your law enforcement officers through. What if they saw for themselves how hard it is to make a deadly force decision and the training and evaluation your law enforcement officers must successfully complete in order to wear their badges? What if they saw statistics for the number of citizen encounters versus the number of arrests made by your agency? What if they were able to look at the crimes-against-children unit through an article on your law enforcement agency blog, understand what they do, and understand the number of times they were forced to intervene and remove a child from a home without incident in the past? Their understanding of the training your crisis and hostage negotiators go through would give them more background in the story of how your SWAT team was forced to take a life during an armed standoff. This is all part of your law enforcement agency's story, and it is worth telling.

You do not need to shoulder the burden to fill the internet and media sources with positive and informative stories. Look around and see that there are plenty of sources to assist. One in particular bears mention. Patrick Shaver is a law enforcement officer who went to film school and took it upon himself to create a documentary about the reality of officer-involved shootings. You can find more about his movie, *Officer Involved*, on his website, www.officerinvolvedproject.com. The movie is excellent and provides a stark reality about these events, the officers who use deadly force, and the effect the use of force has upon them. Like any other source of information, take the time to look and you will learn something. Journalists and officers will learn a lot from the film.

So it is up to you. Hopefully this book has demonstrated and persuasively argued that the choice is yours and the future of your law enforcement agency's media image and public perception is in your hands. You can lead by example and be the first in your state or region to become rabidly proactive, or wait until everyone else makes the change. You can wait until the career of one of your officers is destroyed by media attention following a critical incident, in which they were eventually cleared of any wrongdoing, or act now to change the dialogue and prepare for the media scrutiny that will come from such an event. Attacks on law enforcement officers are increasing. This is especially true of ambushes. The year 2016 may prove to be the deadliest year for law enforcement officers in history. This makes the likelihood of an officer-involved shooting in your jurisdiction involving your agency highly foreseeable. Are you prepared to be under the media microscope to the extent and for the duration of time faced by the law enforcement agencies in and around St. Louis, Missouri, during the summer and fall of 2014?

There is a lot at stake beyond the careers of your officers. As stated many times in this book, there are people and organized groups actively trying to destroy the relationship between law enforcement agencies and the communities they serve. At the same time, they are criticizing agencies for not reaching out to their communities. Law enforcement agencies must act to safeguard and strengthen not only the relationships, but also the perception of the relationships in the communities and in the media.

Finally, if law enforcement agencies do not get a handle on their media responses during and after critical incidents and learn to maximize media opportunities, I fear we will be facing a law enforcement crisis in the United States within ten years. Recruiting numbers are down. I hear this from law enforcement contacts all over the United States. While I have not seen any scientific surveys, I do not need one to understand the importance of what I hear directly from officers: they are telling their children not to go into law enforcement. They are no longer encouraging the people they meet who ask about their jobs to go into law enforcement. Why would they? Pensions are under attack; law enforcement officers are accused of brutality by presidential candidates even when polls by mainstream media sources show 99.1 percent of law enforcement officers every year never even have a complaint filed against them;[207] and videos abound of law enforcement officers being followed around and cursed at while performing their jobs.

Perhaps the most serious point, at least as serious as a recruiting crisis, is the desire of twenty-year veteran law enforcement officers to retire as quickly as possible. At one time, many officers worked past their retirement eligibility date and through to their thirtieth year of service. Some took this course based upon pride, some wanted to keep working, but many who I've known did so because they were in positions that allowed them to make a difference. They were in the ranks of the command staff or senior patrol and training positions. They were willing to stay on in those positions because they believed they made a difference. While they still believe they make a difference, many are retiring because they are tired of the anticop rhetoric.

I do not blame any law enforcement officer for leaving the profession, although I've been sad to see many of them go. One of the number-one complaints I hear is that law enforcement agencies do not back officers anymore and the media seems to be against all law enforcement officers. Like anyone else, their perceptions will drive their actions. Statements like that drove me to write this book.

To the journalists who cared enough to read this book, I want to thank you for taking the time to do so. If we sat down over coffee or a beer and discussed the issues contained herein, we might not agree, but we will at least have listened to each other. I hope you received an insight into the world behind the doors of the law enforcement agency, not only following an officer-involved shooting, but every day. Yours is an honorable profession, and without it there would be no United States of America. As you seek to hold law enforcement officers to their oaths and their obligations to the public, it is only fair that you are held to a standard of fairness, candor, and open-minded investigation. Be the person who dares to disagree with your peers. Research the law as well as the facts. Make the effort to become educated beyond the ken of the average person on the street so that your knowledge and experience will lead to journalism of the highest order, provoking thought and discourse of the peaceful sort. Finally, when a law enforcement officer is cleared of all wrongdoing following an officer-involved shooting, be true to the guiding principles and ethics enumerated in this text and those with which you are familiar, and give appropriate, if not equal, coverage to the fact that his actions have been determined to be lawful, as you did when that question was unclear. Finally, reach across the table and meet the law enforcement officers in your community. You will form professional relationships that will help your mission and your career. Don't be surprised if you also form a friendship or two that lasts a lifetime.

To the law enforcement officers who made it through to the last page of this book, I say this: be proud of your law enforcement service and be loud about your actions in fulfillment of that service. Do not shy away from media attention. Learn to tell your agency's story, and tell it to anyone who will listen in whatever venue and format possible. As there is honor in your work, there is honor in your efforts to inform people and change the tide of negative media attention about law enforcement officers.

There is a popular motivational phrase attributed to many authors: "If it's to be, it's up to me."[208] There you have it. Words to live by.

APPENDIX A

Open-Record Laws in the United States

Jurisdiction	Code Section
Alabama	Code of Ala. § 36-12-40
Alaska	AS § 40.25.110
Arizona	AZ Revised Statutes § 39.101-39.221
Arizona	A.C.A. § 25-19-101, et. Seq.
California	Cal. Gov't Code § 6250-6276.48
Colorado	C.R.S. §24-72-201 to 206
Connecticut	Conn. Gen. Stat. § 1-200 et seq.
Delaware	29 Del. C. § 10001-10007
Florida	Fla. Stat. A.C.A. § 119
Georgia	O.C.G.A § 50-18-70
Hawaii	Haw. Rev. Stat. § 92-1 et seq.
Idaho	I.C. § 74-106
Illinois	5 ILCS 140/1
Indiana	Ind. Code § 5-14-1.5
Iowa	Iowa Code Ann. § 22.1 et seq.
Kansas	K.S.A. § 45-215 et seq.
Kentucky	KRS § 61.872 et seq.
Louisiana	LSA-R.S. 44:1 et seq.
Maine	1 M.R.S. § 402
Maryland	Md. Gen. Prov. Code Ann. § 4-101[209]
Massachusetts	MGL c.66 § 1 et seq.[210]
Michigan	Mich. Comp. Laws Ann. § 15.231-.246
Minnesota	Minn. Stat. § 13.01 et seq.
Mississippi	Miss. Code Ann. § 25-61-1 et seq.
Missouri	Mo. Rev. Stat. § 610.010 et seq.
Montana	Mont. Code Ann. § 2-6-101
Nebraska	Neb. Rev. Stat. § 84-712
Nevada	Nev. Rev. Stat. § 239.010
New Hampshire	N.H. Rev. Stat. Ann. § Ch. 01-A et seq.
New Jersey	N.J. Rev. Stat. § 47:1A-1 et al.
New Mexico	N.M. Stat. § 14-2-1

Jurisdiction	Code Section
New York	N.Y. U.C.C. Law § 6-89
North Carolina	N.C. Gen. Stat. § 132 et seq.
North Dakota	N.D. Cent. Code § 44-04-18 et seq.
Ohio	Ohio Rev. Code § 149.43
Oklahoma	Okla. Stat. tit. 51 §§ 24A.8
Oregon	Or. Rev. Stat. § 192 et seq.
Pennsylvania	P.S. § 67.101
Rhode Island	R.I. Code R. § 38-2-3
South Carolina	S.C. Code Ann. § 30-4-10
South Dakota	S.D.C. § 1-21-1
Tennessee	Tenn. Code Ann. § 10-7-501 through 515
Texas	TGC § 552
Utah	Utah Code § 63G-2
Vermont	1 V.S.A. §§ 315 through 320
Virginia	Va. Code Ann. § 2.2-3700 through 3714
Washington	RCW § 42.04 through 42.56
West Virginia	W. Va. § 29B
Wisconsin	Wis. Stat. §§ 19.31-19.39
Wyoming	Wyo. Stat. § 16-4-201
Washington, DC	DC Code §2-531 through 539

APPENDIX B
Reporter's Privilege Laws and Provisions in the United States

State	Statute or Other Reference
Alabama	Ala. Code § 12-21-142
Alaska	AS 09.25.300 through .390; and Evid. R. 501
Arizona	A.R.S. § 12-2237
Arkansas	Ark. Code Ann. § 16-85-510
California	Cal Evid Code § 1070; and Cal Const, Art. I § 2
Colorado	C.R.S. 13-90-119
Connecticut	Conn. Gen. Stat. § 52-146t
Delaware	10 Del. C. § 4320-26
Florida	Fla. Stat. § 90.5015
Georgia	O.C.G.A. § 24-9-30
Hawaii	Act 210, Hawaii's shield law expired in 2013, and has not been reenacted.
Idaho	N/A
Illinois	735 ILCS 5/8-901
Indiana	Ind. Code Ann. § 34-46-4-2
Iowa	N/A
Kansas	K.S.A. § 60-480
Kentucky	KRS § 421.100
Louisiana	La. R.S. § 45:1452
Maine	16 M.R.S. § 61
Maryland	Md. Courts and Judicial Proceedings Code Ann. § 9-112
Massachusetts	N/A
Michigan	For Grand Jury Proceedings: MCL 767.5a; and for Subpoenas Issued by Prosecutors: MCL 767A.6
Minnesota	Minn. Stat. § 595.021
Mississippi	N/A
Missouri	N/A

State	Statute or Other Reference
Montana	26-1-902, MCA
Nebraska	R.R.S. Neb. § 20-144
Nevada	Nev. Rev. Stat. Ann. § 49.275
New Hampshire	N/A
New Jersey	N.J.S.A. 2A:84A-21
New Mexico	N.M. Stat. Ann. § 38-6-7
New York	NY CLS Civ R § 79-h
North Carolina	N.C. Gen. Stat. § 8-53.11
North Dakota	N.D. Cent. Code, § 31-01-06.2
Ohio	ORC Ann. 2739.04 (broadcasters); and § 2739.12 (newspapers)
Oklahoma	12 Okl. St. § 2506
Oregon	ORS § 44.520
Pennsylvania	42 Pa.C.S. § 5942
Rhode Island	R.I. Gen. Laws § 9-19.1-1 *et seq.*
South Carolina	S.C. Code Ann. § 19-11-100
South Dakota	N/A
Tennessee	Tenn. Code Ann. § 24-1-208
Texas	Tex. Civ. Prac. & Rem. Code § 22.021-22.027; and Tex. Code Crim. Proc. Art. 38.11 and 38.111
Utah	N/A, but see Utah Rule of Evidence 509.
Vermont	N/A
Virginia	N/A
Washington	Rev. Code Wash. (ARCW) § 5.68.010
Washington, DC	D.C. Code § 16-4701-4704
West Virginia	W. Va. Code § 57-3-10
Wisconsin	WSA Const. Art. 1 § 3 has been interpreted by appellate courts to include a journalist privilege.
Wyoming	N/A

ENDNOTES

1 Lance J. LoRusso, *When Cops Kill: The Aftermath of a Critical Incident* (Alpharetta, GA: BookLogix, 2012).

2 "FOP Foundation," Fraternal Order of Police, accessed September 22, 2016, www.fop.net (under "causes" and "FOP Foundation"); also see http://www.georgiafop.org/georgia-foundation/.

3 Henry Campbell Black, *Black's Law Dictionary*, 6th ed. (n.p.: Springer, 1994).

4 *Menuel v. City of Atlanta*, 25 F.3d 990, 997 (1994). (Quoting *Plakas v. Drinski*, 19 F.3d. 1143 [7th Cir. 1994].)

5 *Jacobellis v. Ohio*, 378 U.S. 184, 197 (1964). (Emphasis added.)

6 *Graham v. Connor*, 490 U.S. 386, 396 (1989).

7 *Deshaney v. Winnebago County Dept. of Social Services*, 489 U.S. 189 (1989).

8 Alan Blinder, "Georgia Police Officer Indicted for Murder of Unarmed Black Man," *New York Times*, January 21, 2016.

9 The AP is one of the largest and most trusted sources of independent newsgathering, supplying a steady stream of news to its members, international subscribers, and commercial customers. AP is neither privately owned nor government funded; instead, as a not-for-profit news cooperative owned by its American newspaper and broadcast members, it can maintain its single-minded focus on newsgathering and its commitment to the highest standards of objective, accurate journalism.

AP's commitment to independent, comprehensive journalism has deep roots. Founded in 1846, AP has covered all the major news events of the past 170 years, providing high-quality, informed reporting of everything from wars and elections to championship games and royal weddings.

Today, AP employs the latest technology to collect and distribute content. It is in the process of overhauling its video and photography content: transitioning to high definition, expanding its coverage, and building a new, flexible, powerful infrastructure. AP has the industry's most sophisticated digital photo network; a twenty-four-hour, continuously updated online multimedia news service; a state-of-the-art television news service; and one of the largest radio networks in the US. Its commercial digital photo archive is one of the world's largest collections of historical and contemporary imagery. AP Mobile, the AP's award-winning news app, has been downloaded over nine million times since its launch in 2008, and AP has a strong social media presence, building new connections between AP and its members, customers, and consumers.

Since the Pulitzer Prize was established in 1917, AP has received fifty-one Pulitzers, including thirty-one photo Pulitzers.

AP, which is headquartered in New York, operates in more than 280 locations worldwide, including every statehouse in the US. Two-thirds of its staffers are journalists. For more information, visit http://www.ap.org/company/about-us.

[10] Id.

[11] "AP News Values & Principles," Associated Press, accessed September 22, 2016, http://www.ap.org/company/news-values.

[12] City of Philadelphia Police Department Directive 4.16.

[13] The presence of video of the shooting may also have reduced the rush to judgment that was poised to occur.

[14] An ante litem notice is a pre-suit notice to a government entity announcing an intent to sue as well as a demand for settlement. The ante litem notice must typically be sent in accordance with strict procedures and within strict time constraints. *Black's Law Dictionary*, 10th ed.

[15] See *When Cops Kill: The Aftermath of a Critical Incident*, 109.

[16] FBI Uniform Crime Reporting (UCR) statistics.

[17] David J. Krajicek, "The rise of the crime beat 'news nerds,'" *The Crime Report*, February 9, 2016, http://www.cbsnews.com/news/the-rise-of-the-crime-beat-news-nerds/.

[18] *Terry v. Ohio*, 392 U.S. 1 (1968).

[19] Sonya Smith, "Beat Guide: Your First Beat," accessed August 21, 2016 http://www.spj.org/rrr.asp?ref=41&%3Bt=.

[20] This is known as justification. *Black's Law Dictionary* defines "justification" as (1) a lawful or sufficient reason for one's acts or omissions; any fact that prevents an act from being wrongful; (2) a showing, in court, of a sufficient reason why a defendant did what the prosecution charges the defendant to answer for. Under the Model Penal Code, the defendant must believe that the action was necessary to avoid harm or evil and that the harm or evil to be avoided was greater than the harm that would have resulted if the crime had been committed. *Black's Law Dictionary*, 10th ed.

[21] Vernon J. Geberth, *Practical Homicide Investigation: Tactics, Procedures, and Forensic Techniques*, 4th ed. (Boca Raton, FL: CRC Press, 2006).

[22] Defamation lawsuits against journalists and media sources are fraught with procedural landmines. Journalists and their employers enjoy privileges and presumptions about the goal of their work, and the burden is high for a litigant to succeed in such a suit. Check with an attorney licensed in your state and proceed with caution before filing a defamation suit against a journalists or media outlet.

[23] LoRusso, *When Cops Kill: The Aftermath of a Critical Incident*, 129, citing In Re: Jeffrey Deal, Superior Court of Laurens County, September 8, 2011, transcript p. 127, lines 9–11.

[24] *Black's Law Dictionary*, 8th ed.

[25] "The Watergate Story: Part 4," *The Washington Post*, accessed June 20, 2016, http://www.washingtonpost.com/wp-srv/politics/special/watergate/part4.html.

[26] Kirk Hanson and Jerry Ceppos, "The Ethics of Leaks," Markkula Center for Applied Ethics, Santa Clara University, n.d., accessed June 20, 2016, https://www.scu.edu/ethics/focus-areas/journalism-ethics/resources/the-ethics-of-leaks/.

[27] "The Woodward and Bernstein Watergate Papers," The University of Texas at Austin Exhibitions, Harry Ransom Center, n.d., accessed June 20, 2016, http://www.hrc.utexas.edu/exhibitions/web/woodstein/.

[28] 1973 Pulitzer Prize Winners, The Pulitzer Prizes, accessed June 7, 2016, http://www.pulitzer.org/prize-winners-by-year/1973.

[29] City of Atlanta Police Department SOP 1060.

[30] City of Philadelphia Police Department Directive 416.

[31] City of Portland, Oregon, Police Department Policy 061.35, Press/Media Relations.

[32] City of St. Louis, Missouri, General Order 11-68.

[33] *Black's Law Dictionary*, 8th ed., s.v. "whistle blower."

[34] *Black's Law Dictionary*, 8th ed., s.v. "whistle-blower acts."

[35] Janet Cook, "Jimmy's World," *The Washington Post*, April 28, 1980, accessed May 26, 2016, https://www.washingtonpost.com/archive/politics/1980/09/28/jimmys-world/605f237a-7330-4a69-8433-b6da4c519120/; Bill Green, "THE PLAYERS: It Wasn't a Game," *The Washington Post*, April 19, 1981, accessed May 26, 2016, https://www.washingtonpost.com/archive/politics/1981/04/19/the-players-it-wasnt-a-game/545f7157-5228-47b6-8959-fcfcfa8f08eb/.

[36] Don Van Natta Jr., Adam Liptak, and Clifford J. Levy, "The Miller Case: A Notebook, a Cause, a Jail Cell and a Deal," *New*

York Times, October 16, 2005, accessed June 29, 2016,
http://www.nytimes.com/2005/10/16/us/the-miller-case-a-notebook-a-cause-a-jail-cell-and-a-deal.html.

[37] In re Grand Jury Subpoena (Miller), 438 F.3d 1141 (2005).

[38] "Confidential Source of Videotape Revealed," Reporters Committee for Freedom of the Press, December 2, 2004, accessed June 29, 2016, http://www.rcfp.org/browse-media-law-resources/news/confidential-source-videotape-revealed; "Taricani Ordered Confined to Home on Criminal Contempt Charge," Reporters Committee for Freedom of the Press, December 9, 2004, accessed June 29, 2016, http://www.rcfp.org/browse-media-law-resources/news/taricani-ordered-confined-home-criminal-contempt-charge.

[39] *Cohen v. Cowles Media Co.*, 501 U.S. 663 (1991) (holding that defendant newspaper publisher had no special immunity from the application of general laws and was therefore liable just as any other for breach of contract based on promissory estoppel).

[40] O.C.G.A. 50-18-70(b)(1)(B). ("A request made pursuant to this article may be made to the custodian of a public record orally or in writing.") See Appendix B.

[41] David Hunn, "Not-so Anonymous: How Hackers Wreaked Havoc in St. Louis," *St. Louis Post Dispatch*, November 1, 2014, accessed May 29, 2016, http://www.stltoday.com/news/local/crime-and-courts/not-so-anonymous-how-hackers-wreaked-havoc-in-st-louis/article_809a5d53-7d67-57ff-96f9-ee5772b395d0.html; Alex Rogers, "What Anonymous Is Doing in Ferguson," *Time*, August 21, 2014, accessed May 26, 2016, http://time.com/3148925/ferguson-michael-brown-anonymous/.

[42] Interview with Colonel Ron Replogle, Missouri State Patrol, Ret. March 18, 2016.

[43] You may choose to use this system to code emails from people above you in the chain of command or significant others.

Missing an email from many sources can lead to a great deal of "wailing and gnashing of teeth" in the biblical sense (Matthew 13:42, KJV).

[44] Summary Disclaimer, Cobb County Department of Public Safety, accessed August 17, 2016, http://p2c.cobbcounty.org/p2c/Summary_Disclaimer.aspx.

[45] *Merriam-Webster OnLine*, s.v. "journalism," accessed August 17, 2016, http://www.merriam-webster.com/dictionary/journalism.

[46] John Breech, "Michael Vick reveals exactly when he's going to retire from the NFL," CBS Sports, March 10, 2016, http://www.cbssports.com/nfl/news/michael-vick-reveals-exactly-when-hes-going-to-retire-from-the-nfl/.

[47] Lilly Workneh, "Photo Of Young Boy Hugging Officer At Ferguson Rally Goes Viral and Becomes 'Icon Of Hope,'" *The Huffington Post*, November 30, 2014, accessed April 19, 2016, http://www.huffingtonpost.com/2014/11/30/young-boy-hugs-officer-viral_n_6244604.html. The young man was walking around with a sign that read "FREE HUGS." Sergeant Bret Barnum was happy to oblige. The image was viewed and shared hundreds of thousands of times.

[48] This quote has been attributed, in various forms, to several people, including William Randolph Hearst and George Orwell. However, the quote has been traced to a speech before parliament quoting Lord Northcliffe—May 10, 1968, Hansard, United Kingdom Parliament, Commons Sitting, Freedom of Publication Protection Bill, Speaking: Mr. Jasper More (Ludlow), HL Deb 19, vol. 764, cc819-26. (Accessed hansard.millbanksystems.com on July 2, 2012.)

[49] Jay Black, Bob Steele, and Ralph D. Barney, *Doing Ethics in Journalism: A Handbook With Case Studies*, 3rd ed. (Boston: Allyn & Bacon, 1999), 218.

[50] *Wikipedia*, s.v. "Shooting of Trayvon Martin," accessed May 26, 2016, https://en.wikipedia.org/wiki/Shooting_of_Trayvon_Martin.

[51] Arelis R. Hernandez, "Trayvon Martin: New Black Panthers Offer $10,000 Bounty for Capture of Shooter George Zimmerman," *Orlando Sentinel*, March 24, 2012, accessed May 26, 2016, http://articles.orlandosentinel.com/2012-03-24/news/os-trayvon-martin-new-black-panthers-protest-20120324_1_sanford-vigilante-justice-black-men.

[52] Kerry Picket, "Spike Lee Retweets Incorrect Address of Trayvon Martin Shooter," *The Washington Times*, March 27, 2012, accessed June 7, 2016, http://www.washingtontimes.com/blog/watercooler/2012/mar/27/picket-spike-lee-re-tweets-incorrect-address-trayv/.

[53] Susan Jacobson, "Elderly Couple Abandon Their Home after Address Is Posted on Twitter as That of George Zimmerman," *Orlando Sentinel*, March 29, 2012, accessed May 26, 2016, http://articles.orlandosentinel.com/2012-03-29/news/os-trayvon-martin-wrong-zimmerman-20120327_1_spike-lee-william-zimmerman-retweeted.

[54] "Spike Lee Pays up for Wrong-address Tweet in Trayvon Martin Case," *Los Angeles Times*, March 30, 2012, accessed May 26, 2016, http://latimesblogs.latimes.com/gossip/2012/03/spike-lee-trayvon-martin-wrong-george-zimmerman-address.html.

[55] "SPJ Code of Ethics," Society of Professional Journalists, September 6, 2014, accessed May 26, 2016, http://www.spj.org/ethicscode.asp.

[56] Sigma Delta Chi's first code of ethics was borrowed from the American Society of Newspaper Editors in 1926. In 1973, Sigma Delta Chi wrote its own code, which was revised in 1984 and 1987. The present version of the Society of Professional Journalists' code of ethics was adopted in September 1996. Jay

Black, Rob Steele, Ralph D. Barney, *Doing Ethics in Journalism: A Handbook With Case Studies* (Boston: Allyn & Bacon, 1999).

[57] "About SPJ," Society of Professional Journalists, accessed May 26, 2016, http://www.spj.org/aboutspj.asp.

[58] American Society of News Editors home page, accessed August 17, 2016, http://asne.org/ (formerly known as the American Society of Newspaper Editors until 2009).

[59] The National Press Club home page, accessed August 17, 2016, http://www.press.org/.

[60] New York Times Company, "Standards and Ethics," *New York Times*, accessed May 26, 2016, http://www.nytco.com/who-we-are/culture/standards-and-ethics/.

[61] *Merriam-Webster OnLine*, s.v. "profession," accessed May 26, 2016, http://www.merriam-webster.com/dictionary/profession.

[62] Earnest Greenwood, "Attributes of a Profession," *Social Work* vol. 2, no. 3 (July 1957).

[63] "Best U.S. Journalism Schools & Programs: Complete State-by-State Listing," College Media Matters, accessed May 26, 2016, http://www.collegemediamatters.com/best-u-s-journalism-schools-programs-complete-listing/.

[64] Ron F. Smith, *Ethics in Journalism*, 6th ed. (Hoboken, NJ: Blackwell Publishing, 2008), 12n8.

[65] Id., 10.

[66] This is a quote from the Fourth Amendment to the United States Constitution. The full text reads, "The right of the people to be secure in their persons, houses, papers, and effects, against unreasonable searches and seizures, shall not be violated, and no warrant shall issue but upon probable cause, supported by oath or affirmation, and particularly describing the place to be searched, and the persons and things to be seized."

[67] *Riley v. California*, 134 S.Ct. 2473 (2014).

[68] Jay Black, Rob Steele, Ralph D. Barney, *Doing Ethics in Journalism: A Handbook With Case Studies* (Boston: Allyn & Bacon, 1999).

[69] Id.

[70] Id.

[71] Id.

[72] Ron F. Smith, *Ethics in Journalism*, 6th ed. (Hoboken, NJ: Blackwell Publishing, 2008), 86–87, citing Ian Mayes, "Trust me—I'm an ombudsman," *British Journalism Review* 2 (2004).

[73] Ron F. Smith, *Ethics in Journalism*, 6th ed. (Hoboken, NJ: Blackwell Publishing, 2008), 133, quoting Gordon McKibben, "A 'friendly' talk that cost a man his job," *The Boston Globe*, July 27, 1992.

[74] Ron F. Smith, *Ethics in Journalism*, 6th ed. (Hoboken, NJ: Blackwell Publishing, 2008), 50, from her remarks in the thirteenth annual Otis Chandler lecture at the University of Southern California School of Journalism, quoted in M. L. Stein, "Here we go again!" *Editor & Publisher*, November 28, 1992.

[75] Id., 43.

[76] Id., 47.

[77] Id., 52.

[78] Id., 62. Quoting Paula LaRocque, "Corrections, however painful or funny, needed for credibility," *Quill*, April 2005.

[79] Id., 60. Quoting Scott Maier, "Accuracy matters: A cross-market assessment of newspaper error and credibility," *Journalism and Mass Communication Quarterly* (Autumn 2005).

[80] Ariel Hart, "Delusions of Accuracy," *Columbia Law Review* 42 (July/August 2003), no. 2, p. 20.

[81] Id., 61. Quoting Ariel Hart, "Delusions of Accuracy," *Columbia Journalism Review* (July/August 2003) and American Society of

Newspaper Editors, *Examining our Credibility: Perspectives of the public and the press* (1999).

[82] Id., 61.

[83] Id., 47.

[84] "A Brief History of Blogging," *Webdesigner Depo*, March 14, 2011, accessed May 26, 2016, http://www.webdesignerdepot.com/2011/03/a-brief-history-of-blogging/.

[85] Id.

[86] Id.

[87] Robert Charles Lee, "How Many Blogs Exist in the World?" *Quora*, March 20, 2015, accessed May 26, 2016, https://www.quora.com/How-many-blogs-exist-in-the-world.

[88] Stats, accessed August 17, 2016, https://wordpress.com/activity/.

[89] "Welcome to CIT International," CIT International, accessed August 17, 2016, http://www.citinternational.org/.

[90] This figure should be tracked as part of the LEA process of monitoring and improving interactions with journalists. See Chapter 5 for more information.

[91] *New York Times* home page, accessed August 17, 2016, www.nytimes.com. The videos on the site are listed on pages containing the heading "TIMESVIDEO" or the heading of the section in which the video appears such as "Business."

[92] David J. Krajicek, "The rise of the crime beat 'news nerds,'" February 9, 2016, http://www.cbsnews.com/news/the-rise-of-the-crime-beat-news-nerds/.

[93] I use #5thstreetjustice because as of the time that I am writing this, there are no posts under this hashtag. That could change. You may also find it interesting that several generic hashtags

that I came up with that were the complete fabrications of my imagination were actual hashtags.

[94] Lymari Morales, "U.S. Distrust in Media Hits New High," *Gallup*, September 21, 2012, accessed June 20, 2016, http://www.gallup.com/poll/157589/distrust-media-hits-new-high.aspx; *Cohen v. Cowles Media Co.*, 501 U.S. 663 (1991).

[95] *Black's Law Dictionary*, 10th ed., s.v. "*stare decisis,*" p. 1626.

[96] Charles L. Ponce De Leon, *That's the Way It Is: A History of Television News in America* (Chicago: University of Chicago Press, 2015). From an excerpt from the chapter titled, "The Beginnings of TV News in America."

[97] "An Excerpt from *That's the Way It Is: A History of Television News in America*: Beginnings," University of Chicago Press Books, accessed August 17, 2016, http://press.uchicago.edu/books/excerpt/2015/De_Leon_Thats_Way_It_Is.html.

[98] Charles L. Ponce De Leon, *That's the Way It Is: A History of Television News in America* (Chicago: University of Chicago Press, 2015). From an excerpt from the chapter titled, "The Beginnings of TV News in America."

[99] "News, Network," The Museum of Broadcast Communications, accessed May 26, 2016, http://www.museum.tv/eotv/newsnetwork.htm.

[100] *Wikipedia*, s.v. "Broadcasting," Section 4, "Recorded broadcasts and live broadcasts," accessed August 17, 2016, https://en.wikipedia.org/wiki/Broadcasting#Recorded_broadcasts_and_live_broadcasts.

[101] Robert Davis, "The 1968 Democratic National Convention," *The Chicago Tribune*, accessed June 20 2016, http://www.chicagotribune.com/news/nationworld/politics/chi-chicagodays-democraticconvention-story-story.html.

[102] "TV Reports of JFK Assassination - Walter Cronkite Announces Death of JFK - CBS News JFK," YouTube video, 5:43, posted by the John F. Kennedy channel, April 26, 2014, accessed May 26, 2016, https://www.youtube.com/watch?v=2B_jJEV25g4.

[103] "SPJ Code of Ethics," Society of Professional Journalists, September 6, 2014, accessed May 26, 2016, http://www.spj.org/ethicscode.asp.

[104] James D. Brown, "Protection Through Written Policies," *CALEA*, accessed May 26, 2016, http://www.calea.org/calea-update-magazine/issue-105/protection-through-written-policies.

[105] "Standards Titles," *CALEA*, accessed May 26, 2016, http://www.calea.org/content/standards-titles.

[106] David Usborne, "Michael Brown Shooting: Ten Things We Know—or Know Better—Now the Ferguson Grand Jury's Work Is Over," *Independent*, November 25, 2014, accessed May 26, 2016, http://www.independent.co.uk/news/world/americas/michael-brown-shooting-ten-things-we-know-or-know-better-now-the-ferguson-grand-jurys-work-is-over-9881046.html; United States Department of Justice, "Department of Justice Report Regarding the Criminal Investigation into the Shooting Death of Michael Brown by Ferguson Police Officer Darren Wilson," March 4, 2015, accessed May 26, 2016, p. 5, https://www.justice.gov/sites/default/files/opa/press-releases/attachments/2015/03/04/doj_report_on_shooting_of_michael_brown_1.pdf.

[107] *Black's Law Dictionary*, 10th ed., s.v. "exemplary or punitive damages," 390.

[108] United States Department of Justice, "Department of Justice Report Regarding the Criminal Investigation into the Shooting Death of Michael Brown by Ferguson Police Officer Darren Wilson," March 4, 2015, accessed May 26, 2016, https://www.justice.gov/sites/default/files/opa/press-

releases/attachments/2015/03/04/doj_report_on_shooting_of_mic hael_brown_1.pdf.

[109] In some cases, we were asked to pay for the production of the policies pursuant to the state's open-record laws. Aside from the cost of doing so, in other cases, the request was treated as something other than a strict open-records request, and I suspect they became lost in the shuffle. However, it is very difficult to gather large numbers of policies on any topic due in large part to the number of law enforcement agencies in the United States. We sincerely appreciate the cooperation of the following law enforcement agencies that readily shared their polices: the City of Atlanta, Georgia; the City of Philadelphia, Pennsylvania; the City of St. Louis, Missouri; Charlotte-Mecklenburg Police Department in North Carolina; the City of Portland, Oregon; and the City of Dallas, Texas.

[110] City of Atlanta Police Department Public Affairs SOP 1060.

[111] Charlotte-Mecklenburg Police Department Policy 800-002.

[112] Philadelphia Police Department Directive 4.16.

[113] St. Louis County Police Department, Missouri Q-1 Departmental General Order 11-68.

[114] Portland Police Department 0631.35 Press/Media Relations.

[115] Atlanta Police Department Public Affairs SOP 1060 Paragraph 4.1.5.

[116] "The Commission," CALEA, accessed August 17, 2016, http://www.calea.org/content/commission.

[117] Id.

[118] "Steps in the Accreditation Process," CALEA, accessed August 17, 2016, http://www.calea.org/content/steps-accreditation-process.

[119] CALEA home page, accessed August 17, 2016, www.calea.org.

[120] Law enforcement agencies seem to use different labels to these units, their functions, and the titles of the law enforcement officers assigned to the units. The City of Atlanta has a public affairs unit, the Charlotte-Mecklenburg Police Department employs a public affairs director, and the Portland Police Department uses the term public information officer. City of Atlanta Police Department Public Affairs SOP 1060; Charlotte-Meklenburg Police Department Policy 800-002; City of Portland Police Department 0631.35 Press/Media Relations. The City of Dallas, Texas, Police Department tasks ranking officers on the scene with providing updates to journalists. City of Dallas, Texas, Police Department Policy 323.00 Press Relations.

[121] Faith Karimi, "Shaq, Florida Officer Surprise Kids with a Basketball Game," CNN, January 24, 2016, accessed May 26, 2016, http://www.cnn.com/2016/01/24/us/florida-shaq-police-officers-game/.

[122] Monique O. Madan, "Shaq Is Back on a Police Force – This Time in Doral," *The Miami Herald*, January 20, 2015, accessed May 26, 2016, http://www.miamiherald.com/news/local/community/miami-dade/doral/article7791585.html.

[123] *Tyson v. Trigg*, 50 F.3d 436 (1995).

[124] For the folks who say this is not a good thing to advertise, I could not disagree more. These LEOs either shoot well or they don't, and their scores are public anyway. Their achievements are a testament to your training program and their dedication to their jobs.

[125] "Table 29 - Estimated Number of Arrests," The Federal Bureau of Investigation, 2015, accessed June 20, 2016, https://ucr.fbi.gov/crime-in-the-u.s/2015/preliminary-semiannual-uniform-crime-report-januaryjune-2015.

[126] I have not been able to find any reliable statistics on this issue, and I suspect that this information is not currently being

gathered. However, I have heard anecdotal statements estimating that for every arrest, LEOs have between six to ten citizen contacts. If law enforcement agencies are being forced to track data on all traffic stops and arrest to document the race of the individual detained, they should also keep statistics on the number of overall contacts. I believe the results would be eye-opening.

127 Ken Blanchard, PhD, and Spencer Johnson, MD, *The New One Minute Manager* (London: HarperCollins, 2015).

128 This Morning home page, accessed August 17, 2016, http://thismorningwithgordondeal.com/.

129 Lori Keeton, "What Is Really Rotten in the Food Lion Case: Chilling the Media's Unethical Newsgathering Techniques," *Florida Law Review* 49.1 (1997), 135.

130 Lymari Morales, "U.S. Distrust in Media Hits New High," *Gallup*, September 21, 2012, accessed June 20, 2016, http://www.gallup.com/poll/157589/distrust-media-hits-new-high.aspx.

131 http://policetraining.net/; "Effective Media Skills for Law Enforcement," Florida Regional Community Policing Institute, accessed September 22, 2016, http://cop.spcollege.edu/Training/MediaSkills/MediaSkills.htm (classes held at St. Petersburgh College); "Public Safety Media Training," Russell Ruffin Communications, accessed September 22, 2016, http://publicsafetymediatraining.com/public-safety-media-training/; https://piobootcamp.com/.

132 471 U.S. 1 (1985).

133 Id.

134 Sir William Watson, "England to Ireland" (1888).

135 Albert Mehrabian, PhD, "A Biographical Sketch of Albert Mehrabian, Ph.D," Personality & Communication: Psychological

Books & Articles of Popular Interest, accessed May 26, 2016, http://www.kaaj.com/psych/bio.html.

[136] *Merriam-Webster OnLine*, s.v. "kinesics," accessed May 26, 2016, http://www.merriam-webster.com/dictionary/kinesics.

[137] *Oxford Dictionary Online*, s.v. "news cycle," accessed May 26, 2016, http://www.oxforddictionaries.com/us/definition/american_engl ish/news-cycle.

[138] *Wiktionary*, s.v. "stop the presses," accessed May 26, 2016, https://en.wiktionary.org/wiki/stop_the_presses.

[139] Tim Jones, "Dewey Defeats Truman," *The Chicago Tribune*, accessed May 26, 2016, http://www.chicagotribune.com/news/nationworld/politics/chi-chicagodays-deweydefeats-story-story.html.

[140] Paul Chantler and Peter Stewart, *Basic Radio Journalism* (Amsterdam: Focal Press, 2013), 109.

[141] Id.

[142] Id.

[143] Mitchell Stephens, "History of Television," *Grolier Encyclopedias*, accessed May 26, 2016, https://www.nyu.edu/classes/stephens/History%20of%20Televisi on%20page.htm.

[144] Id.

[145] Id.

[146] Id.

[147] Id.

[148] Id.

[149] "CNN Is First to Stream 24-Hour News Network Online and On Mobile," CNN, July 18, 2011, accessed May 26, 2016,

http://cnnpressroom.blogs.cnn.com/2011/07/18/cnn-is-first-to-stream-24-hour-news-network-online-and-on-mobile/.

150 LoRusso, *When Cops Kill: The Aftermath of a Critical Incident* (2012), 150.

151 Paul Gillin's blog, *Newspaper Death Watch*, accessed June 20, 2016, http://newspaperdeathwatch.com/.

152 "The Arrest Record of Rodney King," University of Missouri-Kansas City, accessed May 26, 2016, http://law2.umkc.edu/faculty/projects/ftrials/lapd/kingarrests.html.

153 George Bush, "Address to the Nation on the Civil Disturbances in Los Angeles, California," May 1, 1992. Online by Gerhard.

154 Doug Linder, "The Trials of Los Angeles Police Officers in Connection with the Beating of Rodney King," University of Missouri-Kansas City, 2001, accessed May 26, 2016, http://papers.ssrn.com/sol3/papers.cfm?abstract_id=1030560.

155 George Bush, "Address to the Nation on the Civil Disturbances in Los Angeles, California," May 1, 1992. Online by Gerhard.

156 "Los Angeles Riots: Remember the 63 People Who Died," *The Los Angeles Times*, April 26, 2012, accessed May 26, 2016, http://latimesblogs.latimes.com/lanow/2012/04/los-angeles-riots-remember-the-63-people-who-died-.html.

157 "What Are the Best Ways of Finding Stories For Freelance Journalism?" The Writer's Bureau, accessed May 27, 2016, http://www.writersbureau.com/writing/What-Are-the-Best-Ways-of-Finding-Stories-as-a-Freelance-Journalist.htm.

158 Eliott C. McLaughlin, "What We Know about Michael Brown's Shooting," CNN, August 11, 2014, accessed May 27, 2016, http://www.cnn.com/2014/08/11/us/missouri-ferguson-michael-brown-what-we-know/.

[159] Id.

[160] Id.

[161] United States Department of Justice, "Department of Justice Report Regarding the Criminal Investigation into the Shooting Death of Michael Brown by Ferguson Police Officer Darren Wilson," March 4, 2015, p. 7, accessed May 26, 2016, https://www.justice.gov/sites/default/files/opa/press-releases/attachments/2015/03/04/doj_report_on_shooting_of_mic hael_brown_1.pdf.

[162] Vernon J. Geberth, *Practical Homicide Investigation: Tactics, Procedures, and Forensic Techniques*, 5th ed. (Boca Raton, FL: CRC Press, 2006). Recurrent quote.

[163] This quote is widely attributed to Otto Van Bismarck, a Prussian statesman. However, the true origin remains somewhat of a mystery.

[164] "Arranging a Press Conference," Community Tool Box, accessed August 17, 2016, http://ctb.ku.edu/en/table-of-contents/participation/promoting-interest/press-conference/main.

[165] City of Dallas, Texas Police Department 323.00, Press Relations 323.01, News Media Requirements and Privileges.

[166] *Merriam-Webster Dictionary*, s.v. "Standing Order." ("An order or procedure that continues to be followed until it is changed or cancelled.")

[167] I represented a LEO following an officer-involved shooting in which there were no less than five separate crime scenes that were several miles apart. One was at a busy intersection, and another in the parking lot of a popular restaurant. Because it took some time following the officer-involved shooting to determine the evidence to be gathered at the scenes, the need to keep those scenes secure and confidential, to the extent possible, was critical to the preservation of evidence and to prevent

contamination. Therefore, the locations were not released for some time.

168 Olson Parmy, "Man Inadvertently Live Tweets Osama bin Laden Raid," *Forbes*, May 2, 2011, http://www.forbes.com/sites/parmyolson/2011/05/02/man-inadvertently-live-tweets-osama-bin-laden-raid/#a819a037c449.

169 *MacMillan Dictionary*, s.v. "onslaught," accessed May 27, 2016, http://www.macmillandictionary.com/us/dictionary/american/onslaught.

170 *Merriam-Webster OnLine*, s.v. "debrief," accessed June 21, 2016, http://www.merriam-webster.com/dictionary/debrief.

171 "What Is Root Cause Analysis (RCA)?" American Society for Quality, accessed May 31, 2016, http://asq.org/learn-about-quality/root-cause-analysis/overview/overview.html; *Medical Dictionary: The Free Dictionary*, s.v. "peer review," accessed May 31, 2016, http://medical-dictionary.thefreedictionary.com/peer+review.

172 O.C.G.A. §§ 31-7-133(a) and 31-7-143.

173 See Appendix A for a list of open-record laws from around the United States.

174 As of this writing, several media sources are still reporting on the Michael Brown shooting in Ferguson, Missouri, on a national basis nearly two years after the officer-involved shooting.

175 "A Hard Day's Night – 'Interview,'" YouTube video, 1:35, posted by AnaLennon, February 18, 2007, accessed May 31, 2016, https://www.youtube.com/watch?v=fl9k3gL6vxw.

176 *Merriam-Webster*, s.v. "sarcasm." ("A mode of satirical wit depending for its effect on bitter, caustic, and often ironic language that is usually directed against an individual.")

[177] "The Beatles Interviews Database," Beatles Ultimate Experience, accessed May 31, 2016, http://www.beatlesinterviews.org/.

[178] "John Lennon: 'We're More Popular Than Jesus,'" The Beatles Bible, March 4, 1996, www.beatlesbible.com/1966/03/04/how-does-a-beatle-live-by-maureen-cleave.

[179] "The Beatles Album Sales Statistics," Statistic Brain, February 19, 2014, accessed May 31, 2016, http://www.statisticbrain.com/the-beatles-total-album-sales/.

[180] Dave Swanson, "How Paul McCartney Finally Ended the Beatles For Good," Ultimate Classic Rock, April 10, 2015, accessed May 31, 2016, http://ultimateclassicrock.com/the-beatles-called-it-quits-42-years-ago-today/.

[181] Apple Press Info, "Apple Launches the iTunes Music Store," Apple,

April 28, 2003, accessed May 31, 2016, https://www.apple.com/pr/library/2003/04/28Apple-Launches-the-iTunes-Music-Store.html.

[182] 5 USCA Section 552, as amended by Public Law 104-231 110 STAT. 3048. You can learn more at http://www.foia.gov/index.html.

[183] Ron F. Smith, *Ethics in Journalism*, 6th ed. (Hoboken, NJ: Blackwell Publishing, 2008), 129.

[184] Id.

[185] Id., 158.

[186] Id., 158.

[187] Id., 170. Smith discusses a 1999 case from the United States Supreme Court that raises Fourth Amendment concerns about journalists following LEOs into private dwellings on search warrants. The case is *Wilson v. Layne*, 526 U.S. 603 (1999), and the result was confirmed in *Hanlon v. Berger*, 526 U.S. 808 (1999).

This has always presented a problem for the journalists, not only due to the inherent danger of standing next to LEOs performing search warrants or otherwise entering homes or private property, as a landowner, lawful tenant, or proper representative often has the right to order the journalists to leave the property even if they would not be authorized to order the LEOs to leave. See e.g. O.C.G.A. Section 16-7-21. The United States Supreme court, in both cases, found a Fourth Amendment violation likely occurred, but the Court extended immunity to the involved officers as the law was not clearly established at the time of the incidents.

[188] Id., 160. Referencing David Ovalle of the *Miami Herald*, quoted by Meg Martin, "Leaving fingerprints: Inside the police beat," November 22, 2005, http://www.poynter.org/2005/leaving-fingerprints-inside-the-police-beat/72312/.

[189] Id., 161.

[190] Id., 162.

[191] Heather Palmer, "Police Officer Poses as Photographer to Nab Shooting Suspect during Stand-off," *The News Media & The Law* (Fall 2001), online at Reporters Committee for Freedom of the Press, accessed June 1, 2016, https://www.rcfp.org/browse-media-law-resources/news-media-law/news-media-and-law-fall-2001/police-officer-poses-photogra.

[192] "(1990) Klanswoman Kills Husband, Blames Blacks and Goes on Anti-Black Speaking Circuit," YouTube video, posted by NoPawn, April 21, 2010, accessed June 1, 2016, https://www.youtube.com/watch?v=9d4pYpCQiXk.

[193] Peter Applebome, "Atlanta Journal; The Killing Was Real; The Story Was a Lie," *New York Times*, March 29, 1990, accessed June 2, 2016, http://www.nytimes.com/1990/03/29/us/atlanta-journal-the-killing-was-real-the-story-was-a-lie.html.

[194] Roy Rogers, Ret. Police Detective, telephone interview, April 17, 2016.

[195] Georgia Dept. of Corrections Offender Search: Neva Veitch.

[196] Jack Shafer, "Stop or I'll Write! Why Cops Shouldn't Fake Being Journalists," *Reuters*, November 11, 2014, accessed June 2, 2016, http://blogs.reuters.com/jackshafer/2014/11/11/stop-or-ill-write-why-cops-shouldnt-fake-being-reporters/.

[197] Id., 158.

[198] *Westerhold v. City of Little Rock, et al.*, Arkansas, Civil Action Number 60-CV-14-3271 Circuit Court of Pulaski County, Arkansas, Fifth Division.

[199] Dan Reimold, "Otterbein U. Student Media Wins Lawsuit: Campus Police Records Must Be Made Public," College Media Matters RSS, May 21, 2015, accessed June 2, 2016, http://www.collegemediamatters.com/2015/05/21/otterbein-u-student-media-wins-lawsuit-campus-police-records-must-be-made-public/; *State Ex. Rel. Schiffbauer v. Banaszak*, 142 OH. St. 3rd 535, 33 N.E.3d 52 (2015).

[200] *Harki v. Dep't of Crim. Justice Servs.*, 2015 WL 9274066 (Va. Cir. [Nov. 2015]).

[201] Complaint at 13, *Paff v. Office of the Attorney General*, Docket No. L1984-15, New Jersey Superior Court of Mercer County.

[202] Complaint at 18, *Perkins v. Hastings et al.*, No. 4:2015-cv-00310, Arkansas Eastern District Court (June 1, 2015).

[203] Complaint at 2, *Christopher v. City of Tacoma*, No. 16-2-05416-7, Washington Superior Court of Pierce County, February 10, 2016.

[204] The immortal last line of *Casablanca* (1942).

[205] *Restatement (Second) of Torts* § 570 (2013).

[206] Ricky Leroux, "Spokesman: Review Is Closed - U.S. Attorney's Office Determines Smyrna Officer-involved Shooting Was Justified," *The Marietta Daily Journal*, June 2, 2016, accessed June 20, 2016, http://www.mdjonline.com/news/spokesman-

review-is-closed/article_0b5bc5b8-2932-11e6-b4fb-971adbf2558d.html.

[207] Ari Melbor, prod., "The State of Policing in 2015," *Morning Joe*, MSNBC, January 18, 2016.

[208] This quote appears in many forms. In this form, it is widely attributed to William H. Johnsen.

[209] This statute was renamed in 2016; it was formerly codified as Md. Gen. Prov. Code Ann. § 10-611.

[210] See also St.2016, c.121 (H4333), an "Act to Improve Public Records" signed into law in 2016. It provides sweeping changes to public records law. Most provisions are effective January 1, 2017.

About the Author

Lance LoRusso began his law enforce- ment career in 1988 and has been practicing law since 1999. His practice focuses on representing law enforcement officers in all areas, including responding to the scene of officer-involved shootings, employment appeals, administrative and criminal investigations, and state licensing inquiries.  Lance also represents law enforcement officers when they are injured on and off duty. He has obtained settlements for law enforcement officers ranging from a few thousand dollars to over two million dollars. He has litigated cases on behalf of law enforcement officers facing civil, administrative, and criminal charges. Lance serves as an advisor for several agencies and teaches at law enforcement academies and conferences around the state of Georgia, the United States, and internationally. In one twelve-month period, he taught use of force and media issues to over two thousand law enforcement officers from more than twenty-five states and several federal agencies. His articles and blog posts have been featured in law enforcement officer publications, including *SWAT* and websites such as lawenforcementtoday.com and officerresource.com, and he is a freelance writer for Harrison Publications. His first book, *When Cops Kill: The Aftermath of a Critical Incident*, is referenced and used in law enforcement academies and criminal justice programs around the United States. All of the profits from *When Cops Kill* support law enforcement-related charities. His first fiction book, *Peacemaking*, is about a law enforcement officer's walk with Christ. All of his books are available through www.lancelorussobooks.com and Amazon. The profits from *Blue News* will also support law enforcement charities.

Other Books by Lance J. LoRusso

When Cops Kill: The Aftermath of a Critical Incident

When Cops Kill takes you through an officer-involved shooting and the years after. Lance deftly answers questions all law enforcement officers involved in a shooting ask themselves, including what it means to be sued as an officer, what happens during an internal affairs investigation, how to handle the inevitable media coverage, and more. In this powerful book, Lance removes the fear of the unknown and replaces it with the power that comes from knowledge and understanding.

Peacemaking

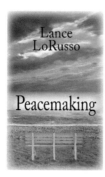

Scotty Painter is the most respected member of his police department, having worked his way up from a street cop to deputy chief. Yet after losing his wife to cancer, he lives alone, haunted by the miserable things he has seen and done while on the force. This misery comes to a head when Scotty finds himself sharing his deepest, most troubling thoughts in a world far apart from his days filled with life and death decisions. His fears, his faith, and ultimately his destiny will be forced to the surface.

Is Scotty ready?

The World Class Rainmaker:
Raising the Bar in Your Law Practice
Lance J. LoRusso & Robin Hensley

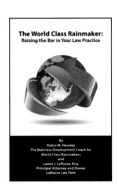

From setting goals that garner real results to igniting old relationships and building successful new ones, *The World Class Rainmaker* lets readers in on the secrets to positioning your law practice to "make more rain." Whether you are an old hand at marketing and building your practice or brand new to rainmaking, Lance and coauthor Robin M. Hensley show you how to do what needs to be done to take your practice to the next level.

For more information, go to www.lancelorussobooks.com